AFRICAN AWAKENING

The Emerging Revolutions

Through the voices of the peoples of Africa and the global South, Pambazuka Press and Pambazuka News disseminate analysis and debate on the struggle for freedom and justice.

Pambazuka Press – www.pambazukapress.org

A Pan-African publisher of progressive books and DVDs on Africa and the global South that aim to stimulate discussion, analysis and engagement. Our publications address issues of human rights, social justice, advocacy, the politics of aid, development and international finance, women's rights, emerging powers and activism. They are primarily written by well-known African academics and activists. Most books are also available as ebooks.

Pambazuka News – www.pambazuka.org

The award-winning and influential electronic weekly newsletter providing a platform for progressive Pan-African perspectives on politics, development and global affairs. With more than 2,500 contributors across the continent and a readership of more than 660,000, Pambazuka News has become the indispensable source of authentic voices of Africa's social analysts and activists.

Pambazuka Press and Pambazuka News are published by Fahamu (www.fahamu.org)

AFRICAN AWAKENING

The Emerging Revolutions

Edited by Firoze Manji
and Sokari Ekine

Pambazuka Press
An imprint of Fahamu

Published 2012 by Pambazuka Press, an imprint of Fahamu
Cape Town, Dakar, Nairobi and Oxford
www.pambazukapress.org   www.fahamu.org   www.pambazuka.org

Fahamu, 2nd floor, 51 Cornmarket Street, Oxford OX1 3HA, UK
Fahamu Kenya, PO Box 47158, 00100 GPO, Nairobi, Kenya
Fahamu Senegal, 9 Cité Sonatel 2, BP 13083 Dakar Grand-Yoff,
Dakar, Senegal
Fahamu South Africa, c/o 19 Nerina Crescent, Fish Hoek,
7975 Cape Town, South Africa

Pambazuka Press gratefully acknowledge the support of the Rosa
Luxemburg Foundation towards the publication of this book.

British Library Cataloguing in Publication Data
A catalogue record for this book is available from the British Library

ISBN: 978-0-85749-021-6 paperback
ISBN: 978-0-85749-022-3 ebook – pdf
ISBN: 978-0-85749-036-0 ebook – epub
ISBN: 978-0-85749-037-7 ebook – Kindle

Printed in the United States

Contents

About the contributors

Charles Abugre is the regional director for Africa, United Nations Millennium Campaign.

Esam Al-Amin is a writer and activist.

Massan d'Almeida is coordinator of Association for Women's Rights in Development.

Samir Amin is the director of the Third World Forum.

Patrick Bond is director of the University of KwaZulu-Natal Centre for Civil Society.

Horace Campbell is a teacher and writer. Professor Campbell's website is www.horacecampbell.net. His latest book is *Barack Obama and 21st Century Politics: A Revolutionary Moment in the USA.*

Lila Chouli is a research associate in the Centre for Sociological Research at the University of Johannesburg.

Sokari Ekine is a Nigerian/British feminist, educator and activist. Sokari is the editor of Black Looks Blog. She writes a regular column for Pambazuka News and is editor of *SMS Uprising: Mobile Activism in Africa.*

Hassan El Ghayesh is a 24-year-old Egyptian. For a long time he thought his only chance of a brighter future would not be in his own country, which he loves dearly. But now, the tables have turned: his faith in people's power has been restored and he feels empowered. For the first time, there is a chance of him contributing to a better Egypt.

Lakhdar Ghettas is a PhD candidate in the International History Department at the London School of Economics and a programme assistant of the LSE IDEAS Centre for Diplomacy and Strategy – North Africa Initiative.

Nigel C. Gibson is an activist and scholar.

Adam Hanieh is a lecturer in the Development Studies Department of the School of Oriental and African Studies (SOAS), University of London. He is author of the forthcoming book, *Capitalism and Class in the Gulf Arab States.*

Konstantina Isidoros is a doctoral researcher in anthropology at the University of Oxford.

Peter Kenworthy has a master of social science in international development studies and is part of Africa Contact's Free Swaziland campaign.

Sadri Khiari is a Tunisian dissident now living in France, where he is a leading intellectual of Le Parti des Indigènes de la République (PIR), an anti-racist political party founded in 2010. He has published a number of books on Tunisia, including *Tunisie. Coercition, consentement, résistance. Le délitement de la cité*, and on the post-colonial situation in France.

Mahmood Mamdani is professor and director of the Makerere Institute of Social Research at Makerere University, Kampala, Uganda, and Herbert Lehman Professor of Government at Columbia University, New York. He is the author, most recently, of *Good Muslim, Bad Muslim: America, The Cold War and the Roots of Terror*, and *Saviors and Survivors: Darfur, Politics and the War on Terror*.

Firoze Manji is founder and editor-in-chief of Pambazuka News and Pambazuka Press.

Imad Mesdoua writes each week on African and Maghreb affairs for *Ceasefire*. His interests include politics, current affairs and Real Madrid FC.

Fatma Naib is a journalist for Al Jazeera English based in the Middle East.

Explo Nani-Kofi is the director of the Kilombo Community Education Project, London and the Kilombo Centre for Civil Society and African Self-Determination, Peki, Ghana, which jointly publish the *Kilombo Pan-African Community Journal* as well as host the 'Another World is Possible' radio programme.

J. Oloka-Onyango is professor and director of the Human Rights and Peace Centre at the Faculty of Law, Makerere University.

Richard Pithouse teaches politics at Rhodes University, South Africa.

Jean-Paul Pougala is a political analyst.

Khadija Sharife is the southern Africa correspondent for *The Africa Report* magazine and a visiting scholar at the Centre for Civil Society (CCS) based in South Africa.

Yash Tandon is former executive director of the South Centre and chairperson of SEATINI.

Melakou Tegegn is an Ethiopian who has lived, worked and studied in the Netherlands.

Kah Walla is the candidate for Cameroon Ô'Bosso in Cameroon's 2011 presidential elections.

1

African awakenings: the courage to invent the future

Firoze Manji

13 July 2011, revised 14 August 2011

We are living today in what is probably one of the most inspiring times in our recent history, reminiscent of the period of the anti-colonial revolutions that followed the Second World War. Our continent is pregnant with hope, but equally it carries hope's twin, despair. This duality, which has remained a characteristic of our post-colonial inheritance, was perhaps best illustrated in the events of 1994: on the one hand we witnessed the rise of the popular movement that brought about the downfall of the apartheid regime in South Africa; and on the other, we saw the massacre of nearly a million people in Rwanda in a period of a few months. Both hope and despair coexist in all our countries. But because of the depth of the current crisis of capitalism, that duality will become ever more polarised in the coming period.

African awakenings

We are all familiar with the extraordinary events that took place in Tunisia and Egypt, leading to the downfall of Ben Ali and Mubarak, and which were followed by popular uprisings in Yemen, Syria, Bahrain and elsewhere in what is known today as the Middle East. Corporate media has christened these events the 'Arab spring'. However, this in not an adequate descriptor as it ignores the widespread expressions of discontent across the continent. Throughout 2011 we have witnessed significant uprisings in a large number of African countries – and we should not forget that Tunisia and Egypt are African countries. Indeed, where does

Africa begin and where does it end? Did the building of the Suez Canal amputate Africa from its intertwined history with the peoples to the east? Is Africa merely a geography? Or should it more correctly be seen as a history, a history that precedes the colonial conquest by millennia.

The uprisings of 2011 have not been confined to the Arab-speaking world. There have also been protests, strikes and other actions in Western Sahara, Zimbabwe, Senegal, Gabon, Sudan, Mauritania, Morocco, Madagascar, Mozambique, Algeria, Benin, Cameroon, Djibouti, Côte d'Ivoire, Burkina Faso, Botswana, Namibia, Uganda, Kenya, Swaziland, South Africa, Malawi and Uganda. Many of these uprisings have been brutally suppressed.

Some of the uprisings have perhaps not (yet) been on the scale that we have witnessed in North Africa, and each has its own aetiologies. But despite the specificities of each, together they can legitimately be considered as the cumulative response to a common experience shared over the last 30 years. Indeed, they have much in common with events we have witnessed this year in Wisconsin (US), Spain, Greece and, indeed, in Italy (where 95 per cent of the population delivered a resounding defeat to the government in a referendum that sought to privatise water, extend impunity to politicians and attempt to expand the use of nuclear power).

The shifting political and social climate in Africa is not limited to the overt, large-scale uprisings. There has been growing evidence in a number of countries of social movements re-emerging during the last 10 years, providing a framework through which the disenfranchised have begun to reassert their dignity, proclaiming – even if only implicitly – their aspiration to determine their own destinies, their own right to self-determination. The emergence and activities of movements such as Bunge La Mwananchi, Bunge Sisters and the Unga Revolution in Kenya, Abahlali baseMjondolo, the Anti-Eviction Campaign and the Landless People's Movement in South Africa, the anti-water-privatisation movement, the growing militancy of the LGBTI movements, the growing women's movement, the formation of alliances of peasant and farmer organisations, the growing demands from organised labour – all these are manifestations of an underlying mood of discontent and disenchantment with the social and political order. Even in South Africa, that so-called democratic success story, 'South African police have conservatively measured an annual average [since 2005] of more than 8,000 "Gatherings Act" incidents by an angry urban populace which remains unintimidated by the superficially populist government of Jacob Zuma' (Bond 2010).

Today, the gathering momentum of these movements for change defines the social and political scene on the continent. We are witnessing not so much an Arab spring as an *African awakening*.

What has given rise to the awakenings?

Conventional wisdom – or more accurately, perhaps, the corporate media – would suggest that the uprisings are happening because the growing middle class have rising expectations for individual freedom, mobility, money, private health and education, luxury commodities, cars, and so on. It is suggested that what is fuelling the discontent with autocratic regimes is middle-class aspiration for an unfettered market and frustration with the regimes that prevent them enjoying these benefits. To give credence to this perspective, the African Development Bank and the World Bank claim that Africa has a burgeoning middle class: apparently one in three Africans are today middle class, based on the ridiculous and laughable definition of that class as being those with an income of \$2–\$20 a day, 'a group that includes a vast number of people considered extremely poor by any reasonable definition, given the higher prices of most consumer durables in African cities' (Bond 2011). Conveniently forgotten, of course, is that 61 per cent of Africans, who are below the \$2-a-day level, are mired in deep poverty (Bond 2011).

However, the mass uprisings and protests that erupted across the continent and in the Middle East, as well as those that we have witnessed in Wisconsin, Ohio, France, Spain, Italy, and the 'sub-clinical' discontent manifested in the emergence of protests by social movements, share a similar impetus.

Whatever one might have to say about the shortcomings of the post-independence governments in Africa – whether of the first or second waves – whatever we might think about the shortcomings of some of the social and political policies, whatever we

3

might say about the undemocratic nature of the regimes that were established, we have to acknowledge their extraordinary achievements over a relatively short period of time after independence. In the space of less than two decades, through the establishment of universal health care, education and social welfare, the expansion and development of transport and communications, and the establishment of grain marketing boards and cooperatives, there were dramatic improvements in life expectancy at birth, infant and child mortality, maternal mortality, university education, and many other parameters of social progress. All these gains were the result of hard-fought independence struggles through which many lives were lost and much blood shed. The regimes of independence had in effect struck a social contract with the mass movements that brought them to power, and in some measure, as part of a modernisation project, they sought to deliver on their promises, albeit in an uneven way (Manji 1998).

But over the last 30 years, countries in the global South, and in particular in Africa, have seen the systematic reversal of the gains of independence. These reversals emerged in the context of a number of major world events: the spiralling worldwide recession of the 1970s; the defeat of the US in Vietnam; the delinking of the dollar from the gold standard and floating of currencies; the emergence of OPEC, which enabled oil-producing states to control the world price of oil, and the resulting glut of capital which flooded the market seeking new avenues for profits; the debt crisis of countries in the global South, as their currencies became devalued; and the establishment of the hegemony of the New Right and its neoliberal policies under the tutelage of Margaret Thatcher in the UK and Ronald Reagan in the US in the 1980s.

Almost without exception, the same set of social and economic policies were implemented under pressure from the international financial institutions across the African continent – the so-called structural adjustment programmes (later rebranded the poverty reduction strategy programmes), all to ensure that African countries serviced the growing debt. But the agenda of the creditors was also to use the debt 'crisis' to open avenues for capital expansion, through extreme privatisation and liberalisation of African economies.

that are being insisted upon by the international finance
ons are the result of the structural needs of financialised
m in the present era, a process that began as early as the
d today dominates all parts of the global economy (Patnaik
here are today, according to Samir Amin, some 500–700
ies that control almost every aspect of our lives, whether
es we wear, transportation, communications, agriculture,
, natural resource extraction and so on (Amin 2010b).
worth quoting Patnaik at length here, for he captures
ly the structural nature of the demands of financialised
hat give rise to demands for specific economic conditions
filled. In the current period, he argues,

nce capital has become international, while the state
ns a nation-state. The nation-state, therefore, willy-nilly
bow before the wishes of finance, for otherwise finance …
ave that particular country and move elsewhere, reduc-
to illiquidity and disrupting its economy.
process of globalisation of finance, therefore, has the
of undermining the autonomy of the nation-state. The
annot do what it wishes to do, or what its elected govern-
has been elected to do, since it must do what finance
s it to do.
s in the nature of finance capital to oppose any state
ention, other than that which promotes its own interest.
not want an activist state when it comes to the promo-
employment, or the provision of welfare, or the protec-
small and petty producers; but it wants the state to be
exclusively in its own interest. It therefore brings about
ge in the nature of the state, from being an apparently
class entity standing above society and intervening in a
lent manner for 'social good', to one that is concerned
exclusively with the interests of finance capital. To
this change, which occurs in the era of globalisation
pressure from finance capital, the interests of finance are
singly passed off as being synonymous with the interests
ety. If the stock market is doing well then the economy is
ed to be doing well, no matter what happens to the level
ger, malnutrition and poverty. If a country is graded well
dit-rating agencies then that becomes a matter of national
no matter how miserable its people are.

The state was declared 'inefficient' (despite its considerable
achievements in the short period since independence), and public
services were run down before being sold off to the oligopolies
for a song. The state was prohibited from subsidising agricultural
production and investing in social infrastructure, with prohibitions on capital investment in health, education, transport and
telecommunications, until eventually public goods were taken
over by the 'private' (read oligopoly) sector. Tariff barriers to
goods from the advanced capitalist countries were removed;
access to natural resources opened up for pillaging; tax regimes
relaxed; and 'export processing zones' established to enable raw
exploitation of labour without any regulations from the state or
trade unions. Over time, privatisation was extended to agriculture, land, and food production and distribution (Manji 1998,
Manji, Free and Mark 2011).

Landlessness, unemployment, increases in child, infant and
maternal mortality rates, decline in life-expectancy rates and
impoverishment on an unprecedented scale came to be the lot
of the majority of citizens, while a minority accumulated and
enriched themselves through their control of the state and alliance with international corporations (Manji 1998). Countries
whose populations were characterised as being more than 80 per
cent rural only two decades ago were transformed so that today
the UN Habitat estimates that some 50 per cent live in the peri-
urban slums with no rights of abode, tenure or any other form of
security. Deregulation of all constraints on capital was the mantra
of the day, justified as the precondition for encouraging foreign
investment, which in turn would supposedly lead to 'development' (Habitat 2010).

The net effect was to reduce the state to having a narrowly
prescribed role in economic affairs, and precious little authority
or resources to devote to the development of social infrastructure.
Its primary role was to ensure an 'enabling environment' for
international capital and to police the endless servicing of debt to
international finance institutions (Amin 2010a).

But the most serious consequence of these policies was
not the reversal of the many gains of independence, but the
erosion of the ability of citizens to control their own destinies.
Self-determination, originally such a powerful motor force for

mobilisation in the anti-colonial movement, was gradually suffocated. Economic policies were no longer determined by citizens and their representatives in government, but by technocrats from the international finance institutions such as the World Bank, with hefty support provided by the international aid agencies. As the state was forced to retreat from the provision of social services, the space was avidly occupied by the development NGOs (nongovernmental organisations). What citizens once had a right to expect by virtue of the gains of independence was replaced by the charitable acts of agencies that were dependent on the support of international aid institutions whose policies were increasingly aligned with those of the international financial institutions (Manji and O'Coill 2002).

This was also a period of significant repression. Political opposition in most countries was discouraged or suppressed; opponents of government were locked up or disappeared. Where progressive developments occurred – as in Burkina Faso under Thomas Sankara – assassinations, support for military coups and economic isolation were some of the weapons used to prevent citizens having the audacity to construct alternatives to the crass policies of neoliberalism. With the collapse of the Berlin Wall and Stalinist 'socialism' in the Soviet Union and Eastern Europe at the end of the 1980s, the credibility of alternatives to capitalist ideologies collapsed too. Without a coherent alternative to the dominant ideologies of capitalism, Thatcher's famous claim of TINA (there is no alternative) became a reality.

Over time, one of the consequences of neoliberal economic policies was the gradual transformation of citizens into consumers. Those with the resources could exercise choice on where they bought their services, education and health care. Power and influence over social policy were increasingly determined by wealth. But those who had no means to participate in consumer society – the pauperised, the landless, the jobless, the never-employed – those unable to consume, were left effectively disenfranchised, and those able to find employment were forced to accept poor working conditions and low wages. Attempts to organise or protest were discouraged by the knowledge that outside stood a reserve army of labour, ever hungry to take jobs from those fortunate enough to have them.

The scale of looting that became possi eral policies is well documented. Each yea of $340 billion flow northwards to serv more than five times the G8's developme 2005). At more than $10 billion a year collectively the citizens of Nigeria, Côte Republic of Congo (DRC), Angola and cially vulnerable to the overseas drain As Brussels-based debt campaigner E 'Since 1980, over 50 Marshall Plans wor been sent by the peoples of the Peripher Centre' (Bond 2005).

Research by the Tax Justice Networ staggering $11.5 trillion has been siphor individuals, held in tax havens where contributing to government revenues. 'A Saharan Africa's GDP is moved offshore (2006) of TJN. 'As several studies have su flight means that Africa – a continent irrevocably indebted – may actually be the world' (Christensen 2006). And finan tions do all they can to hide their wealt UNDP report on illicit funds estimates developed countries have increased fr $20.2 billion in 2008. The top ten export for 63 per cent of total outflows from the while the top 20 account for nearly 83 p

Corruption, far from being the cause consequence of neoliberal ideology the 'incentives' as a necessary part of hum tives ensure that finance capital and olig ture that guarantees compliance to thei a local class that is motivated to collabo has become, therefore, a fundamental s ism in the global South in the era of glo

Many criticise the structural adju their successors, as being the product policies that are said to be dogmatic a fundamentalism. But, as Prabhat Patn

Since the nation-state pursuing trade liberalisation has to cut customs duties, and therefore must restrict excise duties (so as not to discriminate between domestic and foreign capitalists), and since, in the interests of 'capital accumulation' it keeps taxes on corporate incomes ... low, the limit on the fiscal deficit causes an expenditure deflation on its part. And this provides the setting for 'privatising' not only state-owned assets 'for a song' but also welfare services and social overheads like education and health. All this is usually referred to as constituting a 'withdrawal of the state' and its rationale is debated in terms of 'the state' versus 'the market'. Nothing could be more wrong than this. The state under neoliberalism does not withdraw; it is involved as closely as before, or even more closely than before, in the economy, but its intervention is now of a different sort, viz. exclusively in the interests of finance capital. (Patnaik 2011)

What we face across the continent is a process of massive dispossession: dispossession of land through land grabbing, dispossession of the value of our wages, dispossession of our ability to produce what we, rather than what international finance capital, wants. The extent of land grabbing that is occurring across the continent illustrates the scale of what is going on: a recent set of reports from the Oakland Institute shows that 'land grabs encompassing the size of France, displacing thousands of families, building miles of irrigation canals without concern for environmental impacts, allowing crops to be planted that do not improve food security for Africa – done with little or no consultation with those directly impacted, and have no accountability or transparency' (Oakland Institute 2011).

But perhaps the most serious dispossession that we face is a political dispossession. Our governments are more accountable today to the international financial institutions, to the corporations that extract wealth without restriction, and to the international aid agencies that finance institutions such as the IMF, than to citizens. In this sense, our countries are increasingly becoming more akin to occupied territories than democracies.

It is this process of dispossession that was behind the eruption of citizens of Tunisia and Egypt. In both cases it was not only the repressive nature of the Ben Ali and Mubarak regimes, but also the accumulated years of experience of 'pauperisation' or impoverishment of the majority, while a few enriched themselves. When Ben Ali and Mubarak were swept out of power by the popular uprisings, there was an immediate resonance across the continent. While the media sought to portray this as some form of contagious disease, the reality was that the dispossessed across the continent and beyond recognised in the anger and demands of the Tunisians and Egyptians their own demand to reclaim their own dignity, and the aspirations of their own desires. They recognised immediately the common experience of the decades of neoliberalism that had impoverished them. It was no surprise that as far away as Wisconsin, Barcelona, Bahrain, Syria and Yemen the call to establish 'Tahrir Squares' has been on the lips of activists.

Rolling back the gains

What then has been the response of empire to the uprisings?

The sweeping away of Ben Ali in Tunisia and of Hosni Mubarak in Egypt took the imperial governments, who had been ardently supporting those regimes financially, economically, politically and militarily, completely by surprise. The corporate media sought to present the uprisings as sudden and spontaneous, despite the evidence in both countries that the eventual pouring of people on to the streets was the outcome of years of attempts to organise protests that had been brutally suppressed. Corporate media sought to present the mobilisations as being the product of Twitter and Facebook, obscuring the agency of people, and conveniently forgetting that in Egypt the largest mobilisation occurred after both the internet and mobile phone networks had been blocked.

Imperial response to the uprisings has been, in essence, to establish in Tunisia Ben Ali-ism without Ben Ali, and in Egypt, Mubarak-ism without Mubarak. It is instructive to note the profound hypocrisy of US and European governments: in Egypt, they had sought to present Mubarak as a bastion against Islamists in the form of the Muslim Brotherhood. As Samir Amin has pointed out (Amin 2011), Mubarakism comprised the Mubarak family, the military (who control major sectors of the economy) and the Muslim Brotherhood (who, since the days of Anwar Sadat, had been given a direct role in media and in education).

With the fall of Mubarak, it is hardly surprising that the US has been eager to push for the formation of a government comprising the remaining components of Mubarakism – the military and the Muslim Brotherhood. But what is even more instructive are the economic policies now being pushed by the IMF and World Bank: privatisation of the commons, opening up of the economy to the transnational corporations, reduction in social expenditure – in short, the very same worn-out policies that led to the crisis in the first place.

While empire is seeking to contain the mass movements in both Tunisia and Egypt, it is by no means a foregone conclusion that the transformations brought about by the uprisings will be successfully reversed. The military has certainly been active in seeking to intimidate, imprison and torture activists, while the US seeks to apply all kinds of pressures to ensure that compliant regimes are established to protect the interests not only of the oligopolies, but also, of course, of the Zionist state of Israel.

What we have witnessed in Tunisia and Egypt is but Act 1, Scene 1 of a long struggle that may take many decades to reach a transformative conclusion. Revolutions don't happen overnight. They are the product of long struggles over decades that are characterised by upswings and downswings. It is not possible to predict the outcomes of these long struggles, and much will depend on the kind of political programmes that progressive forces within the mass movement are able to advance and how they succeed in organising themselves.

Regime change and military intervention under the guise of humanitarianism

If the events in Tunisia and Egypt inspired hope, its twin, despair, is perhaps what is dominant in relation to Libya, Côte d'Ivoire and Somalia. What may have begun as popular protests in Libya, inspired by the events in neighbouring Tunisia, very soon became captured by the splits within the Gaddafi regime. There appears to be evidence that the rebellion in Libya was nurtured, armed and orchestrated long before there were spontaneous demonstrations, with plans for regime change mapped out well in advance. Ismael Hossein-Zadeh (2011) has pointed out that Gaddafi has much in common with nationalist populist leaders such as Hugo Chavez of Venezuela, Fidel Castro of Cuba, Evo Morales of Bolivia, Salvador Allende of Chile and Jean-Bertrand Aristide of Haiti:

> Gaddafi is guilty of insubordination to the proverbial godfather of the world: US imperialism and its allies. Like them, he has committed the cardinal sin of challenging the unbridled reign of global capital, of not following the economic 'guidelines' of the captains of global finance, i.e. the International Monetary Fund, the World Bank and the World Trade Organisation, and of refusing to join US military alliances in the region. Also, like other nationalist/populist leaders, he advocates social safety net (or welfare state) programs – not for giant corporations, as is the case in imperialist countries, but for the people in need. (Hossein-Zadeh 2011)

Under the now completely discredited excuse of 'humanitarian intervention',[1] the UN-authorised invasion delegated to NATO has involved large-scale bombing, the use of drones and the killing of civilians. Far from protecting citizens, the intervention has created a civil war between the so-called 'rebel' forces and those supporting Gaddafi. All attempts to establish a basis for negotiation have been systematically undermined by NATO and its allies.

Similarly, the UN-authorised intervention in Côte d'Ivoire was a thinly disguised regime-change initiative that has guaranteed corporations control of the lucrative economic resources of the country, in which French and US concerns in particular have gained. What it has failed to resolve are the deep divisions within Ivorian society.

And in Somalia, every attempt to reconstitute a semblance of peace has been systematically undermined with the aid of military intervention by the Meles government of Ethiopia, acting as a proxy of empire.

These events illustrate the growing willingness of empire to intervene militarily to ensure that the regimes that serve its interests are guaranteed. They represent precisely the mirror image of hope that the uprisings demonstrate. They are also consistent with the increasing willingness of empire to engage openly in the barbarism that the world has witnessed in Afghanistan and Iraq, and increasingly in Pakistan.

The state was declared 'inefficient' (despite its considerable achievements in the short period since independence), and public services were run down before being sold off to the oligopolies for a song. The state was prohibited from subsidising agricultural production and investing in social infrastructure, with prohibitions on capital investment in health, education, transport and telecommunications, until eventually public goods were taken over by the 'private' (read oligopoly) sector. Tariff barriers to goods from the advanced capitalist countries were removed; access to natural resources opened up for pillaging; tax regimes relaxed; and 'export processing zones' established to enable raw exploitation of labour without any regulations from the state or trade unions. Over time, privatisation was extended to agriculture, land, and food production and distribution (Manji 1998, Manji, Free and Mark 2011).

Landlessness, unemployment, increases in child, infant and maternal mortality rates, decline in life-expectancy rates and impoverishment on an unprecedented scale came to be the lot of the majority of citizens, while a minority accumulated and enriched themselves through their control of the state and alliance with international corporations (Manji 1998). Countries whose populations were characterised as being more than 80 per cent rural only two decades ago were transformed so that today the UN Habitat estimates that some 50 per cent live in the peri-urban slums with no rights of abode, tenure or any other form of security. Deregulation of all constraints on capital was the mantra of the day, justified as the precondition for encouraging foreign investment, which in turn would supposedly lead to 'development' (Habitat 2010).

The net effect was to reduce the state to having a narrowly prescribed role in economic affairs, and precious little authority or resources to devote to the development of social infrastructure. Its primary role was to ensure an 'enabling environment' for international capital and to police the endless servicing of debt to international finance institutions (Amin 2010a).

But the most serious consequence of these policies was not the reversal of the many gains of independence, but the erosion of the ability of citizens to control their own destinies. Self-determination, originally such a powerful motor force for mobilisation in the anti-colonial movement, was gradually suffocated. Economic policies were no longer determined by citizens and their representatives in government, but by technocrats from the international finance institutions such as the World Bank, with hefty support provided by the international aid agencies. As the state was forced to retreat from the provision of social services, the space was avidly occupied by the development NGOs (non-governmental organisations). What citizens once had a right to expect by virtue of the gains of independence was replaced by the charitable acts of agencies that were dependent on the support of international aid institutions whose policies were increasingly aligned with those of the international financial institutions (Manji and O'Coill 2002).

This was also a period of significant repression. Political opposition in most countries was discouraged or suppressed; opponents of government were locked up or disappeared. Where progressive developments occurred – as in Burkina Faso under Thomas Sankara – assassinations, support for military coups and economic isolation were some of the weapons used to prevent citizens having the audacity to construct alternatives to the crass policies of neoliberalism. With the collapse of the Berlin Wall and Stalinist 'socialism' in the Soviet Union and Eastern Europe at the end of the 1980s, the credibility of alternatives to capitalist ideologies collapsed too. Without a coherent alternative to the dominant ideologies of capitalism, Thatcher's famous claim of TINA (there is no alternative) became a reality.

Over time, one of the consequences of neoliberal economic policies was the gradual transformation of citizens into consumers. Those with the resources could exercise choice on where they bought their services, education and health care. Power and influence over social policy were increasingly determined by wealth. But those who had no means to participate in consumer society – the pauperised, the landless, the jobless, the never-employed – those unable to consume, were left effectively disenfranchised, and those able to find employment were forced to accept poor working conditions and low wages. Attempts to organise or protest were discouraged by the knowledge that outside stood a reserve army of labour, ever hungry to take jobs from those fortunate enough to have them.

The scale of looting that became possible as a result of neoliberal policies is well documented. Each year, third-world payments of $340 billion flow northwards to service a $2.2 trillion debt, more than five times the G8's development aid budget (Dembele 2005). At more than $10 billion a year since the early 1970s, collectively the citizens of Nigeria, Côte d'Ivoire, the Democratic Republic of Congo (DRC), Angola and Zambia have been especially vulnerable to the overseas drain of their national wealth. As Brussels-based debt campaigner Eric Toussaint concludes, 'Since 1980, over 50 Marshall Plans worth over $4.6 trillion have been sent by the peoples of the Periphery to their creditors in the Centre' (Bond 2005).

Research by the Tax Justice Network (TJN) estimates that a staggering $11.5 trillion has been siphoned 'offshore' by wealthy individuals, held in tax havens where they are shielded from contributing to government revenues. 'Around 30 per cent of sub-Saharan Africa's GDP is moved offshore', writes John Christensen (2006) of TJN. 'As several studies have suggested, this rate of capital flight means that Africa – a continent we are continually told is irrevocably indebted – may actually be a net creditor to the rest of the world' (Christensen 2006). And finance capital and the corporations do all they can to hide their wealth in offshore tax havens. A UNDP report on illicit funds estimates that illicit flows from least developed countries have increased from $7.9 billion in 1990 to $20.2 billion in 2008. The top ten exporters of illicit capital account for 63 per cent of total outflows from the least developed countries, while the top 20 account for nearly 83 per cent (UNDP 2011).

Corruption, far from being the cause of the crisis in Africa, is the consequence of neoliberal ideology that sees providing financial 'incentives' as a necessary part of human motivation. Such incentives ensure that finance capital and oligopolies have the infrastructure that guarantees compliance to their needs, and helps nurture a local class that is motivated to collaborate with them. Corruption has become, therefore, a fundamental structural feature of capitalism in the global South in the era of globalisation.

Many criticise the structural adjustment programmes, and their successors, as being the product of bad policy – neoliberal policies that are said to be dogmatic and an expression of market fundamentalism. But, as Prabhat Patnaik has argued recently, the policies that are being insisted upon by the international finance institutions are the result of the structural needs of financialised capitalism in the present era, a process that began as early as the 1970s and today dominates all parts of the global economy (Patnaik 2011). There are today, according to Samir Amin, some 500–700 oligopolies that control almost every aspect of our lives, whether the clothes we wear, transportation, communications, agriculture, industry, natural resource extraction and so on (Amin 2010b).

It is worth quoting Patnaik at length here, for he captures succinctly the structural nature of the demands of financialised capital that give rise to demands for specific economic conditions to be fulfilled. In the current period, he argues,

> [F]inance capital has become international, while the state remains a nation-state. The nation-state, therefore, willy-nilly must bow before the wishes of finance, for otherwise finance … will leave that particular country and move elsewhere, reducing it to illiquidity and disrupting its economy.
>
> The process of globalisation of finance, therefore, has the effect of undermining the autonomy of the nation-state. The state cannot do what it wishes to do, or what its elected government has been elected to do, since it must do what finance wishes it to do.
>
> It is in the nature of finance capital to oppose any state intervention, other than that which promotes its own interest. It does not want an activist state when it comes to the promotion of employment, or the provision of welfare, or the protection of small and petty producers; but it wants the state to be active exclusively in its own interest. It therefore brings about a change in the nature of the state, from being an apparently supra-class entity standing above society and intervening in a benevolent manner for 'social good', to one that is concerned almost exclusively with the interests of finance capital. To justify this change, which occurs in the era of globalisation under pressure from finance capital, the interests of finance are increasingly passed off as being synonymous with the interests of society. If the stock market is doing well then the economy is supposed to be doing well, no matter what happens to the level of hunger, malnutrition and poverty. If a country is graded well by credit-rating agencies then that becomes a matter of national pride, no matter how miserable its people are.

Since the nation-state pursuing trade liberalisation has to cut customs duties, and therefore must restrict excise duties (so as not to discriminate between domestic and foreign capitalists), and since, in the interests of 'capital accumulation' it keeps taxes on corporate incomes ... low, the limit on the fiscal deficit causes an expenditure deflation on its part. And this provides the setting for 'privatising' not only state-owned assets 'for a song' but also welfare services and social overheads like education and health. All this is usually referred to as constituting a 'withdrawal of the state' and its rationale is debated in terms of 'the state' versus 'the market'. Nothing could be more wrong than this. The state under neoliberalism does not withdraw; it is involved as closely as before, or even more closely than before, in the economy, but its intervention is now of a different sort, viz. exclusively in the interests of finance capital. (Patnaik 2011)

What we face across the continent is a process of massive dispossession: dispossession of land through land grabbing, dispossession of the value of our wages, dispossession of our ability to produce what we, rather than what international finance capital, wants. The extent of land grabbing that is occurring across the continent illustrates the scale of what is going on: a recent set of reports from the Oakland Institute shows that 'land grabs encompassing the size of France, displacing thousands of families, building miles of irrigation canals without concern for environmental impacts, allowing crops to be planted that do not improve food security for Africa – done with little or no consultation with those directly impacted, and have no accountability or transparency' (Oakland Institute 2011).

But perhaps the most serious dispossession that we face is a political dispossession. Our governments are more accountable today to the international financial institutions, to the corporations that extract wealth without restriction, and to the international aid agencies that finance institutions such as the IMF, than to citizens. In this sense, our countries are increasingly becoming more akin to occupied territories than democracies.

It is this process of dispossession that was behind the eruption of citizens of Tunisia and Egypt. In both cases it was not only the repressive nature of the Ben Ali and Mubarak regimes, but also the accumulated years of experience of 'pauperisation' or impoverishment of the majority, while a few enriched themselves. When Ben Ali and Mubarak were swept out of power by the popular uprisings, there was an immediate resonance across the continent. While the media sought to portray this as some form of contagious disease, the reality was that the dispossessed across the continent and beyond recognised in the anger and demands of the Tunisians and Egyptians their own demand to reclaim their own dignity, and the aspirations of their own desires. They recognised immediately the common experience of the decades of neoliberalism that had impoverished them. It was no surprise that as far away as Wisconsin, Barcelona, Bahrain, Syria and Yemen the call to establish 'Tahrir Squares' has been on the lips of activists.

Rolling back the gains

What then has been the response of empire to the uprisings?

The sweeping away of Ben Ali in Tunisia and of Hosni Mubarak in Egypt took the imperial governments, who had been ardently supporting those regimes financially, economically, politically and militarily, completely by surprise. The corporate media sought to present the uprisings as sudden and spontaneous, despite the evidence in both countries that the eventual pouring of people on to the streets was the outcome of years of attempts to organise protests that had been brutally suppressed. Corporate media sought to present the mobilisations as being the product of Twitter and Facebook, obscuring the agency of people, and conveniently forgetting that in Egypt the largest mobilisation occurred after both the internet and mobile phone networks had been blocked.

Imperial response to the uprisings has been, in essence, to establish in Tunisia Ben Ali-ism without Ben Ali, and in Egypt, Mubarak-ism without Mubarak. It is instructive to note the profound hypocrisy of US and European governments: in Egypt, they had sought to present Mubarak as a bastion against Islamists in the form of the Muslim Brotherhood. As Samir Amin has pointed out (Amin 2011), Mubarakism comprised the Mubarak family, the military (who control major sectors of the economy) and the Muslim Brotherhood (who, since the days of Anwar Sadat, had been given a direct role in media and in education).

With the fall of Mubarak, it is hardly surprising that the US has been eager to push for the formation of a government comprising the remaining components of Mubarakism – the military and the Muslim Brotherhood. But what is even more instructive are the economic policies now being pushed by the IMF and World Bank: privatisation of the commons, opening up of the economy to the transnational corporations, reduction in social expenditure – in short, the very same worn-out policies that led to the crisis in the first place.

While empire is seeking to contain the mass movements in both Tunisia and Egypt, it is by no means a foregone conclusion that the transformations brought about by the uprisings will be successfully reversed. The military has certainly been active in seeking to intimidate, imprison and torture activists, while the US seeks to apply all kinds of pressures to ensure that compliant regimes are established to protect the interests not only of the oligopolies, but also, of course, of the Zionist state of Israel.

What we have witnessed in Tunisia and Egypt is but Act 1, Scene 1 of a long struggle that may take many decades to reach a transformative conclusion. Revolutions don't happen overnight. They are the product of long struggles over decades that are characterised by upswings and downswings. It is not possible to predict the outcomes of these long struggles, and much will depend on the kind of political programmes that progressive forces within the mass movement are able to advance and how they succeed in organising themselves.

Regime change and military intervention under the guise of humanitarianism

If the events in Tunisia and Egypt inspired hope, its twin, despair, is perhaps what is dominant in relation to Libya, Côte d'Ivoire and Somalia. What may have begun as popular protests in Libya, inspired by the events in neighbouring Tunisia, very soon became captured by the splits within the Gaddafi regime. There appears to be evidence that the rebellion in Libya was nurtured, armed and orchestrated long before there were spontaneous demonstrations, with plans for regime change mapped out well in advance. Ismael Hossein-Zadeh (2011) has pointed out that Gaddafi has much in common with nationalist populist leaders such as Hugo Chavez of Venezuela, Fidel Castro of Cuba, Evo Morales of Bolivia, Salvador Allende of Chile and Jean-Bertrand Aristide of Haiti:

> Gaddafi is guilty of insubordination to the proverbial godfather of the world: US imperialism and its allies. Like them, he has committed the cardinal sin of challenging the unbridled reign of global capital, of not following the economic 'guidelines' of the captains of global finance, i.e. the International Monetary Fund, the World Bank and the World Trade Organisation, and of refusing to join US military alliances in the region. Also, like other nationalist/populist leaders, he advocates social safety net (or welfare state) programs – not for giant corporations, as is the case in imperialist countries, but for the people in need. (Hossein-Zadeh 2011)

Under the now completely discredited excuse of 'humanitarian intervention',[1] the UN-authorised invasion delegated to NATO has involved large-scale bombing, the use of drones and the killing of civilians. Far from protecting citizens, the intervention has created a civil war between the so-called 'rebel' forces and those supporting Gaddafi. All attempts to establish a basis for negotiation have been systematically undermined by NATO and its allies.

Similarly, the UN-authorised intervention in Côte d'Ivoire was a thinly disguised regime-change initiative that has guaranteed corporations control of the lucrative economic resources of the country, in which French and US concerns in particular have gained. What it has failed to resolve are the deep divisions within Ivorian society.

And in Somalia, every attempt to reconstitute a semblance of peace has been systematically undermined with the aid of military intervention by the Meles government of Ethiopia, acting as a proxy of empire.

These events illustrate the growing willingness of empire to intervene militarily to ensure that the regimes that serve its interests are guaranteed. They represent precisely the mirror image of hope that the uprisings demonstrate. They are also consistent with the increasing willingness of empire to engage openly in the barbarism that the world has witnessed in Afghanistan and Iraq, and increasingly in Pakistan.

A period of wars and revolutions

Samir Amin (2010b) has pointed out that the current crisis of capitalism – which he locates as beginning in the 1970s, with the delinking of the dollar from the gold standard – has parallels with the first major crisis of industrial capitalism almost 100 years previously in the 1870s. The consequence of that crisis was the colonisation of the world and the division of Africa into colonial territories, the wide-scale grabbing of land and resources, brutal mass killings and genocide, and the growing concentration and centralisation of capital. The period following that saw the massacre of millions in the inter-imperial war of 1914–18, the depression that led to the rise of fascism in Europe, and the outbreak of the Second World War, which killed millions. But the same period also saw the first successful anti-capitalist revolution in Russia, the successful peasant-led revolutions in China, the rise of the anti-colonial revolutions, the defeat of first the French and then the US in Vietnam, and the revolution in Cuba. But the current crisis of capitalism is different from the earlier one in that the scale of concentration and centralisation of capital is unprecedented; it is also accompanied by a financialisation of capital on an unprecedented scale.

We have entered a new period of wars and revolution, a period of barbarism or social transformation. In Africa we have seen the devastation of Somalia, the destruction of the natural environment in places such as the Niger Delta, the military interventions in Libya and Côte d'Ivoire, to say nothing of the arming of regimes that ensure the illegal occupation of Western Sahara. At the same time we see the emergence of social movements reasserting the dignity of our people through the protests and uprisings that have developed across the continent. The outcome of all these events cannot be foreseen. But there are grounds for optimism.

What way forward?

As our governments genuflect to the corporations and international financial institutions and ignore the wishes of their citizens, the solution on offer is the fetishisation of the ballot box, where citizens are presented merely with choices between different versions of the same comprador elite elements. What this approach ignores is that while citizens may have a chance to vote once every four to five years, finance capital votes every day on the stock markets, a vote that has direct consequences for every aspect of production, and the prices of everyday goods, fuel, land, and so on.

If we are to regain control over our own destinies and dignity, we need to consider not so much how to use the ballot box but rather how we democratise our societies. What kind of processes do we need to allow us to democratise every aspect of our lives? For example, who determines what is produced, how it is produced, by whom it is produced, how much is produced, for whom is it produced and what is done with the product? And how do citizens decide on how the surplus is used? The same goes for all sectors: health, education, social welfare, telecommunications, agriculture, natural resource extraction.

Of course, such decision making would be anathema to finance capital, to the corporations, and to those compliant governments who have neither the courage nor the will to stand up to them. Unless citizens themselves have direct control and say over these critical issues, democracy simply does not exist. Instead we are faced with decision making that is in essence based on the same old structures that ensured colonial domination and control.

We need to be creative. We do not need to go shopping for 'off the peg' answers at the supermarkets of the corporations, banks and finance houses. It is time we had the courage to invent the future. Either we do that, or others will determine our future for us.

There are a number of important features of the present situation that are favourable for beginning to build the kind of world that we want to live in.

First, there is little doubt that because of the extent of the financialisation of capital and its dominance in the current era, the ruling classes face a dilemma: financialised capital demands that neoliberal policies be implemented relentlessly – from the perspective of capital, there is no alternative. Yet these are precisely the policies that have created the current crisis. Einstein's famous statement captures this dead end: 'You can't solve a problem by using the same kind of thinking that created the problem.' There is, in effect, a bankruptcy of ideas. This presents us with an opportunity. In Latin America, ALBA countries (Bolivarian Alliance for the Peoples of Our America) are seeking to develop social, political, and economic integration between the countries of Latin America and the Caribbean, based on a vision of social welfare, bartering and mutual economic aid, rather than trade liberalisation as with free-trade agreements. They are even planning to establish their own currencies. A similar debate needs to be opened up in Africa.

Second, one of the striking features of today's world is the degree to which there is growing recognition across the global South of the commonalities in experience of the dispossessed. Indeed, there is even recognition of those commonalities emerging in the North – as in the recent uprisings in Wisconsin, Spain and Greece. For the first time in many years, we see the potential to create solidarity links with people in struggle based not on charity or pity, but on recognition of the common cause of our dispossession.

Third, whereas for many years social struggles have focused on single issues – for instance, water, energy, environment or health – today the material basis for cooperation between different sectors is greater than it has been for years. Initiatives such as the World Social Forum, for all its shortcomings, provide an exceptional opportunity for forging both cross-sectoral and inter-regional solidarity.

Fourth, since the collapse of Stalinism and the Soviet Union, there has been a crisis of credibility in the dogmas that have so long imprisoned progressive and creative thinking about the kind of world we want to live in. At a time when the credibility of neoliberal ideas is in crisis, this means that there is greater room for creativity as well as learning from the mistakes that have been made by the left internationally.

Finally, while recognising that there are many struggles against those who seek to exploit Africa, there are opportunities also to create today the alternatives to the profit-driven motives of corporations. For example, African farmers' organisations are confronting the onslaught of powerful actors such as the Bill and Melinda Gates Foundation and the Rockefeller Foundation, backed by oligopolies like Monsanto, who are 'pushing agro-chemical crops using multi-genome patents. The objective of the corporations

– or at least the end result – is plain to see: the control over Africa's plant biomass to generate super-profits for mega-chemical and seed corporations' (Tandon 2011). Yet at the same time, farmers and peasant organisations, especially those led by women, have been organising to counter this by launching their own campaign, 'We are the solution: celebrating African family farming systems', in which indigenous knowledge and sustainable farming methods are promoted.

What these movements understand is that now is the time for us to chart a new path towards freedom and justice, ensuring that emancipation is not some distant dream but rather something that we make happen today. The outcome of our struggles for emancipation is not in the hands of the gods, but in our own ideas, struggles and solidarity. We have the capacity to influence, if not determine, the way things will turn out. But to do so, we have to have the courage to invent the future. Let me leave the last words to Thomas Sankara:

> You cannot carry out fundamental change without a certain amount of madness. In this case, it comes from nonconformity, the courage to turn your back on the old formulas, the courage to invent the future. It took the madmen of yesterday for us to be able to act with extreme clarity today. I want to be one of those madmen. (Sankara 1985)

§

This book comprises a selection of essays published in Pambazuka News during the first six months of 2011. Our aim in publishing this volume has been to inform discussions about the nature of the uprisings, their causes and the prospects for the future. Selecting the essays has been a challenge because of the wealth of analyses and commentaries available. We long debated about how to group the essays, whether geographically or thematically. Ultimately, we decided that it would be best to present them chronologically, to give a sense of the growing excitement of catching history on its wings.

Pambazuka News (*pambazuka* in Kiswahili means the 'awakening') has provided probably the most comprehensive coverage to be found of the struggles of African peoples for dignity, self-determination and emancipation that have swept the continent during 2011. Pambazuka News provides a unique and dynamic platform for a voluntary network of more than 2,800 writers, thinkers, activists, artists, bloggers and organisations. Inevitably, without paid stringers across the continent, there has been some unevenness in the coverage of the uprisings. That unevenness is reflected in this collection.

There is no doubt that, given the unpredictable speed of unfolding revolutions, by time the book is published there will have been further developments of significance on the continent. That does not mean that the perspectives provided in this collection will have become 'dated'. On the contrary, these essays will provide an essential basis for understanding the dynamics of the emerging revolutions. To continue following events since July 2011, we invite you to be a regular visitor to the Pambazuka News website: www.pambazuka.org.

http://pambazuka.org/en/category/features/74882

Note

1. Interestingly, 'humanitarian intervention' was also the excuse used to justify King Leopold's brutal colonisation of the Congo (see Hochschild 2011).

References

Amin, S. (2010a) 'Millennium Development Goals: a critique from the South', Pambazuka News, http://pambazuka.org/en/category/features/67326, accessed 28 July 2011

Amin, S. (2010b) *Ending the Crisis of Capitalism or Ending Capitalism*, Oxford, Pambazuka Press

Amin, S. (2011) '2011: an Arab spring?', in *African Awakening: The Emerging Revolutions*, Manji, F. and Ekine, S. (eds), Oxford, Pambazuka Press

Bond, P. (2005) 'Dispossessing Africa's wealth', Pambazuka News, http://www.pambazuka.org/en/category/features/30074, accessed 28 July 2011

Bond, P. (2010) 'South African's financial bubble and boiling social protest', paper presented at the *Socialist Register* workshop on crisis, Toronto, February, http://ccs.ukzn.ac.za/files/Bond%20SA%20financial%20bubble%20and%20boiling%20protest.pdf, accessed 7 September 2011

Bond, P. (2011) 'Latest fibs from world financiers', Pambazuka News, http://pambazuka.org/en/category/features/73149, accessed 28 July 2011

Christensen, J. (2006) 'Tax justice for Africa: a new development struggle', Pambazuka News, http://www.pambazuka.org/en/category/comment/31903, accessed 28 July 2011

Dembele, D.M. (2005) 'Aid dependence and the MDGs', Pambazuka News http://www.pambazuka.org/en/category/features/29376, accessed 30 September 2011

Habitat (2010) *State of the World's Cities*, Nairobi, UN Habitat

Hochschild, A. (2011) *King Leopold's Ghost*, London, Pan Books

Hossein-Zadeh, I. (2011) 'Why regime change in Libya?', Pambazuka News http://www.pambazuka.org/en/category/features/74278, accessed 28 July 2011

Manji, F. (1998) 'The depoliticisation of poverty', in Eade, D. (ed), *Development and Rights*, Oxford, Oxfam: 12–33

Manji, F. and O'Coill, C. (2002) 'The missionary position: NGOs and development in Africa', *International Affairs*: 78(3): 567–83

Manji, F., Free, A. and Mark, C. (2011) 'New media in Africa: tools for liberation or means of subjugation', in *New Media, Alternative Politics*, Working Paper 2, Cambridge (in press)

Oakland Institute (2011) 'Why did the Oakland Institute publish its findings on land grabs in Africa?', http://media.oaklandinstitute.org/why-did-oakland-institute-publish-its-findings-land-grabs-africa, accessed 28 July 2011

Patnaik, P. (2011) 'Notes on imperialism: phases of imperialism', Pambazuka News, http://www.pambazuka.org/en/category/features/70060, accessed 28 July 2011

Sankara, T. (1985) 'Daring to invent the future: interview with Jean-Phillippe Rapp', in *Thomas Sankara Speaks: The Burkina Faso Revolution 1983–1987*, New York/London, Pathfinder Press

Tandon, Y. (2011) 'Kleptocratic capitalism: challenges of the green economy for sustainable Africa', Pambazuka News, http://www.pambazuka.org/en/category/features/74507, accessed 28 July 2011

UNDP (2011) 'Illicit financial flows from the least developed countries (LDCs) 1990–2008', http://www.beta.undp.org/undp/en/home/librarypage/poverty-reduction/illicit-flows-1990-2008.html, accessed 14 August 2011

2

The never-ending revolution: perspectives from the African blogosphere

Sokari Ekine

In February three things became clear to the editors of Pambazuka News. First, keeping abreast of the numerous uprisings and protests[1] across the continent was becoming a challenge; second, coverage of the uprisings and protests in Africa was uneven and selective; and third, the social media – Twitter, YouTube, blogs and Facebook – were fast becoming crucial sources of information on the uprisings. In response Pambazuka News began a series of weekly summaries, covering both the high-profile 'revolutions' and the less overt uprisings which were happening in countries in the east, west and south of the continent. The aim was to show that voices of revolution do not have to be highly vocal and visible. On the contrary, there are thousands of activists and social justice movements from across Africa and the diaspora who are totally committed to changing the socio-political landscape in their countries.

Revolutions are a complex process of competing interests and multiple tensions, as we witnessed in the chaotic militarisation following the removal of Mubarak. The street protests and associated cyber activism that remove a dictator are but one small step towards liberation. What has to follow is a decolonisation of the figuratively decolonised, a process which Fanon (1963) asserts:

> demands a sustained, quotidian commitment to the strug-
> gle for national liberation, for when the high, heady wind of
> revolution loses its velocity, there is no question of bridging
> the gap in one giant stride. The epic is played out on a difficult

day-to-day basis and the suffering endured far exceeds that of the 'colonial' period'.

The back story, which helps to explain the sustainability (so far) of the Egyptian uprising, is the movement building and networking which took place over the previous five years between political activists both within Egypt and across the whole Middle East North Africa (MENA) and Middle East regions.

Cynthia Boaz of the International Center on Nonviolent Conflict had been in touch with many of the activists at the forefront of the 25 January movement in Egypt. She is emphatic that there was nothing spontaneous about the uprising, although even the organisers of the 25 January protest in Tahrir Square could not have known it would lead to the overthrow of Hosni Mubarak:

'[W]hat is now known as the January 25 Movement, while sparked by a similar revolt in Tunisia, was anything but impromptu.

'I didn't know they were planning … to start on Jan. 25,' she said, 'but I knew the movement had planned for a major action. It's an organized, planned, disciplined movement.'

'It isn't like these movements have emerged overnight. They've just been waiting for an opportunity,' Boaz said.

Libya is an exception because 'it's not organized, there's not a coherent, unified message,' she said. 'It's not disciplined, and it's not non-violent.'

Egyptian activists worked for years to identify and neutralize the sources of power in the nation of 83 million. Their effort extended to having coffee with members of the Army…

'It's a very nuanced divide and conquer strategy,' Boaz said. 'You genuinely build real relationships with people, and you begin to help them question the legitimacy of the ruler and the system they're upholding.' (NAN 2011)

Much of the activism took place around supporting and documenting the numerous strikes, protests and campaigns during the period. In this way activists were able to build a solid foundation based on collective consciousness and shared skills, which has led to a strong popular movement. With the creative and non-instrumental uses of new media technologies, the emperor is made naked and his secrets exposed and what appears to be spontaneous is in fact 'a movement waiting for a strategic moment in time' (NAN 2011).

But the process of revolution cannot be limited to nationalistic actions of solidarity. There must also be a transformation in social consciousness, otherwise struggles will be appropriated/co-opted by the elite within the state and the interests of foreign governments. The protests to remove Hosni Mubarak succeeded but in his place, the military elite have attempted to appropriate the revolution in the name of nationalism and have to a large extent replicated the repression and excesses of the Mubarak regime. The Egyptian activists have begun to recognise this as they witness the fragmentation of consensus, and old formations of solidarity and alliances begin to weave themselves back into the frame.

> Fanon is clear that if national consciousness does not turn into social consciousness then a predatory elite can capture the state and enrich themselves in the name of the nation. He is clear that when the national bourgeoisie is given the freedom to claim that it represents the people it is a real danger to the people. For Fanon the national bourgeoisie can never liberate the people. The people have to liberate themselves by a second struggle to turn national consciousness into a social consciousness. (Kota 2011)

During the first six months of 2011, protests, strikes and other actions took place in Zimbabwe, Senegal, Gabon, Sudan, Mauritania, Morocco, Algeria, Benin, Cameroon, Djibouti, Côte d'Ivoire, Burkina Faso, Botswana, Namibia, Uganda, Kenya, Malawi and Swaziland. Some protests have been single 'days of rage', others have lasted a few days or, as in the case of Gabon, Mauritania and Morocco, sporadically for months (Ekine 2011a). Others are like Zimbabwe, which has been in a state of revolt against the Mugabe regime since before the 2008 elections (Sokwanele 2008). Zimbabwe has a revolutionary history borne out in the Chimurenga war of independence, so it is not surprising that there is a vibrant civil society, with a strong female presence, which has a history of resistance to Robert Mugabe and Zanu-PF. Members of WOZA (Women of Zimbabwe Arise) have demonstrated over and over again; their members have been beaten, arrested and tortured but still they continue to take to the streets; for example in 2010 some members (Sokwanele 2011) were detained for celebrating International Peace Day. In February 2011, in a bizarre act of censorship, the Zimbabwean government arrested and tortured 52 social justice activists for watching and discussing a video on the Egyptian uprisings (Kubatana 2011):

> Zimbabwe is neither Tunisia nor Egypt. Far from it! In fact, Zimbabwe's political predicament is far worse than that of these two North African countries before their recent revolutions. But events in the two countries have certainly planted ideas in Zimbabweans' minds that may influence the country's future in a significant way. (Ncube 2011)

Trevor Ncube's points raise a number of questions on the character and timing of the present wave of protests strikes and actions (excluding Tunisia and Egypt) across the continent. First, how do we contextualise the protests historically; second, what connections can we make between the uprisings across the continent; and third, how has the level of repression impacted on the nature of the protests and their intensity? Activist and academic Katsiaficas (2011) presents an excellent example. In a recent interview on the Middle East uprising, he recounts a conversation with a member of the Karen Liberation Movement, who reflected that calling people to mass protests on the streets was inviting them to a massacre so to do so would be a mistake. Another way has to be found that works in a local context – some states are more repressive than others and, crucially, the armed forces do not always side with the people as in Tunisia and Egypt.

Here is the second set of questions. Are we noticing these protests because of what is happening in Egypt and Tunisia? After all, protests, strikes and campaigns have been ongoing for years. Are the protests happening in isolation or are activists working across national borders? What is it that is different about the present set of protests? In a sense these questions answer themselves. There is no doubt that the uprisings in Tunisia and Egypt, as we shall see, have influenced the wave of continental and regional protests and strikes, setting a benchmark for revolutionary imperatives and strategies. There is a uniqueness about these uprisings: they are taking place at this time – not last year or the next but in the now – and this is irrespective of the duration or outcome. There is a degree of synchronisation and cross-border action; a set of new technology tools have helped facilitate action and information is being disseminated in new ways. Fanon acknowledges the significance of new technology in 'changing consciousness' when he refers to the emergence of Radio Free Algeria which, like the social media of the time, became the voice of the revolution and changed how people accessed knowledge and information (Fanon 1963: 9).

In *A Dying Colonialism*, Fanon states that each generation will approach revolution in the context of their moment in history:

> Fanon insists that praxis must be rooted in the temporal, that each generation must confront the living reality of its own situation, accept its own call to battle, gather its own weapons, and, in the vortex of struggle, from within the collective mutation of popular political empowerment, produce its own truths. But while we do confront each situation straddling infinity, with its prospects for new secrets to be revealed, and nothingness, which condemns us to absolute responsibility for our choices in the face of the void, we do not step into that situation from nowhere. The contribution made by our ancestors in struggle is part of what makes us, and it provides us with some of our weapons. (Pithouse 2010: 3)

To some extent the protests appear in clusters of two or more, with often similar formation and ideals. Take for example Kenya and Uganda, which both have a large and vibrant civil society. Kenya's 'Unga Revolution' is focused on economic realities such as rising prices and high unemployment: '[A] collection of civil society groups, including Bunge La Mwananchi, campaigning for economic and social rights, have been formed in response to the rising cost of living and loss of social benefits' (Ekine 2011b).

Similarly, rising prices was the primary focus of the 'walk to work' campaign in Uganda, which began after the elections in April 2011. However, the response to both actions was significantly different. In Kenya a proposed May Day rally was banned while in Uganda protestors were met with live bullets, teargas and mass arrests (Kagumire 2011).

What seems like a brief moment in the history of Uganda represents a fundamental change in the power relations between state and citizens. A Ugandan reporter expressed this succinctly when she spoke of a new awareness of rights: '[M]any Ugandans are now aware of their rights to speak out. This right is provided by the state through the constitution that guarantees freedom of speech. So this time many Ugandans are supporting what the opposition is doing because they want the government to listen to their pleas' (Your Commonweatlh 2011).

West Africa, Burkina Faso and Senegal – possibly along with Swaziland further south – are the countries most desperate for political and social change (as opposed to having expressly economic concerns). While the Ugandan and Kenyan protests have focused on rising prices, Senegal and Burkina Faso are closer to Egypt and Tunisia geographically as well as having many 'structural similarities':

> Events in Tunisia, Egypt and Libya certainly have encouraged mobilisation in Burkina Faso, where people also want the current regime 'out'. From slogans such as 'Tunisia is in Koudougou' and 'Burkina will have its Egypt' to caricatures on Facebook, there are echoes of the Arab spring in the country and some youth groups in Koudougou have even compared Justin Zongo to Mohamed Bouaziz. In contrast to Ben Ali's Tunisia and Mubarak's Egypt, Burkina Faso has always had a certain degree of freedom of information and expression and the right to organise. It is easier for young people from underprivileged classes to meet and plan their actions in person rather than on the net.
>
> Essentially, the resemblance to the uprisings in the north lies in structural similarities – an unequal society, high unemployment, the lack of future perspectives, police violence, impunity, a closed political system, a bourgeoisie tied in with a nonfunctioning political administration and the longevity of the regime. (Chouti 2011)

The formation of the protests in Burkina Faso have been quite different and in a sense more complex than others on the continent. While in some situations the police have apologised to protestors for violence, the government, traders and unemployed

youth have at various times been in confrontation with the muti-
nous armed forces, who at the same time turned against the state:

> Its appropriation of the state for its own profit has confirmed
> the true nature of a regime which starves its population and
> represses its youth, re-electing itself some four times since
> 1991 despite outcomes contested by its opponents – 24 years
> of a regime of tyranny and a highly effective mission to defend
> strategic French neocolonial interests in West Africa until its
> power becomes obsolete.
>
> In this context, the youth's frustrations and the general social
> disintegration have crystallised dangerously in the shape of
> coordinated confrontations with the symbols of the regime.
> The mutiny of the presidential guard on 14 April (and then
> in other military camps in Kaya, Po and Tekodogo) has met
> a violent response from local traders furious at the looting of
> rebel soldiers, leading ultimately to demonstrators from vari-
> ous sectors coming together to burn down the headquarters
> of the party in power – the CDP (Congress for Democracy and
> Progress) – and the government and the mayor of Ouagadou-
> gou. In response, Compaore imposed a curfew in the capital,
> retreated to his hometown, dissolved the government and
> dismissed the army chiefs. On 27 April, it was the turn of
> the police to rebel, as the school pupils, students and youth
> broaden their movement. (Pierre Sidy 2011)

Nonetheless, events in both Senegal and Burkina Faso have their
roots in local conditions, and mobilisation of the protests has not
been led by political and tech-savvy internet users but through
civil society and activists on the ground. On 5 March, Senegalese
blogger, Basile announced on his blog (I blog, therefore I am) and
on Twitter (@basileniane #19mars) that a demonstration 'We are
fed up' would take place on 19 March 2011, which made a direct
reference to Egypt and Tahrir Square:

> The winds of revolution from 'Arabic' countries are blowing
> towards Senegal. Indeed the head of the press group Walfadjri
> (fr) just kicked it off. In a press conference on Thursday, Sidy
> Lamine Niasse called all Senegalese to a demonstration on
> March 19 – the anniversary of the Senegalese political alterna-
> tive – to denounce the injustice reigning in the country. The

sit-in will take place at the Protêt square or the Independence Square, rechristened the highly symbolic name of 'Tahrir Square' by Sidy Lamine Niasse. (Basile 2011)

A further statement made on the website Afrik explained the disillusionment of the youth with 40 years of mismanagement, corruption, rising prices, high unemployment and, most importantly, the belief that 86 year-old President Abdoulaye Wade was seeking to change the constitution to allow him a third term and priming his son Karim to succeed. The statement also condemned the arrest of rap group Keur Gui after their denouncement of the president and his failures (Global Voices 2011).

On 19 March, 3,000–5,000 protesters gathered in Independence Square in what turned out to be a peaceful rally, despite the government announcement the night before that it had foiled an attempted coup and made 15 arrests. Many doubted the truth of this and felt it was a ploy to destabilise the protests by reaching out to nationalist sympathies. This may have worked because a separate group of some 10,000 demonstrators marched to the presidential palace in support of Wade.

Three months later, on 23 June, thousands of Senegalese in cities across the country and from all walks of life took to the streets with the chant 'Don't touch my constitution' in opposition to a proposed law which would allow a presidential candidate to take power with just 25 per cent of the vote and create a vice-president, which position people feared Wade would give to his son. Within hours, Wade had capitulated and abandoned the proposed 25 per cent vote, but not the plans for a vice-president and not before human rights activists Alioune Tine (who had previously received death threats) and Oumar Diallo were seriously wounded in a brutal attack (West African Democracy Radio 2011).

The reference to Tahrir Square was both a rallying call to enact a dream of a different Senegal and a declaration that says 'we are here' and things are no longer as they were.

The massive street protests in Dakar and cities across Senegal forced an almost immediate turnaround as the government quickly withdrew some of the proposed constitutional changes. In December 2010, in 'Twilight of a regime or dawn of a new era', Sidy Diop

(2010) warned of a looming instability in Senegal as the regime 'confronted by threats to its survival' struggled to keep a hold:

> The choice for President Wade is transparency and engagement with voters or as he has attempted to do, violate the constitution. If, on the other hand, it is a question of taking another path, violating the constitution and republican values, this project would be very dangerous for national cohesion and might incur civil war. And any politician, of whatever political stripe, whose acts and gestures above all serve his personal ambition, would commit an enormous blunder and cause his country to slide into violence and chaos. This is why we dare to hope that those who believe Wade has this intention are mistaken. Such an enterprise would not only be very risky but also his compatriots would put into question his whole life and his political career, which has been for the most part dedicated to changeover among parties, to commitment without concessions, to a continuous struggle for the defence of public liberties and democracy. (Diop 2010)

Diop refers to an emerging movement and 'new ways of expression through petitions', which he suggests should be institutionalised as a way of both rejecting decisions and as instruments for creating new laws:

> The present situation in Senegal is at a decisive turning point in its history. We have, on the one hand, a power that is very uncertain about its survival and that seeks solutions of all kinds for its continuity but which, of its own accord, has deprived itself of the bases that can guarantee it. On the other hand, there is an opposition that is trying hard to elaborate concepts and strategies in order radically to change the nature of the state and of power but which must overcome the difficulties and obstacles that lie in the path of a sustainable unity.
>
> And then, between these traditional forces, a civil society has emerged that brings real hope to those that now doubt the capacity of the parties to get the country going again, because they themselves have contributed to create the present difficult situation. (Diop 2010)

In the wake of the 23 June protests, Senegalese civil society (Slate Afrique 2011) made the expedient decision to create a new movement incorporating some 60 groups – parties, associations, NGOs, civil society. Their first demand is for the president not to contest the 2012 elections, although they realise that political and social change requires substantial organisation and cannot rely on the short-term impact of street protest.

However, what kind political and social change can take place within a framework of activism built on the elitisms, exclusions and hierarchies of mainstream civil society and whose interest is not necessarily in line with the aspirations of the people? Pithouse takes the criticism of NGOs further, suggesting that they undermine popular movements on numerous levels:

> It has been argued that NGO-based civil society is often fundamentally unable or unwilling to recognise popular agency. Iran Asef Bayat has argued that 'the current focus on the notion of "civil society" tends to belittle or totally ignore the vast array of often uninstitutionalized and hybrid social activities – street politics – that have dominated urban politics in many developing countries'. Englund reports that in Malawi, NGOs operate in such a way that 'dissent … must take a prescribed form before it is recognised'. In South Africa, Abahlali baseMjondolo assert that 'some of the NGOs are always denying and undermining the knowledge of the people'. The official modes in which dissent can be recognised are, precisely, those in which NGOs are structurally strong and poor peoples' organisations are structurally weak. It has also been argued that NGO- and donor-based civil society often 'channel' dissent in ways that remove it from the popular realm. (Pithouse 2010: 8)

Pithouse's criticisms become more relevant in a political environment where the 'left' engage in 'double speak'. Using the language of the left and the actions of liberals or the right, they confuse the landscape with talk of 'friendly capitalism', which is similar to suggesting it is better to die from friendly fire than from that of the enemy – when either way you are dead! The world is full of the liberal noise of the Google 'ideas' crowd, who laud a host of new social entrepreneurship ideas where, in a meritocratic society of affirmative action, a few are chosen and hailed as examples of black economic empowerment and the rest are left searching for the same old crumbs.

Moving further east geographically, there have been months of continuous protest in Gabon. On 29 January thousands began protesting against the leadership of President Ali Bongo Ondimba, the son of former President Omar Bongo. Although they were faced with the brutal forces of the regime, the protests spread across Gabon. Despite the intensity and longevity of the Gabonese protests they were hardly reported, as these tweets point out:

@cletusrayray: Is anyone listening? 'Pambazuka - #Gabon: The forgotten protests, the blinkered media' #Egypt #Libya #Bahrain #Yemen'.

@eDipAtState explained one possible reason for this:

'Media won't cover Cameroon/Gabon much. Protesters need to use Twitter/Facebook & send reports to AJE. #Gabon #Cameroon'. (Ekine 2011b)

It is hard to imagine that the global corporate media were unaware of Gabon and other African protests; it is clear that choices are made as to which conflicts and revolutions are covered. These choices need to be challenged, as do other silences, such as the voices of women, sexual minorities, refugees, landless people and migrants across the continent. Ethan Zuckerman points out in Pambazuka News the danger in selective reporting:

The danger of ignoring Gabon's revolution isn't just that opposition forces will be arrested or worse. It's that we fail to understand the profound shifts underway across the world that change the nature of popular revolution. The wave of protests that swelled in Tunisia may not break just in the Arab world, but across a much larger swath of the planet ... And as audiences around the world watch in wonder as Christian and Muslim protesters pray together in Tahrir Square, they wonder why struggles in Gabon can't command at least a fraction of this attention. (Zuckerman 2011)

In neighbouring Cameroon there was a brief uprising against President Biya, again largely unreported. Kah Walla, the founder of Cameroon Ô'Bosso (Cameroon lets go), describes the protests:

They wanted to stop us from protesting, we protested. We have a non-violent philosophy, which we maintained in the face of extreme violence. An incredible force of young Cameroonians. We started out almost 300 and ended up less than 50 but [being a] nugget has banished fear, for ourselves and for many other Cameroonians. The population did not join us in droves, but: not one person out of hundreds complained about the blocking on the road. If we ever doubted it, we now have extreme clarity on the absolute need for change and the absolute need for unwavering determination in bringing it about in our country. (Walla 2011)

It is hard to read Kah Walla's report without seeing the shadow of Tunisia and Egypt. There may not be a formal network of activists working across borders but there is no doubt that at least in some cases, the MENA and Middle East uprisings are influential.

One significant change from five or even three years ago is the technological landscape, not just the internet, which remains at an average of 5 per cent across the continent but, more importantly, satellite television, which has made Al Jazeera, BBC World and CNN accessible to the masses. The other technology is the mobile phone and its instrumental uses – SMS, camera, video and, to a lesser extent, the mobile internet and access to Twitter and Facebook. African citizens are far more informed than ever before and, crucially, they have been able to use information in more timely and creative ways. People have reached a self-understanding and a belief that they can bring about change, but doing so needs building a strong movement and network within national borders and regionally.

At the time of writing, a group of secret bloggers based in Equatorial Guinea announced they would be using social media platforms to get rid of President Obiang Nguema:

1. The Equatorial Guinean Youth Collective, we are a youth organization, born in Equatorial Guinea in secret, to organize and fight for our legitimate rights and interests, joining the youth, strengthening the youth movement.
2. We have teamed up to find the exchange of news, views and the effective support of workers and democratic organizations in the imperialist countries and mainly of Central African countries, as young people and workers who have brought down dictatorships in Tunisia and Egypt. (Colectivo Jovenese de Guinea Ecuatoria 2011)

Two years ago it would have been difficult to imagine that a small group of online activists could have a significant contribution to toppling a government, but Tunisia and Egypt have shown that with time this is a real possibility. For the people of Equatorial Guinea, the collective is the beginning of a much-needed movement which, with commitment, has the potential to create a global awareness of the abuses of the Obiang regime and eventually lead to an uprising.

The majority of protests we are witnessing across the continent are very much in an embryonic stage. Some countries are more organised than others, for example Swaziland has a strong trade union base with connections to COSATU (the Congress of South African Trade Unions) in South Africa. It is also in the process of developing a strong civil society, many members of which were active in organising the protests of 12 April. However, none of this is new. History is full of revolutions, many of which led to totalitarian states and imperialist republics that went on to colonise more than half the world. Take Europe in 1848:

> [E]very country in Europe had a revolution. And they happened very quickly one upon the other. People were riding on horses with broadsides to the next town. It's not like social contagion is a brand new thing. And I'm not saying that to minimize the significance of the new things, but just to put them into context to appreciate what they enable us to do and what they do not. (Movement.Org 2011)

After the layers of repression and corruption have been stripped away, what then? To destroy is easier than to rebuild. The former can happen in a moment, the latter, as history informs us, may take forever and if we are not careful may end with confusion: one day we wake up and find there is a Napoleon. 'How do you translate mobilisation into organisation?' (Movement.Org 2011).

Discussing the implications and possibilities of a different world in the context of a 'continuous revolution' is part of the process of transformation. Leonhard Praeg uses Derrida's notion of the 'messianic' to explain how this cannot be attained yet must be continually struggled for:

He (Derrida) reads democracy, justice, love and friendship as promises of fulfillness or plenitude and our lives, laws, desires and commitments as mere finite attempts to calculate their incalculable plentitude...

The Africa-that-will-always-remain-yet-to-come is the African messianic; and the excess of nomination the recognition, both that it won't come as well as the insistence that it must. (Praeg 2011)

In other words there is an ever-present contradiction in the reality of our lives because the dream of a different African future can never be realised. But at the same time we must engage with our struggles 'under the promise' that transformation 'must and will happen'. Thus we need the never-ending revolution, which requires a constant rethinking and reshaping of our vision that is not based on short-term actions and limited to problems of the now.

Note

1. The term 'uprisings' is used to indicate sustained, organised series of protests such as witnessed in Tunisia, Egypt, Mauritania and Libya and which could also be described as revolutions. The term 'protests' is used to describe those events which are sporadic and/or short lived, at an embryonic stage of development and consist of protests, campaigns, strikes, riots.

References

Chouti, Lila (2011) 'Popular protests in Burkina Faso', Pambazuka News, 30 March, http://www.pambazuka.org/en/category/features/72114, accessed 1 July 2011

Colectivo Jovenese de Guinea Ecuatoria (2011) 31 May, http://colectivojovenesecuatoguineanos.blogspot.com, accessed 2 July 2011

Diop, Sidy 'Senegal: twilight of a regime or dawn of a new era?', Pambazuka News, 28 December http://www.pambazuka.org/en/category/features/68183, , accessed 1 July 2011

Ekine, Sokari (2011b) 'Defiant in the face of brutality', Pambazuka News, 2 June, http://pambazuka.org/en/category/features/73738, accessed 2 July 2011

Ekine, Sokari (2011a) 'Uprising, imperial and uncertainty', 7 April, http://bit.ly/lSV1yx, accessed 2 July 2011

Fanon, Frantz (1963) The Wretched of the Earth, New York, NY, Grove Press

Global Voices (2011) 'Senegal: March 19, national day of action', 16 March, http://bit.ly/gGADT8, accessed 1 July 2011

Basile (2011) 'Senegal: the wind will blog from the revolution March 19 at the Independence Square', I blog, therefore I am, 5 March, http://bit.ly/lA90ve and http://bit.ly/gGADT8, accessed 1 July 2011

Kagumire, Rosebell (2011) 'Those who said you would never see war were wrong', 29 April, http://bit.ly/mLAmXD, accessed 2 July 2011

Katsiaficas, George (2011) 'North Africa now, Asia then', radio interview on Against the Grain, 29 March, http://bit.ly/izy3iQ, accessed 2 July 2011

Kota, Ayanda (2011) 'Ayanda Kota on Julius Malema and the pitfalls of national consciousness in contemporary South Africa', 26 June, http://bit.ly/lSV1yx, accessed 2 July 2011

Kubatana (2011) 'SAMWU condemns arbitrary arrest of 52 socialist activists in Harare', 22 February, http://www.kubatanablogs.net/kubatana/?m=201102&paged=3, accessed 1 July 2011

Movement.Org (2011) 'Has technology changed organising? A conversation with movement scholar, Marshall Ganz', 21 June, http://bit.ly/iVMi5P, accessed 3 July 2011

Ncube, Trevor (2011) 'Zimbabweans are their own liberators', 21 February, http://www.kubatanablogs.net/kubatana/?p=4894, accessed 1 July 2011

Nonviolent Action Network (NAN) (2011) 'SSU professor: Egypt revolt not spontaneous', 15 March, http://nonviolentaction.net/?p=3888, accessed 2 July 2011

Pithouse, Richard (2010) 'Fidelity to Fanon', http://churchland.org.za/padkos%20articles/Pithouse%20Fidelity%20to%20Fanon.pdf, accessed 7 September 2011

Praeg, Leonhard (2011) 'Rethinking everything', *Thinking Africa Newsletter*, June

Sidy, Pierre (2011) 'Burkina Faso: people no longer afraid', Pambazuka News, 26 May 2011, http://www.pambazuka.org/en/category/comment/73584, accessed 1 July 2011

Slate Afrique (2011) 'Broad coalition against the candidacy of President Wade', http://bit.ly/kIs5eU, accessed 2 July 2011

Sokwanele (2008) 'Mapping terror in Zimbabwe: political violence and elections 2008', 18 June, http://www.sokwanele.com/map/electionviolence, accessed 1 July 2011

Sokwanele (2011) 'The power of love can conquer the love of power', 14 February, http://www.sokwanele.com/thisiszimbabwe/archives/6326, accessed 1 July 2011

Walla, Kah (2011) 'The power is within us: a protest diary from Cameroon', Pambazuka News, 24 February 2011, accessed 1 July 2011

West African Democracy Radio (2011) 'Senegal: group to stop 3rd term, HRW wants probe, Tine on ordeal', 3 July, http://bit.ly/my8rJx, accessed 1 July 2011

Your Commonwealth (2011) 'The high cost of living in Uganda at the moment is alarming', 11 May, http://bit.ly/mcfITG, accessed 1 July 2011

Zuckerman, Ethan (2011) 'Gabon: the forgotten protests, the blinkered media', Pambauzka News, 17 February, http://www.pambazuka.org/en/category/features/70961, accessed 1 July 2011

3

Crisis in Côte d'Ivoire: history, interests and parallels

Explo Nani-Kofi

13 January 2011

One thing that is interesting about Côte d'Ivoire is that two of its heads of states, the first and the present one, have a trade union background but their leadership of the country has not helped strengthen trade unions or the labour movement's influence.

Houphouët-Boigny was involved in organising the African Agricultural Union in 1944 and the union was active in the founding of his party, Parti démocratique de Côte d'Ivoire (PDCI). Boigny was also a leading member of its predecessor, Rassemblement démocratique africain (RDA), which was in an alliance with the French Communist Party during the colonial period. The present head, Laurent Gbagbo, was detained during the Houphouët-Boigny regime for his activities in the National Trade Union of Research and Higher Education. In between the two the only elected leader was Houphouët-Boigny's chosen successor, Henri Konan Bedie, so he could be regarded as an extension of Houphouët-Boigny's politics. It was during his period of trade union activities that he formed the Ivorian Popular Front (FPI). His party was seen to be friendly with the social democrats of the Socialist Party of France.

Politics in Côte d'Ivoire since independence and the current crisis have never given the labour movement any weight in decision making, participation in or the direction of affairs. The dominant force in the politics of the country has been France – the colonial power. The French first came to what is now Côte d'Ivoire in 1637 and formalised their control around 1842.

Despite this, as early as 1959, Houphouët-Boigny expelled his deputy, Jean-Baptiste Mockey for leading a group of people within Boigny's own party and government who openly opposed the government's Francophile policies. He was accused of plotting to kill Boigny through the use of voodoo. In 1963, there were more than 100 secret trials in which Mockey and others such as Ernest Boka, head of the Supreme Court, were implicated.

Houphouët-Boigny had a poor relationship with governments in West Africa that were not the favourites of the West. Houphouët is alleged to have supported rebels and plotters against the regimes of Kwame Nkrumah in Ghana, Sekou Toure in Guinea and Patrice Lumumba in the present-day Democratic Republic of Congo (DRC). He is also associated with the coup against the pro-Soviet Matthieu Kerekou in Benin in January 1977. He supported Jonas Savimbi's UNITA when the ruling government in Angola was pro-Soviet and UNITA was the favourite of the US in Angola. It is believed that he worked closely with Blaise Compaore in the overthrow of Thomas Sankara in Burkina Faso. He influenced French backing for Charles Taylor's rebel forces in Liberia.

Laurent Gbagbo also said in July 2008 that he received support from Blaise Compaore, current president of Burkina Faso, during the period that he organised against Houphouët-Boigny. Blaise Compaore is widely seen as the person who intervened on behalf of the French and other Western interests to bring to an end the radical anti-imperialist politics led by Thomas Sankara when he was head of state in Burkina Faso. This means that no matter the labels, the politics of Côte d'Ivoire were heavily influenced by pro-French interests and forces close to them.

It was only in 1990, when the anti-incumbent[1] movement in Africa took off after the collapse of the Berlin Wall, that the first election since independence was held in Côte d'Ivoire in which somebody stood against Felix Houphouët-Boigny; this man was Laurent Gbagbo. While friends of the West fraudulently present Ghana under Nkrumah as a tyranny, the presidential election in Ghana on 27 April 1960 had two candidates: Kwame Nkrumah and J.B. Danquah. Côte d'Ivoire, which was praised, had nobody opposing Houphouët-Boigny.

In 1969, the Students and Pupils Movement of Côte d'Ivoire

(MEECI) was founded and its founding congress was held in the PDCI's (the ruling party) offices. This provoked riots from Ivorian students in opposition to this body, which was seen as a puppet organisation of the one-party state, which was trying to stifle student representation and voices. Boigny interpreted these student riots as an action masterminded by foreign pro-communist forces and had a group of students arrested.

The World Confederation of Labour (WCL) continued to make complaints about the harassment of trade unionists and the obstruction of the free operation and functioning of trade unions in Côte d'Ivoire under the regime of Houphouët-Boigny. There are two umbrella trade union bodies in Côte d'Ivoire: Dignité and the General Union of Workers of Côte d'Ivoire (UGTCI); the latter is seen as being favoured by the regime.

From 1978, unfavourable cocoa prices contributed to a worsening economic situation. Student demonstrations took place in 1982 of which some lecturers, including Laurent Gbagbo, were seen as the instigators. The end of the cold war in 1989 freed the West to reduce its support for puppet regimes, so the anti-incumbent movement renewed both trade union and student militancy. Even the army mutinied in 1990 and 1992. Houphouët-Boigny died in 1993.

The suppression of functioning democratic bodies representing social groups and classes as well as the virtual monopoly of pro-France politics meant there was no culture of mass organisation and mass intervention based on ideological differences. As a result politics were dominated by differences that were supported or driven by anti-incumbent movements or ethnic groups.

The first visible struggle was for the succession to Boigny's throne. It emerged between Alassane Ouattara, the prime minister, and Henri Konan Bedie, the president of the National Assembly. Bedie's regime introduced the policy of differentiating between full Ivorians and non-Ivorians. In 1995, the word Ivoirité emerged to refer to 'full' Ivorians. Although this originally meant those who had both parents from Côte d'Ivoire, it degenerated to become the people from the south and east of the country. Ouattara, whose parents come from the north, was now alleged to be a Burkinabé (a national of Burkina Faso). People from the north were affected by this xenophobic policy as a large number of migrants from Mali and Burkina Faso had come to live in the north as workers on the cash-crop farms.

Those of us in places such as Britain, where we campaign against immigrants being declared illegal, will be shocked that Africans in an African country face this type of discrimination – an idea totally hostile to the principles of Pan-Africanism. In October 1995, there was an election which Ouattara was not allowed to contest because of a governmental review of the electoral code that alleged he was not eligible; the review was seen by some as having targeted him. The anti-incumbent movement was also poorly organised and Bedie won the elections with 96 per cent of the vote.

Ivoirité discriminates not only on ethno-regional grounds, but also against class; for example, the rural agricultural working class – which has contributed to the cocoa farms which have brought hard currency – are disregarded and not considered as citizens. The government also banned the Student Federation of Côte d'Ivoire (FESCI), which was formed in 1990. Following allegations of corruption and repression, the Bedie regime was overthrown by a *coup d'état* on 24 December 1999, which brought General Robert Guei to power as the military ruler of Côte d'Ivoire. Henri Konan Bedie fled into exile.

The military regime of Robert Guei continued promoting Ivoirité and also the exclusion of those who were seen as corrupt politicians of the past. The Guei junta organised elections in 2000, which were characterised by violence, in which about 200 were killed. A Supreme Court decision excluded 14 of the 19 people who wanted to contest the presidential elections. Those disqualified included Ouattara and Bedie. Guei attempted to declare himself the winner of the elections but popular street protests and the lack of support from the military forced him out of power.

Gabgbo, who was shown to be leading in the votes, was installed as president. Ouattara's supporters continued to demand a new and inclusive election. The atmosphere of impunity created by Ivoirité became institutionalised. A forum for reconciliation was set up in 2001 which included Robert Guei, but he withdrew from it in September 2002. A number of members of the Ivorian Armed Forces of northern origin mutinied on 19 September 2002, declaring that they were dissatisfied with the lack of representation through the discriminatory Ivoirité. Robert Guei, his wife and some members of his family were killed during the mutiny. There is a strong suspicion that the rebellion was supported by Burkina Faso.

As the rebellion spread the new forces came to control 60 per cent of the Ivorian landmass. It is alleged that Gbagbo also brought in mercenaries from Belarus and former combatants of the Liberian war. The country then divided into two, with the north under the control of the rebels while the Gbagbo government controlled the south. The French brokered a peace agreement on 24 January 2003 and sent troops to protect a buffer zone between the government- and the rebel-controlled territories. In July 2004, the UN, the African Union (AU) and the Economic Community Of West African States (ECOWAS) organised a summit in Accra, Ghana, to prevent a renewal of hostilities and reinvigorate the French-brokered peace.

The post-cold war era was dominated by pro- and anti-incumbent movements and now the power had shifted to Gbagbo and the FESCI forces allied to him. This can be seen from the visibility of former FESCI leaders such as Charles Ble Goude of the Young Patriots (Congres Panafricain des Jeunes Patriotes – COJEP), Moussa Zeguen Toure of the Patriotic Group for Peace (Groupe Patriotique pour la Paix – GPP) and Guillame Soro of the Patriotic Movement of Côte d'Ivoire (Mouvement Patriotique de la Côte d'Ivoire – MPCI) who have been split by Ivoirité. While Soro is the leader of the rebel movement his former colleagues, who are pro-Gbagbo, are at the head of pro-Gbagbo militias.

The formal FESCI structure has become an extension of the Gbagbo government's forces. There have been allegations of abuses by FESCI activists and that the police have been unable to take any action against them. Human Rights Watch investigations found out that FESCI activists ransacked the headquarters of the two leading human rights organisations, the Ivorian League for Human Rights (Ligue Ivorienne des Droits de l'Homme – LIDHO) and Actions for the Protection of Human Rights (Actions pour la Protection des Droits de l'Homme – APDH). They were targeted for supporting striking university lecturers. Horrific crimes are alleged to have been committed by all parties in the conflict; Human Rights Watch, Amnesty International and the

UN investigations have uncovered the use of death squads, mass executions, torture and rape.

In November 2004, the Gbagbo government bombed the rebel-controlled city of Bouake, killing civilians and French soldiers, leading to reaction from French soldiers as well. In April 2005, there was another peace agreement among the forces in the conflict mediated by the then president of South Africa, Thabo Mbeki, in Pretoria. On 29 July 2005, the parties reaffirmed their support for the Pretoria agreement. Arrangements were made about how to organise the elections in 2005 when Gbagbo's controversial tenure of office as president would end. The instability in the country resulted in the elections being postponed several times until the recent elections in 2010. A government of national unity was set up, co-opting the rebels in 2007; the electoral code was amended in 2008 to prepare for elections.

The elections were finally held on 31 October 2010, but no candidate won outright so a run-off was organised between the two leading candidates, Laurent Gbagbo and Alassane Ouattara on 28 November 2010. In the imperfect conditions of Côte d'Ivoire today, election results reflect the control of the forces of violence – the National Army and the New Forces rebel group. According to the Electoral Commission, Alassane Ouattara received 2,483,164 votes (54.1 per cent) and Laurent Gbagbo 2,107,055 (45.9 per cent). After looking at voting irregularities, the Constitutional Court declared that the votes properly cast amounted to 2,054,537 (51.45 per cent) for Laurent Gbagbo and 1,938,672 (48.55 per cent) for Alassane Ouattara.

The Ouattara group regard the disproportionate cancellation of votes from the north, which they control, as fraud perpetrated by the Gbagbo-controlled Constitutional Court. The UN, AU and ECOWAS have endorsed the Electoral Commission's results and are demanding that Gbagbo should hand over power. ECOWAS has also threatened to use force to remove Gbagbo if he does not step down in favour of Alassane Ouattara.

The threat to use force is a very ill advised; it would appear as an invasion and could worsen the situation. It is worth noting that both sides are protected by the forces of violence. The Gbagbo government is protected by the armed forces, which have been loyal to it during the crisis, and the Alassane Ouattara group controls the north through the rebels of the New Forces, while he is also being protected by the UN peacekeepers in Abidjan, the capital of Côte d'Ivoire.

On 26 December 2010, Alassane Ouattara called for a national strike of workers until Gbagbo hands over, but this was ignored by most workers in Abidjan and work at the main ports, Abidjan and San Pedro, went on normally, with just some shopkeepers in Bouake, capital of the rebel-held north, closing their shops (but even there banks and public transport functioned without disruption). Both Gbagbo and Ouattara have had themselves sworn in and set up governments, with Gbagbo controlling the government media while the rebels depend on pirate radio broadcasts.

Various forces have taken sides on who has won the elections. Some start from the position that the Ivorian government should be respected, and that not respecting the Gbagbo government is to disregard the sovereignty of Côte d'Ivoire, but that ignores the fact that the situation in Côte d'Ivoire is a crisis and has not been normal since the elections of 2000. Some have even tried to give the impression that Alassane Ouattara is a neoliberal representative of external forces. To this Horace Campbell answered in an interview with Democracy Now's Amy Goodman that if the Gbagbo regime is such a pro-people government how come it has made an agreement with Trafigura and March Rich to dump toxic waste in Côte d'Ivoire?

Every effort needs to be made to resolve the matter peacefully. The International Trade Union Confederation (ITUC) has also appealed to its two affiliates in Côte d'Ivoire to make efforts for a peaceful resolution of the crisis. A delegation of ECOWAS made up of the presidents of Sierra Leone, Cape Verde and Benin, together with an AU representative in the person of the prime minister of Kenya, have been to Côte d'Ivoire to meet the two groups. Ouattara's ambassador to the UN said on the 'Hard Talk' programme on 11 January 2011 that talks are going on behind the scenes.

For a permanent solution, it must be seen clearly that this problem is not just about Côte d'Ivoire but another manifestation of the crisis of post-colonial Africa. The issue of the population of countries being uncompromisingly divided along ethnic, religious or geographical territories has become a common feature of various elections, including even the apparently peaceful ones like Ghana. The post-colonial arrangement whereby the elite have inherited the colonial status quo while presenting black faces to manage the colonial structure fails to address the aspirations of the masses of the people.

During the anti-colonial struggles the mass of people were mobilised in unity to fight the external forces. However, independence has meant that the masses have not played any further role in democratisation beyond endorsing one among rival groups to share the remaining spoils of the colonial arrangements. This requires structures that involve the masses of the African people in grassroots decision making and political involvement. There needs to be cross-border cooperation among them with the support of forces which are struggling to end the unjust global system which marginalises the majority of people in the supposed advanced countries and the lesser-developed countries as a whole. The lessons have to be learnt from Zimbabwe, Kenya and Côte d'Ivoire to guide future elections since the factors which contributed towards the crisis in Côte d'Ivoire are present in all the other African countries.

http://pambazuka.org/en/category/features/70058

Copyright © 2011 Explo Nani-Kofi

Note

1. I have used the word anti-incumbent here to describe the movements pushing for change in Africa from the end of the 1980s and early 1990s. Sometimes they have been referred to as pro-democracy movements but I have decided to describe them as anti-incumbent as their mobilisation focused so much on achieving the use of the ballot box and the need to remove the incumbent government.

4

Tunisia: the fall of the West's little dictator

Esam Al-Amin

20 January 2011

When people choose life (with freedom)
Destiny will respond and take action
Darkness will surely fade away
And the chains will certainly be broken

Tunisian poet Abul Qasim Al-Shabbi (1909–1934)

On New Year's Eve 1977, former President Jimmy Carter was toasting Shah Reza Pahlavi in Tehran, calling the Western-backed monarchy 'an island of stability' in the Middle East. But for the next 13 months, Iran was anything but stable. The Iranian people were daily protesting the brutality of their dictator, holding mass demonstrations from one end of the country to the other.

Initially, the Shah described the popular protests as part of a conspiracy by communists and Islamic extremists, and employed an iron fist policy, relying on the brutal use of force by his security apparatus and secret police. When this did not work, the Shah had to concede some of the popular demands, dismissing some of his generals, and promising to crack down on corruption and allow more freedom, before eventually succumbing to the main demand of the revolution by fleeing the country on 16 January 1979.

But days before leaving, he installed a puppet prime minister in the hope that he could quell the protests, allowing him to return. As he hopped from country to country, he discovered that he was unwelcome in most parts of the world. Western countries that had hailed his regime for decades were now abandoning him in droves in the face of popular revolution.

Fast forward to Tunisia 32 years later.

What took 54 weeks to accomplish in Iran was achieved in Tunisia in less than four. The regime of President Zine al-Abidine Ben Ali represented in the eyes of his people not only the features of a suffocating dictatorship, but also the characteristics of a mafia-controlled society riddled with massive corruption and human rights abuses.

On 17 December 2010 Mohammed Bouazizi, a 26-year-old unemployed graduate in the central town of Sidi Bouzid, set himself on fire in an attempt to commit suicide. Earlier in the day, police officers had taken away his stand and confiscated the fruits and vegetables he was selling because he lacked a permit. When he tried to complain to government officials that he was unemployed and that this was his only means of survival, he was mocked, insulted and beaten by the police. He died 19 days later in the midst of the uprising.

Bouazizi's act of desperation set off the public's boiling frustration over living standards, corruption and lack of political freedom and human rights. For the next four weeks, his self-immolation sparked demonstrations in which protesters burned tyres and chanted slogans demanding jobs and freedom. Protests soon spread all over the country, including to its capital, Tunis.

The first reaction by the regime was to clamp down and use brutal force, including beatings, tear gas and live ammunition. The more ruthless the tactics the security forces employed, the more people got angry and took to the streets. On 28 December the president gave his first speech, claiming that the protests were organised by a 'minority of extremists and terrorists' and that the law would be applied 'in all firmness' to punish protesters.

However, by the start of the new year tens of thousands of people, joined by labour unions, students, lawyers, professional syndicates and other opposition groups, were demonstrating in over a dozen cities. By the end of the week, labour unions called for commercial strikes across the country, while 8,000 lawyers went on strike, bringing the entire judicial system to an immediate halt.

Meanwhile, the regime started cracking down on bloggers, journalists, artists and political activists. It restricted all means of dissent, including social media. But following nearly 80 deaths by the security forces, the regime started to back down.

On 13 January Ben Ali gave his third televised address, dismissing his interior minister and announcing unprecedented concessions while vowing not to seek re-election in 2014. He also pledged to introduce more freedoms and to investigate the killings of protesters during the demonstrations. When this move only emboldened the protestors, he then addressed his people in desperation, promising fresh legislative elections within six months in an attempt to quell mass dissent.

When this ploy also failed, he imposed a state of emergency, dismissing the entire cabinet and promising to issue the army with a shoot-to-kill order. However, as the head of the army General Rachid Ben Ammar refused to order his troops to kill the demonstrators in the streets, Ben Ali found no alternative but to flee the country and the rage of his people.

On 14 January his entourage flew in four choppers to the Mediterranean island of Malta. When Malta refused to accept them, he boarded a plane heading to France. While in mid-air he was told by the French that he would be denied entry. The plane then turned back to the Gulf region where he was finally admitted and welcomed by Saudi Arabia. The Saudi regime has a long history of accepting despots including Idi Amin of Uganda and Parvez Musharraf of Pakistan.

But a few days before the deposed president left Tunis, his wife Leila Trabelsi, a former hairdresser known for her compulsive shopping, took over a ton and a half of pure gold from the central bank and left for Dubai along with her children. The first lady and the Trabelsi family are despised by the public for their corrupt lifestyle and financial scandals.

As chaos engulfed the political elites, the presidential security apparatus started a campaign of violence and property destruction in a last-ditch attempt to sow discord and confusion. But the army, aided by popular committees, moved quickly to arrest them and stop the destruction campaign by imposing a night curfew throughout the country.

A handful of high-profile security officials such as the head of presidential security and the former interior minister, as well as business oligarchs including Ben Ali's relatives and Trabelsi family members, were either killed by crowds or arrested by the army as they attempted to flee the country.

Meanwhile, after initially declaring himself a temporary president, the prime minister had to back down within 20 hours in order to assure the public that Ben Ali was gone forever. The following day, the speaker of parliament was sworn in as president, promising a national unity government and elections within 60 days.

Most Western countries, including the US and France, were slow to recognise the fast-paced events. President Barack Obama did not say a word as they were unfolding, but once Ben Ali was deposed, he declared: 'the US stands with the entire international community in bearing witness to this brave and determined struggle for the universal rights that we must all uphold.' He continued: 'We will long remember the images of the Tunisian people seeking to make their voices heard. I applaud the courage and dignity of the Tunisian people.'

Similarly, the French president, Nicolas Sarkozy, not only abandoned his Tunisian ally by refusing to admit him to the country while his flight was in mid-air, but he even ordered Ben Ali's relatives, staying in expensive apartments and luxury hotels in Paris, to leave the country.

The following day the French government announced that it would freeze all accounts that belonged to the deposed president, his family, or in-laws, in a direct admission that the French government was already aware that such assets were the product of corruption and ill-gotten money.

Corruption, repression and Western backing

A recently published report from Global Financial Integrity (GFI), titled 'Illicit financial flows from developing countries: 2000–2009,' estimates Tunisia was losing billions of dollars to illicit financial activities and official government corruption, in a state budget that is less than $10 billion and with a GDP of less than $40 billion per year.

Economist and co-author of the study, Karly Curcio, notes: 'Political unrest is perpetuated, in part, by corrupt and criminal activity in the country. GFI estimates that the amount of money illegally lost from Tunisia due to corruption, bribery, kickbacks, trade mispricing and criminal activity between 2000 and 2008 was, on average, over one billion dollars per year, specifically $1.16 billion per annum.'

A 2008 Amnesty International study, titled 'In the Name of Security: Routine Abuses in Tunisia,' reported that 'serious human rights violations were being committed in connection with the government's security and counter-terrorism policies'. Reporters Without Borders also issued a report that stated Ben Ali's regime was 'obsessive in its control of news and information. Journalists and human rights activists are the target of bureaucratic harassment, police violence and constant surveillance by the intelligence services.'

The former US ambassador in Tunis, Robert Godec, has admitted as much. In a cable to his bosses in Washington, dated 17 July 2009, recently made public by Wikileaks, he stated in regard to the political elites: 'they rely on the police for control and focus on preserving power. And, corruption in the inner circle is growing. Even average Tunisians are now keenly aware of it, and the chorus of complaints is rising.'

Even when the US Congress approved millions of dollars in military aid for Tunisia in 2010, it noted 'restrictions on political freedom, the use of torture, imprisonment of dissidents, and persecution of journalists and human rights defenders'.

Yet, ever since he seized power in 1987, Ben Ali has counted on the support of the West to maintain his grip on the country. Indeed, General Ben Ali was the product of the French Military Academy and the US Army School at Fort Bliss, Texas. He also completed his intelligence and military security training at Fort Holabird in Maryland.

Since he had spent most of his career as a military intelligence and security officer, he developed, over the years, close relationships with Western intelligence agencies, especially the CIA, as well as the French and other NATO intelligence services.

Based on a European intelligence source, Al Jazeera recently reported that when Ben Ali served as his country's ambassador to Poland 1980–84 (a strange post for a military and intelligence officer), he was actually serving NATO's interests by acting as the main contact between the CIA and NATO's intelligence services and the Polish opposition in order to undermine the Soviet-backed regime.

In 1999 Fulvio Martini, former head of Italian military secret service SISMI, declared to a parliamentary committee that 'In 1985–1987, we (in NATO) organised a kind of *golpe* [*coup d'état*] in Tunisia, putting president Ben Ali as head of state, replacing Burghuiba', in reference to the first president of Tunisia.

During his confirmation hearing in July 2009 as US ambassador to Tunisia, Gordon Gray reiterated the West's support for the regime as he told the Senate Foreign Relations Committee, 'We've had a long-standing military relationship with the government and with the military. It's very positive. Tunisian military equipment is of US origin, so we have a long-standing assistance program there.'

Tunisia's strategic importance to the US is also recognised by the fact that its policy is determined by the National Security Council rather than the State Department. Furthermore, since Ben Ali became president, the US military delivered $350 million in military hardware to his regime.

As recently as 2010, the Obama administration asked Congress to approve a $282 million sale of more military equipment to help the security agencies maintain control over the population. In his letter to Congress, the president said: 'This proposed sale will contribute to the foreign policy and national security of the United States by helping to improve the security of a friendly country.'

During the Bush administration the US defined its relationship with other countries not with grandiose rhetoric on freedom and democracy, but rather according to how far each country embraced its counter-terrorism campaign and pro-Israel policies in the region. On both accounts Tunisia scored highly.

For instance, a Wikileaks cable from Tunis, dated 28 February 2008, reported a meeting between Assistant Secretary of State David Welch and Ben Ali in which the Tunisian president offered his country's intelligence cooperation 'without reservation', including FBI access to 'Tunisian detainees' inside Tunisian prisons.

In his first trip to the region in April 2009, President Obama's special envoy to the Middle East, George Mitchell, stopped first in Tunisia and declared that his talks with its officials 'were excellent'. He hailed the 'strong ties' between both governments, as well as Tunisia's support of US efforts in the Middle East. He stressed President Obama's 'high consideration' of Ben Ali.

Throughout his 23-year rule, hundreds of Tunisian human rights activists and critics such as opposition leaders Sihem Ben Sedrine and Moncef Marzouki, were arrested, detained, and sometimes tortured after they spoke out against the human rights abuses and massive corruption sanctioned by his regime. Meanwhile, thousands of members of the Islamic movement were arrested, tortured and tried in sham trials.

In its August 2009 report 'Tunisia, continuing abuses in the name of security', Amnesty International said: 'The Tunisian authorities continue to carry out arbitrary arrests and detentions, allow torture and use unfair trials, all in the name of the fight against terrorism. This is the harsh reality behind the official rhetoric.'

Western governments were quite aware of the nature of this regime. But they decided to overlook the regime's corruption and repression to secure their short-term interests. The State Department's own 2008 Human Rights Report detailed many cases of 'torture and other cruel, inhuman, or degrading treatment', including rapes of female political prisoners, by the regime. Without elaboration or condemnation, the report coldly concluded: 'Police assaulted human rights and opposition activists throughout the year.'

What next?

'The dictator has fallen but not the dictatorship,' declared Rachid Ghannouchi, the Islamic leader of the opposition party al-Nahdha, or Renaissance, who has been in exile in the UK for the past 22 years. During the reign of Ben Ali, his group was banned and thousands of its members were tortured, imprisoned or exiled. He himself was tried and sentenced to death in absentia. He has announced his return to the country soon.

This statement by al-Nahdha's leader has reflected popular sentiment, cautioning that both the new president, Fouad Mebazaa, and prime minister, Mohammad Ghannouchi, have been members of Ben Ali's party – the Constitutional Democratic Party – so their credibility is suspect. They have helped in implementing the deposed dictator's policies for over a decade.

Nevertheless, on the day Ben Ali fled the country, the prime minister promised a government of national unity. Within days he announced a government that retained most of the former ministers (including the most important posts of defence, foreign, interior and finance), while including three ministers from the opposition and some independents close to the labour and lawyers' unions. Many other opposition parties were either ignored or refused to join on principled protest against the ruling party's past.

In less than 24 hours, on 18 January, huge demonstrations took place all over the country in protest against the inclusion of the ruling party. Immediately, four ministers, representing the labour union and an opposition party, resigned from the new government until a true national unity government is formed. Another opposition party suspended its participation until the ruling party ministers are either dismissed or resign their position.

Within hours the president and the prime minister resigned from the ruling party and declared themselves as independents. Still, most opposition parties are demanding their removal and their replacement with reputable and national leaders who are truly independent and have 'clean hands'. They question how the same interior minister who organised the fraudulent elections of Ben Ali less than 15 months ago could supervise free and fair elections now.

It is not clear if the new government will survive the rage of the street. However, perhaps its most significant announcement was a general amnesty and the promise to release all political prisoners in detention and in exile. It also established three national commissions.

The first commission is headed by one of the country's most respected constitutional scholars, Professor 'Ayyadh Ben Ashour, and will address political and constitutional reforms. The other two are headed by former human rights advocates, one to investigate official corruption, while the other will investigate the killing of the demonstrators during the popular uprising. All three commissions were appointed in response to the main demands by the demonstrators and opposition parties.

14 January 2011 has indeed become a watershed date in the modern history of the Arab world. Already, about a dozen

would-be martyrs have attempted suicide by setting themselves ablaze in public protest against political repression and economic corruption in Egypt, Algeria and Mauritania. Opposition movements have already led protests praising the Tunisian uprising and protesting at governments' repressive policies and corruption in many Arab countries, including Egypt, Jordan, Algeria, Libya, Yemen and the Sudan.

The verdict on the ultimate success of the Tunisian revolution is still out. Will it be aborted by either infighting or the introduction of illusory changes to absorb the public's anger? Or will real and lasting change be established, enshrined in a new constitution that is based on democratic principles, political freedom, freedoms of press and assembly, independence of the judiciary, respect of human rights and an end to foreign interference?

As the answers to these questions unfold in the next few months, the larger question of whether there is a domino effect on the rest of the Arab world will become clearer. But perhaps the ultimate lesson for Western policymakers is this: real change is the product of popular will and sacrifice, not imposed by foreign interference or invasions.

To topple the Iraqi dictator, it cost the US over 4,500 dead soldiers, 32,000 injured, a trillion dollars, a sinking economy, at least 150,000 dead Iraqis, a half-million injured and the devastation of their country, as well as the enmity of billions of Muslims and other people around the world.

Meanwhile, the people of Tunisia toppled another brutal dictator with less than 100 dead. They will forever be remembered and honoured by their countrymen and women as heroes who paid the ultimate price for freedom.

http://pambazuka.org/en/category/features/70247

This chapter was first published by *CounterPunch*.

5

Gabon's lords of poverty

Khadija Sharife

27 January 2011

Gabon's Ba'aka pygmy population may soon be saying *au revoir* to smoked fish and *nihao* to tofu, if the $3.5 billion Belinga iron-ore mining deal, awarded to a Chinese consortium in 2006, goes off without a hitch. The ore, billed as one of the world's last remaining major untapped deposits, was first discovered in 1885 in a remote forested region located in the Ogooue-Ivindo province. It is estimated to hold one billion tons of ore with iron content of 64 per cent.

According to the deal struck by Gabon's former lifetime dictator – and Africa's longest standing president – Omar Bongo, China received a 25-year tax holiday, despite profits projected within eight years, and 90 per cent of the profits thereafter as well as environmental and other para-fiscal exemptions such as significant control over national infrastructure.[1]

Except that Gabon has little or no infrastructure – just 10 per cent of the roads are paved and an estimated 70 per cent of the population lives below the poverty belt. Political and civil rights are limited to laminated constitutions, and economic, social and cultural rights, such as state services ranging from healthcare to waste sanitation, are unheard of.

But it would be wrong to conclude that Gabon's development policy has failed: over 120 French multinationals in addition to Gabon's venal political elite take development very personally indeed, collaborating on the kind of corporate–state partnerships glimpsed in the Elf Affair.

Though Gabon scores in the top 33 per cent of countries with high-ranking per capita GDP ($14,000) – averaging four times that

51

of sub-Saharan Africa – Gabon's political elite lord over the country's wealth as they do the artificially manufactured poverty. And just in case the population rebels, France's strong Marine Infantry Battalion, based in the capital Libreville, will swiftly intervene, via France's 'Africa' policy of Francafrique. Gabon, renowned as the focal point of Francafrique, composed of secretive defence agreements, multinationals and handpicked black governors, has existed in a state of forced peace since decolonisation.[2]

Despite the Elysee's internal recommendations in a June 2008 defence policy paper advising the closure of France's military unit based in Libreville, French President Sarkozy has yet to do so.[3]

'The French protect our system against internal and external threats. In exchange, we support their policies in Africa and elsewhere,' revealed Gabon's presidential adviser.[4]

Yet, despite continuing the tradition of power through patronage, the country's new 'electoral' dictator – Ali Ben Bongo Jr – has signalled a shift in the country's allegiance, moving away from the West, toward the East. Bongo Jr's success was the product of 'locked down' cities, and widespread harassment and violence, targeting opposition parties and civil society, as well as the already oppressed media, such as *L'Union*, whose editor Albert Yangari was arrested before being transported to the army's intelligence headquarters.[5] None of this will come as a surprise to Gabon's citizens in a country where public security is the mandate of the army and the president has the power to veto any legislation at will.[6]

Tellingly, Bongo Jr's choice of personal assistant happens to be Chinese, a trend proliferating throughout the continent, which has received over $29.3 billion since 2002 through development projects geared at the exploitation of finite resources financed by the state-owned Export-Import Bank of China (China Exim). And this is where China gets really smart: instead of establishing donor relationships with cash-strapped corrupt African states, China – itself an emerging nation all too aware of socio-economic challenges – collateralises finite natural capital in exchange for development and revenue. This barter system has not only redefined Africa's 'risk' profile – leading to the World Bank's support of China Exim-led investments – but additionally generates a positive perception disconnected from that of the 'Western colonialists'.

The deal could not come at a better time: presently oil accounts for 80 per cent of export earnings, but production has sharply declined, standing at 270,000 barrels per day (bpd), down from 351,890 barrels in 1998. Paradoxically, though the country remains one of sub-Saharan Africa's top five oil producers, Gabon holds just two billion barrels in dwindling reserves – unlike Nigeria's 36 billion.[7]

Belinga's iron-ore project, wholly financed by the state-owned China Exim, includes the $790 million Belinga mining facility; two hydro-electric dams designed to electrify the mine (Grand Poubara and Kongou Falls, the latter with a price tag of $754 million); and the 560km railway and planned deep-water port at Santa Clara, engineered to transport resources from north-east Gabon to the Atlantic and then Beijing. The first shipments are scheduled to leave for China in 2011, with an estimated 30 million tons extracted each year.[8]

But profits from finite resources are largely derived from taxes – including mineral tax (royalties) and corporate tax – via region-specific resources. Meanwhile, the proposed 26,850 jobs appear unlikely to materialise as China's leitmotif is generally to export Chinese labour, save that of mining. Transmission lines, supplying power to end destinations, often amount to half the project's costs, bypassing populations in favour of mining facilities.

The proposed Kongou Dam, situated in the Invindo National Park – Gabon's share of the Central African rainforest, inhabited by unique and endangered species such as the forest elephant – jeopardises the 'ecological commons', primarily used by indigenous people for survival and income. Long before environmental impact assessments were conducted, China began paving the 42km road to Kongou Falls, facilitating poaching, wildlife trafficking and the logging of one of the world's last remaining ancient rainforests and carbon sinks, absorbing 20 per cent minimum of emissions annually. The letter of agreement was signed by Gabon's mines minister Richard Onouviet.

What does Gabon and the world stand to lose?

The subsidy, according to 40 years of research conducted in Gabon by fellows from the University of Leeds, is economically valued at £13 billion each year. Globally, the Central African rainforest is second only to the Amazon. Ironically, the loans violate

China Exim's own social and environmental guidelines – articles 6 and 12 – referring to social, ecological, employment, security, health, migrant and land acquisition.

Thanks to a network of local civil society groups, headed by Brainforest, a Gabon-based NGO environmental organisation, China Exim appears to have postponed financing until the China National Machinery and Equipment Import and Export Corporation (CEMEC) is investigated for alleged ecological violations. Brainforest's efforts have resulted in concessions initially marked at 5,000sq km, reduced to the actual size required: 600sq km.

But Belinga remains the only hope for the export earnings required by Bongo and Co, as well as resource-hungry China.

'Whatever happens and whatever anyone says, Belinga will go ahead,' stated Omar Bongo in 2007.[9] Bongo Sr's extraordinary ability to undermine and 'purchase' opposition parties has rendered Gabon a nation of imprisoned citizens, lubricating the fiction of 'flag independence' – a situation benefitting the 'khaki coup' of Bongo Jr in the recent elections.

Yet Beijing's footprint, if properly engaged, may just be the catalyst needed to inspire a movement toward liberation from internal and external colonialists, whatever their skin colour.

http://pambazuka.org/en/category/features/70398

This chapter was first published in May 2010 in the *Harvard World Poverty and Human Rights* journal where the author is assistant editor.

Notes

1. BankTrack, 'Belinga iron ore project – Gabon, http://www.banktrack.org/show/dodgydeals/belinga_iron_ore_project, accessed 16 September 2011.
2. Xan Rice (2009) Gaobon's President Bongo confirmed dead at 78', *Guardian*, 8 June, http://www.guardian.co.uk/world/2009/jun/08/gabon-omar-bongo-death-reports, accessed 16 September 2011.
3. Christophe Boisbouvier (2010) '50 years later, Françafrique is alive and well', rfi english, 16 February, http://www.english.rfi.fr/africa/20100216-50-years-later-francafrique-alive-and-well, accessed 16 September 2011.
4. Ibid.
5. Reporters Without Borders (2009) 'Fear in Libreville after leading daily's editor is arrested and questioned for several hours', 25 September, http://en.rsf.org/gabon-fear-in-libreville-after-leading-25-09-2009,34598.html, accessed 16 September 2011.
6. Amnesty International, 'Gabon human rights', http://www.amnestyusa.org/all-countries/gabon/page.do?id=1011274, accessed 16 September 2011.

7. Energy Information Administration (2009), http://www.eia.doe.gov/
    emeu/international/reserves.html, accessed 16 September 2011.
8. Antoine Lawson (2007) 'Gabon's greens fret over China iron ore project',
    http://www.reuters.com/article/idUSL1174482620071012, accessed 16
    September 2011.
9. Ibid.

b

Tunisia's revolution: self-organisation for self-emancipation

Horace Campbell

27 January 2011

The full explosion of the Tunisian revolutionary process is now taking root across Africa, far beyond the town of Sidi Bouzid, from where Mohammed Bouazizi had sent a message to youths all across the world that they should stand up against oppression. The overthrow and removal of the dictator Zine al-Abidine Ben Ali on 14 January 2011 was an important stage in this revolution. When this dictator (who was a top ally of the US and France) fled to Saudi Arabia, dictators and corrupt party leaders all over the world trembled as the popular power in the streets found support in all parts of Africa, the Middle East and parts of Europe. This revolution in Tunisia is a typical example of the self-mobilisation of ordinary people for their own emancipation, independent of a vanguard party or self-proclaimed revolutionaries. The iteration of the Tunisian revolution in other parts of Africa and the Middle East is fast becoming a pattern that speaks volumes about the nature of 21st century revolutions.

At the time of writing, the revolution is going through its third stage, where the popular forces are seeking a drastic change in the politics of the society and demanding a new order in Tunisia, based on freedom, democracy and social justice. In short, the people are calling for a form of popular democracy that moves beyond aliena-tion and beyond the separation of politics and economics.

The first stage of the revolution started with the self-immo-lation and self-sacrifice of Mohammed Bouazizi in the region of

Sidi Bouzid. The unemployed graduate Bouazizi set himself on fire to protest against police brutality after they harassed and stopped him from selling fruits and vegetables, which was his only means of livelihood. The second stage involved the mass organisation and the deployment of new networks for revolution among the youth and the working people, leading to the popular overthrow of the dictator. The third stage involved the merger of the caravans of liberation into the capital Tunis with the break in the ranks of the forces of coercion. It was at this stage that the true revolutionary character of the self-organisation started to emerge. At this third stage, the prolonged popular protest of the organised poor emerged, with women and youth taking the lead in calling for the arrest of the dictator and for a new government of the people. It is at this delicate stage of this revolution that it is most necessary for revolutionaries all over the world to stand together with the Tunisians, and to draw the positive lessons that can spread the revolution like a fire to burn off the corruption and destruction of capitalism and neoliberalism.

The capitalist classes have been wounded in Tunisia and they want to do all within their power to contain this new wave of revolution. However, their ability to undermine this revolution will depend on the vigilance and support of revolutionaries internationally. We must remember that revolutions are made by ordinary people and that there are millions who want a new form of existence where they can live like decent human beings. In another era of capitalist depression and war, it was C.L.R. James who commented: 'That is the way a revolution often comes, like a thief in the night, and those who have prepared for it and are waiting for it do not see it, and often only realise that their chance has come when it has passed.'

James was referring to the Chinese masses who had led the way in the revolutionary process in China. The real point of Tunisia, as in China, is that in every revolutionary situation it is the real action of human beings taking to the streets, defying the police and fighting with courage and imagination that changes society. Revolutionaries should grasp the epoch-making process that is now underway in the world. How this epoch-making process will mature across Africa, Europe and Asia will depend on the politics and organisations that shape the movement in the coming weeks and months. Revolutionaries must learn the positive lessons: the new pattern of 21st century revolution, the new forces of revolution and the new tools of revolutionary struggles that are being fashioned by those who are making sacrifices for a new mode of social existence.

Self-immolation, sacrifices and self-organisation

In a month, the narrative in the international media on Tunisia has changed completely. Prior to the present uprising against the capitalist classes and the dictator, Tunisia was represented in the Western media as a stable, free-market economy that was a symbol of the success of capitalism, a top ally of the US in the war against terrorism. Tunisia was a choice destination for European tourists as the same European states shut their doors to migrants from Africa. Behind the image of Tunisia as a stable tourist resort where Europeans could relax was the reality of repression, corruption, censorship and massive exploitation of the people. The concentration and centralisation of wealth and power in the hands of the ruling family alienated even members of the capitalist classes who were locked out of the inner circles of opulence and obscene wealth. In the midst of struggle, there was unemployment and suffering. Mohammed Bouazizi, a youth who had sought to dignify his existence by becoming a fruit and vegetable seller, decided to sacrifice himself to make a stand against oppression and break with the politics of obedience.

Mohammed Bouazizi, like millions of youths across the world, wanted a new world. He had studiously gone through school only to find that the economy did not have a place for him. He created his own space by becoming a fruit and vegetable vendor in the town. But even in this capacity, the society had no room for the creativity of the youth so the police harassed him continuously and on 17 December 2010 confiscated his vegetable cart. Bouazizi was the principal breadwinner of his family and decided to make a stand against oppression. After unsuccessfully complaining to the local authorities, he burnt himself as an act of protest. He did not die immediately and his sacrifice was an inspiration for others to resist oppression and popularise his action.

The other youths in Sidi Bouzid took up his cause and carried messages of his self-immolation across Tunisia and beyond. As the youth mobilised and took to the streets with 'a rock in one hand, a cell phone in the other', their message cracked the walls of censorship to the point where the dictator himself sought to mollify this rebellion by going to the hospital to try to contain the anger of the youth and blunt the rising protest. In an effort to gain their support, the government declared 2011 the year of the youth. But the youths were not waiting for a dictator to declare a year for them; they were bent on taking the year and making the break for a new decade.

Mohammed Bouazizi joined his ancestors on 4 January, expiring from the self-immolation, but his act of sacrifice acted as a spark to impress on the youths the importance of intentionality to make a break with the old forms of oppression. The rebellion that had been sparked by the action of Bouazizi took over the region of Sidi Bouzid and moved from spontaneous actions of solidarity to an organised resistance that brought in new forces who recognised the determination of the youths. The rebellion took on an all-class character as teachers, lawyers, workers, trade unionists, small-scale entrepreneurs and other social forces joined in this first phase of the revolution. Within a week, the revolution had spread to Tunis and the masses had joined in the streets to topple the dictatorship.

The fall of the Ben Ali regime

Ben Ali was like the many other African leaders who had joined the anti-colonial struggles only to take over the habits and behaviour of the colonialists. Tunisia had become independent in 1956 and the ruling party developed authoritarian principles as it sold itself as a base for Western capitalism. The more the society ingratiated itself with the West, the more the ruling sections of the political class felt a sense of impunity, believing that Western support could shield them from popular opposition. In the case of Ben Ali, he had not only supported a rabid form of corruption, his regime earned praise as one of the firmest supporters of the war against terrorism.

This support from France and the US concealed the economic terrorism of capitalism, but as the global economic depression took its toll on the people, there were protests to reveal the extent of the terror and corruption of the dictator who had been in power since 1987. The ruling party was dominated by the national capitalist class, as well as the foreign multinationals and banks that cooperated to establish free-trade zones where workers could not organise. Unemployment and poverty among the youth had made them a pool of cheap reserve labour to be manipulated by religious and political leaders, but youths such as Mohammed Bouazizi had risen above the politicisation of religion. When by 10 January the rebellion had spread to Tunis, the maturation of years of agitation immediately manifested itself in the slogans of the rebellion: 'Down with the party of thieves, down with the torturers of the people.'

These slogans of rebellion resonated with all sections of the oppressed and initially, as the police shot and killed unarmed civilians, Ben Ali dismissed the demonstrators as terrorists. Ben Ali called the demonstrations the work of masked gangs 'that attacked at night government buildings and even civilians inside their homes in a terrorist act that cannot be overlooked'. This reflex summoning up of the bogey of terrorism did not scare the people, and by Thursday 13 January the anger of the families of those shot in cold blood was buttressed by the maturation of the popular resistance to the dictatorship. The president's billionaire son-in-law ran away and by Friday Ben Ali, who had promised the masses that he would not stand for the presidency in 2014, fled the country. While in flight, even his imperialist allies deserted him. It was only the Libyan dictator Mu'ammer al-Gaddafi who had the temerity to castigate the Tunisian people for removing Ben Ali from power. Gaddafi spoke for the other dictators across Africa and the Middle East when he said in a televised address that, 'You [Tunisians] have suffered a great loss. There is none better than Zine [Ben Ali] to govern Tunisia.'

Gaddafi exposed the fact that the African unity that he represented was the unity of dictators. But even as he spoke the revolution was moving to the third stage as the caravans of liberation converged on Tunis, as the ideas and principles of self-organisation and self-emancipation spread across Africa. Initially, other European leaders were silent, but as the gravity and seriousness of the Tunisian workers and youth became a force in international politics, the government of Switzerland froze the accounts of Ben Ali and his family. Former allies of Ben Ali such as the leaders of the US and France distanced themselves from his rule as the images of revolution from Tunisia spread through mainstream media, rising from the networks of social media to the mainstream. In this information warfare, the news outlet Al Jazeera acted as a source of information, connecting the struggles throughout the world of dictators and despots.

Intentionality, self-organisation, self-mobilisation and self-empowerment

When the second stage of the revolution was maturing, the interim government closed schools and universities in an attempt to blunt the youth's energy. After the universities reopened, there were new demonstrations across Tunisia as teachers and students called a general strike. The full expression of a worker–student alliance was beginning to take shape as workers occupied workplaces and set up committees to run them. It is this advanced consciousness of worker control that is slowly taking shape as the revolution of Tunisia experiments with networks of networks beyond the old standards of democratic centralism and other worn ideas of revolutionary organisation and the vanguard party. Social media and social networking may represent one of the forms of this revolutionary process, but its character is still embedded in the self-organisation and self-emancipation of the oppressed. It is this powerful force of self-emancipation that is acting as an inspiration and beating back vanguardists, whether secular or religious.

In order to discredit this revolutionary process, the Western media has been promoting the bogey that Islamists will be the beneficiaries of the revolution. But the women of Tunisia have demonstrated clearly that they are not going to be sidelined in a revolutionary process. These women, within and outside Tunisia, have been organising for decades against patriarchy and other forms of male domination and will not be silenced in this moment of revolution. What was visible from the images from Tunisia was the centrality of women and youths in this revolutionary process. Tunisian society is one where the women had stood firm against the fundamentalists who wanted to control the bodies and minds of women. These women made common cause with the youths and other sections of the working people to form the backbone of the revolution. Their presence and firmness acted as a barrier to the kind of vanguardism that could be claimed by sections of the opposition. Hence, as Ben Ali fled, all the socialists, communists, Islamists, trade unionists, human rights workers, rappers and other social forces emerged on the political stage of Tunisia. The placards and slogans that proclaimed 'vive la révolution' were a manifestation that all over the country, from south to north, there had been a burning desire for change.

This burning desire for change was most clearly expressed in the expressions of workers and poor farmers from the rural areas, who converged on Tunis as they chanted: 'We have come to bring down the rest of the dictatorship.' They did this in defiance of a curfew and a state of emergency. They had travelled through the night in a caravan of cars, trucks and motorcycles from towns across the rocky region far from Tunisia's luxurious tourist beaches.

I was in West Africa as this revolution unfolded. Everywhere I went, youths and other workers were anxiously following the revolution as the mass resistance spread to Algeria, Egypt, Jordan and Yemen. In all of the societies I visited there were young people who wanted to know more about what was happening in revolution. Bouazizi's action sends a major lesson to youths across Africa and the pan-African world. This lesson is embedded in the significance of his self-immolation. Bouazizi's self-immolation signifies self-sacrifice, different from the actions of suicide bombers. In a world where disgruntled elements take to suicide bombing as a weapon of coercion and protestation, Bouazizi stands out as an oppressed and disgruntled youth who wanted to make a sacrifice for revolution without violence and the killing of innocent souls. Youths do not have to embark on self-immolation as a sacrifice for a better tomorrow. But ultimately, they must be ready to make some sacrifices for self-emancipation, instead of being passive or offering themselves as tools of manipulation and suppression in the hands of the ruling elites.

In a period when alienated youths are open to manipulation by conservative forces so that they shoot innocent people or turn themselves into suicide bombers, the action of Mohammed Bouazizi marked a new phase of youth action. This new phase was manifest in the statement by some Tunisian revolutionaries: 'Mohammed Bouazizi has left us a testament. We will not abandon our cause.'

Whither the revolutionary process?

Far from retreating from the streets, the demonstrations and positive actions of the people have galvanised others in Algeria, Libya, Egypt, Jordan and Yemen. The more the Tunisians demanded the arrest of Ben Ali and his family, the more Western leaders sought to limit the damage and call for stability and social peace – but what they are really calling for is the protection of local and international capital. The Western capitalists fear the socialists, progressive feminists, trade unionists and youths who are determined to build a new basis for economic relations, where the wealth of the society is organised for the well-being of the people. Already, there is a discussion of the full nationalisation of the assets that were previously owned by the Ben Ali family. This talk of nationalisation stirs fear in the ranks of other capitalists, who want to inherit the politics and economic base of Ben Ali.

How this process will develop in Tunisia will depend on the politics and organisations that shape the movement in the coming weeks and months. As one socialist organ proclaimed:

Tunisia needs a new democratic government which represents the national and popular will of the people and represents its own interests. And a system of this type cannot emerge from the current system and its institutions or its constitution and its laws, but only on its ruins by a constituent assembly elected by the people in conditions of freedom and transparency, after ending the tyranny.[1]

Revolution is a process, not an event. The revolutionary process in Tunisia is maturing through twists and turns. Progressive forces in the imperialist centres must organise so that the militarists in the West do not prop up the dictators to hijack the process as the people begin to register a new historical era. The people have risen with confidence. They want a break with capitalist exploitation and corrupt leaders. Self-organisation and self-emancipation for social and economic transformation will take the popular forces from one stage of consciousness to the next.

http://pambazuka.org/en/category/features/70472

Note

1. Statement of the Communist Workers Party of Tunisia, http://www.socialistunity.com/?p=7544, accessed 14 August 2011.

7

Aslema ya Tunis, *au revoir* Ben Ali

Melakou Tegegn

3 February 2011

Only a few dates enter the history books of a country, to be remembered by future generations for their significance in bringing freedom and democracy. The latest such date to enter the history books is 14 January 2011, the day the people of Tunisia overthrew the 23-year dictatorship of Ben Ali.

Dictators, who appear invincible and who think they can surmount any crisis with the use of brutal force and who still threaten to use the same brute force to quell an ongoing rebellion by the people who, abhorring the conditions of their lives have finally said enough and taken to the streets not only for themselves but also for their children, these dictators suddenly turn coward and flee. Mengistu Haile Mariam, the hangman and blood-thirsty killer, fled Ethiopia when the going got tough. When the going got tough, the coward dictator wet his pants. The Tunisian dictator did the same.

As in February 1974, Ethiopia's most unforgettable days, Tunisia is still in a dilemma after a historic victory yesterday. In the way that Haile Selassie's brutal dictatorship suppressed liberties that prevented an organised opposition, Ben Ali's suppression of liberties also prevented the country from having an organised and viable opposition on the day after the historic victory. Now, the big question is whether or not the Tunisian political elite, who were groomed by Ben Ali, will be able to circumvent the people's victory and impose its rule in such a way as to prevent the people's alternative from reigning. Mengistu managed to do that for 17 years, only to be swept away in 1991. We hope nothing like that will take place in Tunisia. The revolution should be crowned with freedom and democracy and the establishment of a democratic state that guarantees the people of Tunisia the freedom and democracy they have fought for. That was exactly what Mengistu prevented from happening in Ethiopia in the wake of the 1974 Revolution. Ethiopia was not lucky even after Mengistu; the ruling coalition, the EPRDF, still stopped the people of Ethiopia from having the freedom and democracy that they demanded, fought and died for in 1974.

Like Ethiopia, Tunisia is a country with a rich history. A number of 'civilisations' have reigned in Tunisia, starting with the Phoenicians and extending to the Greek, Roman and the Ottoman empires. It is home to Carthage, the famous 'civilisation' in North Africa that later gave way to Arab 'civilisation'. Tunisia is the home of the indigenous Amazigh people, commonly known as the Berbers, as are Algeria and Morocco. Historical relics of these various 'civilisations' are still found in the country. A Roman town is found intact in a place called Duga on the Mediterranean. Tunisia's proximity to Europe greatly influenced its late history, with an impact on its livelihood systems, social organisation and economy. Tunisia is the largest producer and exporter of olives; it has a dynamic economy and social organisation that can only be compared to Southern Europe. It has one of the largest middle classes in the world and is a middle-income country, scoring very highly on the Human Development Index.

Abject poverty such as prevails in Africa is not the problem in Tunisia despite a very high rate of unemployment among educated people. Tunisian poverty is similar to European poverty. The biggest problem that has throttled Tunisian society has been the dictatorship. The state was a typical police state as in the dictatorships that reigned in Latin America in the 1960s and 70s. The revolt of the people of Tunisia once more confirmed the natural dictum that humans, unlike animals, cannot live without the freedom to express what they think. That is why freedom to human beings is a natural construct. It is not a gift or something that drops from heaven; humans simply cannot live without freedom. Suppressing freedom is, in the first place, artificial: it came with the emergence of the state. In traditional systems of governance that still prevail in pastoral and hunter–gatherer societies, there is no repression of the right to expression. The Tunisian revolution once more confirmed that freedom and democracy are essential ingredients of life for humans.

The events in Tunisia should interest us Ethiopians a great deal. Some time ago, there was a report that Meles' regime was studying the system in Tunisia as a successful example of a one-party state. Undoubtedly, Meles should be the one most disappointed by what happened in Tunisia yesterday. His idol, Ben Ali, the champion of a one-party state who also claimed an election victory by more than 86 per cent (he seems to be a bit more modest than Meles, who claimed a 99.6 per cent victory) has just been swept away by a revolution that was ignited less than a month ago. If Ben Ali with his 86 per cent election victory claim is swept away, what can happen to Meles, who unashamedly claimed a 96 per cent victory? Under Ben Ali's rule, expressions of opposition were so rare that the international community wrongly thought of it as one of the most stable countries with a dynamic economy. The people of Ethiopia, on the other hand, have always expressed their disgust with Meles' regime ever since it came to power. The 2005 elections confirmed that the overwhelming majority of our people wanted his regime out of office. It is a political irony of immense proportions that Meles Zenawi claimed that 99.6 per cent of the same population switched their votes to him in a matter of five years. The word shame does not seem to exist in his vocabulary. At the end of the day, Meles has to look elsewhere for a role model for a one-party rule. But where?

What is crucial for Ethiopians is to draw lessons from what has happened in Tunisia over the last month, culminating in the overthrow of the dictatorship there. We cannot rule out a similar event taking place in our country too, sooner or later. But better assume it can than it cannot as the historical dilemma that bedeviled us in 1974 will not be repeated.

In 1974, when the people of Ethiopia revolted, they did not have a political organisation that would lead them to freedom and democracy. Almost 40 years later, we still face the same dilemma. What will happen if Woyane is overthrown by a popular revolt? Just think of it, who will reign in power? Will the same military come to power in a name other than the Derg? As the

Amharic saying goes, '*ayhonimin titesh, yihonalin yaszi*' (roughly translated as: 'better think that something will happen than it won't'). Certainly, any group that assumes power in the wake of the overthrow of Woyane will proclaim political amnesties and invite all refugees to come back, liberalise the political situation, organise elections, and so on – promises that they think will thrill the public.

It is important for Ethiopians to get better organised now than ever, patch up our differences, stop the squabbling and embark on the serious political work of discussion and debate on issues that we will unavoidably grapple with sooner or later. We need political courage and realism to cross the Rubicon and embark on this kind of political work. At stake are the lives of 80 million people and the future of our children. What will we bestow on the next generation? Rivalry or modesty? Personal grandeur or serving the people? We have to choose now. You never know what will happen tomorrow. Did we know last November that the heroic people of Tunisia would overthrow Ben Ali in January 2011?

http://pambazuka.org/en/category/features/70657

8

Tunisia and Egypt: revolutions without self-proclaimed revolutionaries

Horace Campbell

3 February 2011

> It was a victory parade – without the victory. They came in their hundreds of thousands, joyful, singing, praying, a great packed mass of Egypt, suburb by suburb, village by village, waiting patiently to pass through the 'people's security' checkpoints, draped in the Egyptian flag of red, white and black, its governess eagle a bright gold in the sunlight. Were there a million? Perhaps. Across the country there certainly were. It was, we all agreed, the largest political demonstration in the history of Egypt, the latest heave to rid this country of its least-loved dictator. Its only flaw was that by dusk – and who knew what the night would bring – Hosni Mubarak was still calling himself 'President' of Egypt.

This is how Robert Fisk of the UK's *Independent* newspaper captured the mood of optimism of the peoples in Tahrir Square (also called Liberation Square) in Cairo before the veiled fist of counter-revolution unleashed its whip to reverse the initiative of the popular uprising in Cairo. On Tuesday 1 February there were over 2 million people gathered on Liberation Square to demand the removal of Hosni Mubarak, and on Wednesday 2 February plain-clothes police and armed thugs mounted on camels and horses stormed the unarmed citizens, attempting to kill and brutalise those who want to be free. The people stood their ground and beat back the government thugs.

The peoples of Egypt and Tunisia have made their mark on the world stage and they have shifted the balance of power back to ordinary people. They have re-established the essence of popular democratic participation and elevated the issues of the politics of inclusion. This shift is bringing back the sense of power to the exploited all over the world. Oppressed peoples all over the world now take courage from the new sense of purpose of the demonstrators. Their confidence and freedom from fear have been so inspiring that there are already popular uprisings and protests in Jordan, Yemen and Sudan. Not far behind are citizens in Algeria, Cameroon and Libya, who are slowly stirring and demanding political and social change.

Indisputably, youths are rewriting the meaning of revolutionary organisation and at the same time exposing the hollowness and hypocrisy of the liberal 'democratic' posture of Western imperialists. It is this same Western liberal force that supported the regime in Egypt as a bulwark of 'stability and counter-terrorism' in North Africa and the Middle East. By unleashing thugs and state-security personnel to attack the unarmed civilians, the Egyptian revolution now poses a challenge to the fourth stage of the revolution: how to harness the ideas of revolutionary non-violence to be able to stand firm and fight back against internal and external provocations. In this standoff, the army will be put to the test as the external supporters of the moribund Mubarak regime seek to crush the revolutionary spirit of the people. One of the important tasks of the peace and justice movements internationally is to oppose the militarists, who will seek to exploit the moment of transition to foment war and military interventions.

Millions in Liberation Square and across Egypt

As millions of people surge on to the streets of Alexandria, Aswan, Cairo, Port Said, Suez and other Egyptian cities, the anti-dictatorship protest in Egypt built on the third stage of the revolutionary process in Tunisia and brought an entirely new force: the power of numbers and the test of creative means of self-defence. On Tuesday 1 February, there were reports that an estimated more than two million people were on the streets of Cairo demanding the removal of the dictatorial regime of Mubarak. Millions more amassed in every city and community in Egypt. In Chapter 6 of this book, I outlined three basic stages of the Tunisian revolution. In my analysis I identified the first stage as the self-immolation and sacrifice of Mohammed Bouazizi. The second stage involved the self-mobilisation of the popular forces of Tunis, leading to the removal of the Ben Ali government. The third stage involved the caravans of liberation, when people from even the most rural parts of Tunisia rode to Tunis to hasten the dismantling of the remnants of the Ben Ali regime.

The massive outpouring of popular energy for social justice not only moved the ideas of liberation from town to town but across borders. This week, we seek to grasp how the Tunisian revolution intersects with the Egyptian uprising, and what this means for 21st century revolutions. In Egypt, the people have declared very clearly that theirs is a popular revolt of a revolutionary character. In both places, the potential revolutionary character could mature to the extent that winning the rank and file of the military and police to create a new society could be the foundation for a quantum leap in the move away from dictatorship and brutal repression.

One thing that stands out in both revolutions is the search by people from all walks of life to end a system that represses their human dignity and generates fear and submission. The Egyptian and Tunisian revolts are also uprisings against neoliberal capitalism and the medicines of the International Monetary Fund (IMF) and Bretton Woods institutions that pushed the trickle-down prescription for the economic health of society. Not only did implementing a neoliberal economic programme supported by the IMF and World Bank in 2004–05 directly foster the income inequality and conditions which the Tunisians and Egyptians are seeking to change, but during this period, these same institutions 'applauded' the governments for the success of these programmes because they achieved higher rates of GDP growth and increased foreign investment. Just as Ireland was applauded for its 'successful' economic model before imploding, it is evident that the 'success' being achieved occurred as impoverishment and unemployment for the majority of citizens were increasing.

Both Tunisians and Egyptians have witnessed massive unemployment, poor living conditions, a lack of decent housing, exploitation and low wages, state corruption, police repression and brutality, inflation and other forms of state terrorism. These conditions persisted in societies of billionaires, massive expenditure on the state security apparatus and a general climate for providing the conditions for capitalists to accumulate vast amounts of wealth.

The dehumanisation of Egyptian youths has been consistent with the dehumanisation of the people of the region. This dehumanisation is most advanced in the Palestinian territory. And it was not by accident that the same Egyptian government that dehumanised these people assisted Israel in blockading Gaza in an effort to starve and subdue the Palestinians.

The massive gap between the rich and the poor in Egypt is now in the open, taking this rebellion beyond the Western media's narrative about rage, anger, chaos and Islamic extremism. The transformation of the consciousness of the Egyptian and Tunisian peoples places the issues of social transformation at the centre of politics. Thus for the people of Egypt, it is not simply about the removal of Mubarak, it is also about the removal of the local and international apparatus that kept Mubarak in power for 30 years. This understanding is important because one narrative being told is that people are rebelling for greater political and economic freedom, as if poverty and unemployment were caused by the political dictators 'controlling' the economy. This is false. Under the neoliberal programmes in Tunisia and Egypt, the economies were 'liberalised' and state-owned enterprises were 'privatised' in the name of promoting economic freedom. In such environments, political and economic elites (foreign and local) were able to capture the majority of whatever gains were produced by the greater economic freedoms introduced by neoliberal policies.

From the murder of Khaled Said in Alexandria in June 2010 to the self-immolation of the Tunisian Mohammed Bouazizi, there is a new generation of youths able to mobilise social-networking tools to light up the imagination of other youths so that they too had to take a stand against police brutality. We now know that the police beating of Khaled Said 'ignited protests in Cairo and Alexandria and demands for justice spread like wildfire on blogs and social-networking sites'. With the deployment of new social media tools for organising by the youths and the collective security efforts of the people to defend their communities in Egypt, there is a pattern of self-organisation that contains the seeds of a new strategy for 21st century revolutions. How the seeds will germinate will depend on the extent to which the organisation for revolutionary non-violence and self-defence can take root and beat back the organised state violence that has been unleashed to destabilise the popular revolt.

Revolutions without self-proclaimed revolutionaries

Khaled Said had been killed because he dared to expose the depth of the corruption of the police and the operatives of the ruling political party, the National Democratic Party (NDP). Originally founded by Anwar Sadat to provide legitimacy for a military dictatorship, the NDP has dominated politics, pushing out other social forces from the centre of the legal political stage. Mubarak dominated this party and treated it as his personal fiefdom, promising to place his son as his heir, as if Egypt had become a monarchy. This example of a leader usurping the role of the party in society undermined the meaning and essence of political parties as vehicles of popular organisation.

A prominent feature of the revolutions in Tunisia and Egypt so far has been the absence of vanguard parties or personalities as leaders of the revolts. Throughout the 20th century, there was the conception that revolutions required vanguard parties or groups comprised of the most advanced sections of the working class and intelligentsia. This vanguard in the past had to be prepared to wage armed struggles to capture state power. The basic thesis on the need for advanced elements of the working class to lead revolution were spelt out by Lenin in two important documents, 'What is to be done' and *The State and Revolution*. These documents provided a guide for revolutionaries, and there were successful revolutions in China, Cuba and Vietnam, which were different from the deformities of vanguardism that had developed in the Soviet Union under Joseph Stalin and which were copied by Mubarak. The negative experiences of vanguardism were not confined to despots such as Mubarak and Stalin. Non-socialists and non-communists in societies such as Zaire under Mobutu and Iran practised vanguardism.

73

In Iran the mullahs adopted some of the tactics of vanguardism with disastrous results for the people of Iran after the overthrow of the Shah, thus undermining the emancipatory goals of the revolutionary process. As though the experiences of vanguardism had been studied by the young people of Egypt and Tunisia, they were careful not to elevate any individual or party that could hijack or personalise their struggle for freedom. These youths worked to build trust and cooperation among the networks of social forces that were fighting for freedom.

As the momentum of the Egyptian revolution gathered strength, Nobel laureate Mohamed ElBaradei left Vienna and joined the movement, offering himself up as a leader of the popular revolt. By the seventh day of the popular uprising, the coalescence of the opposition forces around ElBaradei was a defensive act because the Western media had insisted on placing the stamp of Islamic extremism on this peaceful opposition to dictatorship.

These experiences make it essential to spell out the importance of revolutions carried out without self-proclaimed revolutionaries and leaders. In Egypt, youths and women from what is now called the April 6 Movement emerged to organise and connect the networks of networks. It could be argued that they were aware of the positive and negative lessons of vanguardism, whether in the former Soviet Union or in Iran. It is for this reason that we hear the slogan in the streets of Egypt, 'This is the revolution of all the people.'

We now know that this uprising in Egypt came after years of patient and consistent work by young men and women who have been organising in the April 6 Movement. This is a group of young persons who had used the social-networking instrument of Facebook to call on the youths of Egypt to support the workers in their struggles. From 6 April 2008 these youths have been meeting and organising to build a movement linking their work to communities all across Egypt and linking up with grassroots activists in other parts of the world. By establishing the principles of sharing and cooperation instead of competition, they worked to be more effective in building a new kind of campaign for political change.

In my book *Barack Obama and 21st Century Politics*, I offered the principles of ubuntu – the philosophy of shared humanity – as a basic revolutionary ideal for the 21st century. At the core of this idea is the struggle to be human, and to rise above human hierarchies, divisions, xenophobia and compartmentalisations. The echoes of ubuntu reverberated from the actions and words of the ordinary people at the forefront of the Tunisian and Egyptian revolutions. At some points during the protests when Islamist sections of the protesters shouted 'Allahu Akbar!', a louder chant echoed, 'Muslims, Christians, atheists, we are all Egyptians.' Behind these chants lay the acts of Christians who offered to guard Muslims as they prayed during the demonstrations. These small acts of ubuntu and recognition of each other's humanity have to be celebrated, elevated and cascaded across Africa and the Middle East for transformation in the 21st century.

The youths had carried forward a long tradition of struggle that had come from the working people of Egypt. Egypt has one of the strongest social movements for peace and justice in Africa. Umm Kulthum is still revered in her nationalistic songs of self-determination and dignity. Leading African thinkers and activists from Egypt such as Samir Amin and Nawal El Saadawi are household names among progressives in all parts of the world. Eighty years old, Nawal El Saadawi, in particular, spoke for millions of women, narrating how she had been incarcerated twice – once in the cells of the regime and then in the prison that is Egyptian society. Her book *Woman at Point Zero* called for women in all parts of Africa and the Middle East 'to mobilise against gender oppression'.

The youths and women who have been organising day and night are the inheritors of organising traditions that had been undertaken by trade unionists, writers, journalists, farmers, artists, progressive intellectuals, women, religious forces and patriotic business-people. The strength of these social forces is so remarkable that the ruling elements resorted to violence. The closing down of the internet and shutting down of cell-phone services and non-government media were only the more modern manifestations of a long tradition of repression that had placed conservative militarists at the top of the political ladder in Egypt. Anwar Sadat had been explicit in his efforts to reverse the populist efforts of Gamal Abdel Nasser, one of the foremost nationalists in the independence period in Africa. When Sadat was gunned down in cold blood by elements from within the military itself, Hosni Mubarak became president in 1981.

The Mubarak dictatorship was an alliance between local oppressors and the US and Israel to beat back the legitimate demands of the peoples of Egypt. In the past century there has never been a moment when the peoples of Egypt have not been organising and protesting for better conditions. With the entrenchment of militaristic rule, political parties were banned, leaders were arrested, killed or sent into exile and genuine political expression stifled. The youths were studying the positive and negative lessons of political organising in order to fashion new tools for political struggle.

Revolutionary self-organisation and non-violence

All of the evidence of young men and women, rich and poor, organising in communities points to the level of social and political consciousness that has motivated the people to mobilise themselves to defend their interests. These millions of Egyptians are not afraid to stand up for their rights. These people have provided crucial revolutionary leadership and developed tactics that have now won over the majority of the Egyptian people to the cause of revolution. In the process, they have broken the cohesion of the Egyptian political and economic ruling class that had been built up with the help of the military–industrial complex and the Wall Street elements of the US. It is not by accident that as the revolution was unfolding, army chiefs from Egypt were in Washington DC consulting with the joint chiefs of staff of the US military. The billions of dollars that have gone from US citizens to support the dictatorship of Hosni Mubarak had supported divisions in the Egyptian military so that there was a class of officers whose interests were allied with those of the US and Israel against the interests of the Egyptian people. It is to this group that the sections of US and European leaders are turning in order to break the cohesion of the revolutionary forces in the streets. With the Western media presenting the popular revolt as scenes of chaos and anger, the Mubarak regime unleashed armed elements in the streets to fit into the template of the Western image while seeking to destroy the popular power that had occupied Tahrir Square. When the forces of the state stormed the people on Liberation Square the people stood their ground, defending themselves. Hundreds were wounded but this test brought out the fourth major stage of the revolution: the reconsolidation of the popular forces to sharpen the tools of revolutionary non-violence and self-defence.

These revolutionary forces in the streets have understood the social divisions in the military and have made direct appeals to the rank and file of the armed forces. These appeals have been consistent with not only the tools of organising, but the manner of organising. Having conceptualised the manner of self-organisation in advance, the revolutionaries have been ahead of the government so that even when the internet was shut down, the tactics of self-organisation gave way to sophisticated and creative means of communication. It is this sophisticated organisation that defeated the attempts of the government to crush the mass movement. This sophisticated organisation will also be needed if the counter-revolutionary forces consider war as the weapon of choice to reverse the revolution.

Indeed, the pattern of revolutionary organisation and revolutionary leadership in the Tunisian and Egyptian revolutions have so far neutralised the scheming of counter-revolutionary elements in Egypt and the US, who were bent on using anti-Islamist and counter-terrorism propaganda to beat back the popular revolts. The centrality of the Egyptian military to regime legitimacy in Egypt has been consistent for the past 50 years. However, at the height of the cold war, the US moved to support the most conservative fundamentalists in Egypt in order to bolster the US's cold war goals. Younger readers may not remember that it was in Egypt that the US recruited many of its mujahideen fighters to fight the Soviet Union in Afghanistan. The mujahideen fighters were also deployed against trade unionists, socialists, women and other social justice networks in Egypt. Sectarianism and fundamentalism served both the dictators and their imperial backers.

It is imperative to note that one of the positive lessons from both Egypt and Tunisia is the unity of the people across regional lines. In this process, the women of Tunisia and Egypt have emerged among the foremost and clearest section of the revolution. For decades, Egyptian women have been struggling against a government that suppresses Islamic fundamentalism, but mobilised the ideas of Islamic fundamentalism to dominate women. The images of forthright women outlining the goals of the mass movement sweeping Egypt and Tunisia remain an inspiration across Africa and the Middle East. We want to repeat that the struggles for reproductive rights, bodily integrity and opposition to sexual oppression elevated the democratic struggle beyond the rights to freedom of speech, to assemble and for workers to organise.

Iterations of 21st century revolutions in Africa and the Middle East

The Egyptian and Tunisian revolutions have now changed the political calculus and the discourse on politics and revolution. Not only have these revolutions transformed the consciousness of the people, they have also given rise to a new burst of creative energies and become a school for new revolutionary techniques for the 21st century. These energies could be translated into numerous actions geared toward revolutionary transformations across Africa and the Middle East. Clearly, the changes in economic conditions which the people are calling for will not be achieved by the types of reforms financed by foreign donors to promote 'more' economic freedom. They will only be achieved by the peoples electing new leaders and governments with the courage to implement alternative economic policies which focus on addressing the conditions of life as opposed to the interests of foreign investors and local elites.

The uprising in Egypt reached a tipping point where the counter-revolutionary forces are in disarray and cannot keep up with the pace of change. There is a pattern of popular outpouring which is cascading from Tunisia and Egypt to all societies under dictatorial rule in Africa and the Middle East. The task of progressives is to celebrate the positive lessons of self-organisation and the wind of self-emancipation blowing across Africa. Progressives cannot be on the sideline and have to find their own method of showing solidarity with the people who are now being mowed down in the streets.

We have spelt out what we are learning from some of the

characteristics of these 21st revolutions. The highlights so far are:

- The revolutions are made by ordinary people, independent of vanguard parties and self-proclaimed revolutionaries
- The nature of independent networks of networks and the sophistication of the tools of the revolution
- The leadership of ordinary people who displayed self-mobilisation for the revolution
- The building of revolutionary non-violence for self-defence
- The revolutionary ideas of the people whose ultimate goal is to be dignified human beings and not to be dictators' robots or zealots.

It is now up to us progressives to embrace and support this pattern of revolution, to initiate a quantum leap beyond neoliberalism, capitalism, militarism and dictatorship in Africa and the Middle East.

http://pambazuka.org/en/category/features/70670

9

Egypt: free at last, an inside look

Hassan El Ghayesh

17 February 2011

It's Thursday 10 February, and we are waiting for what we think will be the last speech by Egyptian president Hosni Mubarak: his resignation. We become tenser, as his speech was scheduled for 18.00, but we have to wait for hours. By being late, Mubarak continues to show his disrespect for the Egyptian people. He is an expert at it and has been doing it for 30 years. At last he is on. The speech is delivered in a paternal tone, as would a father confronting his ungrateful children. I am not listening closely to what he has to say, I am just waiting for one statement: 'I resign.' He never says it; instead he passes his responsibilities to the newly appointed vice-president, Omar Suleiman, but stays on.

This is by far Mubarak's weakest speech. You can tell that it has been poorly written; it was not filmed as one shot, but instead as a series of shots that were edited together, and it was just too late. I believe he broke down under stress and sadness during his speech and that they had to film it in many takes and then fix the whole thing together in a montage. This is probably why the broadcasting of the speech was delayed a few hours.

If this speech had been 12 days earlier, on 28 January, the protesters might have settled down and accepted everything Mubarak said. But his stubbornness was met with even stronger determination by the protesters. I was furious at the speech. After 17 days of solidarity and the deaths of more than 300, we would accept nothing less than the resignation of Mubarak.

Thursday's speech was the last chance to deter people from

joining the protests the next day. Over the previous two weeks, Friday and Tuesday had witnessed huge protests, with numbers exceeding the one million mark. Mubarak's last chance to calm people down didn't have the desired effect.

I was in Hurghada, 450km south of Cairo. I went to the bus station, bought myself a ticket and was on the first bus to Cairo to join protesters in Tahrir Square, determined to stay there until he left. I was convinced that one more week of protests would be sufficient for him to step down. The unions were already in, institutions all over the nation were showing solidarity and employees in both the private and public sectors threatened to go on strike. The questions that were in my mind were: will Mubarak step down before we slip into total chaos? Will the army take Mubarak's side and confront the protesters? I thought at the time that Mubarak's lust for power had no limits and I expected very pessimistic scenarios if he did not step down any time soon.

It's Friday 11 February, the Friday of the martyrs, and we are heading to downtown Cairo on the metro. It is filled with people heading to Tahrir, from the ages of 18 to 30. We arrive at Tahrir where we're searched by three civil committees. Graffiti artists immortalise the revolution on the walls of 19th-century buildings in downtown Cairo; burnt police cars are changed to artefacts as people write their names and demands in colourful calligraphy on them.

At last we are at the square, and once you are there you can't really move. People move around the square in a manner reminiscent of Mecca – Tahrir Square is a Mecca for those seeking freedom. Many stages fill the perimeter of the square. I can't really see or hear those on the stages; I can only hear cheers of approval of what they have to say. Huge posters of the martyrs dangle down from balconies of buildings around the square; every traffic light in the square has a poster attached to it. Tents are mainly in the middle of the square – every tent has a sign indicating where the occupants are from, and they are from all over Egypt.

Tahrir Square becomes a microcosm of Egypt with all its crowdedness, noise, overflowing human emotion and, most importantly, its hate for Mubarak. Protesters from Menoufeya, Mubarak's birthplace, hold signs that read 'Menoufians apologise'. The army units are alert and are preventing the protesters from coming anywhere near their tanks. Still, I see no worries on the faces of protesters, who firmly believe the army is on their side.

In the meantime, another protest is taking place in front of the presidential palace – tens of thousands show up. It is the biggest in Cairo after the protests at Tahrir. Still, nobody is waiting for a statement by the president. He gave a statement the day before. I am back home at around 17.00. The communication blackout is still in force in the Tahrir Square area and I am in dire need of making some phone calls.

I switch on the TV. Omar Suleiman is scheduled to make a statement. I say to myself 'Oh man … not this guy again.' I had watched his interview with ABC and it was absolutely horrific. He said things such as: 'Those protesters are being pushed by the Islamic current'; 'Egyptians don't have the culture of democracy'; and 'I would advise those protesting to get back to their jobs if they want what's better for Egypt.' He later said in Egyptian national newspapers that his statements had been misunderstood and taken out of context. We just laughed. We didn't expect much from Suleiman – it's Mubarak who chose him – but we expected some decency at least.

I decide to watch the statement by Suleiman at home and head to Tahrir afterwards. The family gathers around the TV in anticipation. Suleiman is on. 'Mubarak resigns.' Can the feeling be described?

For 10 seconds, you totally forget about who you are, what you do or where you are – it's pure euphoria. Then it all comes back to you slowly. I am Hassan, an Egyptian who was part of a revolution that brought down a dictator. We fought to get to Tahrir, as we saw Egyptians pay with their lives in tribute to freedom. We were peaceful and we stood for something we believe is right. We are the people and our will must prevail; how couldn't we realise that from the beginning?

My phone doesn't stop ringing for 30 minutes and I don't stop calling all those who had been at Tahrir with me for another hour. We made it! Congratulations, we made it! Most of Egypt is in the street celebrating. I can't remember the number of smiles and hugs exchanged. I do remember, though, how the older generation looked at us with absolute admiration and gratitude. We did something of which they never dreamed. The flame of youthful demonstrations hasn't been ignited in Egypt since the early 1970s.

And then all of a sudden, we hit so strongly that we shake the foundation of this regime. I will forever remember the first day, the first morning I wake up to the smell of freshly baked freedom, the first shower that rinses away all the corruption and stench of the former regime.

Former ministers, former members of parliament and those close to the regime, start falling one by one. They are denied permission to travel abroad and their bank accounts are frozen.

The military council is now in control. People in Egypt generally trust the military. They like to say it's the only institution in this country not being invaded by corruption. They have stated on many occasions they are in power to protect the revolution's requests and to make sure they are met. Everything they've done so far proves them true to their words. The parliament is dissolved; the constitution is in the process of being changed. They give exact dates for handing power to a civilian president. The government is the same one Mubarak brought to power in his last days, headed by Prime Minister Ahmed Shafiq.

We are not sure if they are going to form a new transitional government or not. In his last speech Shafiq stated that restoring order and security was his priority, which isn't promising at all. Shafiq, I don't want your security. I want my freedom.

Will things get better, or will they get worse? I am not sure. I sometimes even have my doubts about the revolution. What if things go wrong again? But I always remind myself: we stood against tyranny and corruption and that cannot be wrong. We shall rise again if we see the slightest tendency by those in power to kill our dream of change.

I have my doubts about the six months of military rule in Egypt. I have my doubts about conducting fair presidential elections in six months' time. We shouldn't think it is over yet. The fight for democracy is never ending. We have all become keepers of democracy and freedom. I am honoured to be given such responsibilities and am willing to stay true to what we stood up for. There is no going back.

http://pambazuka.org/en/category/features/70963

This chapter first appeared in *Daily Maverick*. It has also been published by Free African Media, from where it is licensed under Creative Commons.

Chronicles of an Egyptian revolution: a protester's first-hand account

Hassan El Ghayesh

17 February 2011

Imagine that for 24 years you don't ever have hope of things getting better. Mubarak is ruling Egypt with an iron fist, while the people are captured in a cycle of paralysing fear and hopeless apathy. We are kept from even daring to imagine a different reality from the poverty, inequity, government corruption and indignity we know. The only hope for a fresh graduate like me will be to look for chances elsewhere. Through school and university, I have already met enough bureaucracy and corruption to make me realise there is probably no way a young professional would ever make it in such an atmosphere without becoming everything I've always despised.

So what led to the revolution in such an unpromising situation? The call for protests started on Facebook through the group 'We are all Khaled Said'. Said was a 28-year-old Egyptian from Alexandria who was beaten to death on 6 June 2010 for refusing to show his ID to two policemen. He was abducted in a police vehicle, taken to a police station, tortured to death and his corpse was later dumped in the street.

But still, the call for protests through Facebook had been going on for three years and it never really worked out for Egyptian activists. So why did the Egyptians show up in the streets in such great numbers? The success of the Tunisian revolution was the key factor. Some other factors may include the illegitimate parliamentary elections in November 2010, the rampant unemployment and corruption and a strong sense of solidarity among the Egyptian population after the bombing of the Saints Church in Alexandria on New Year's Eve. The bombing also showed that, apart from terrorising and torturing innocents, the police force wasn't doing much.

I am from the middle class, a class that will disappear in Egypt if things keep going the way they are. We are the educated few who get better chances and who get to spend a year or two abroad while studying. I got to see that things can operate on a different level, that we do not have to settle for what we have. I strongly believe that if the Egyptian people are given the chances of a better education, a better healthcare system and a better model to follow they will shine. I might not have suffered the most from Mubarak's regime, but I will stand for those who suffer the most. The middle class has a responsibility towards the working class, no matter how the regime tried to widen the gap between us or how it frightened us from ever interacting on a meaningful level. I knew that one day we would stand up against the regime to represent a working class that had no voice.

I currently work and reside in Hurghada, a tourist town by the Red Sea, 450km south of Cairo. I took a vacation from work for nine days, starting on Tuesday 25 January, to travel to Cairo and join the protests. As I was preparing to catch the bus to Cairo on the morning of the 25th I heard the news about how a few hundred thousand people had showed up at Tahrir (literally 'liberation') Square. I was more determined than ever to join the protests. Unfortunately, the first bus to Cairo arrived at midnight. I kept in contact with friends in the square, who told me they were able to get to Tahrir despite being attacked by the police, who were using sticks and tear gas to separate them.

Until, suddenly, phone calls to my friends at Tahrir Square were all met with the same message: 'This phone cannot be reached at the moment.' The government had managed to shut down all cell-phone communication in Tahrir Square.

As I arrived in Cairo I received a call from a friend who told me that at about 12.30 the anti-riot police, who had surrounded the protesters for a few hours, viciously attacked the square and evacuated all protesters. Egyptian TV showed nothing of the protests. National newspapers run by the government totally ignored the protests, as if they never happened.

I was eager to join the protests the next day. As we went to Tahrir we were met by thousands of anti-riot police stationed to secure the square. Anyone between the ages of 18 and 45 was asked to show their ID. One policeman approached me and my friend and asked us why we were at Tahrir and if we were going to join any of the protests. He then went on about how much trouble we would get into and, in a threatening tone, added: 'You seem like you come from good families. Your parents wouldn't like it if you were arrested.' I met his remarks with a few laughs and told him we were just hanging out in one of the cafes I knew nearby.

We walked around downtown Cairo and checked Facebook and other social websites trying to find out where the protests were. Along the way we met a few protests taking place. The biggest was in front of the lawyers' syndicate and had about 1,000 protesters. They were stopped at the gate of the syndicate by the anti-riot police and everything was kept under control. As the sun was setting, a few thousand protesters started to burn tyres along the Corniche (the main road along the Nile). They were trying to make their way to the national TV building. Again the anti-riot police had complete control of the situation. Even though they had control, they had to use violence through police in civilian clothes, who suddenly held their sticks in the air and started chasing protesters.

I was about 100m away from the protest and was taking pictures when two policemen in civilian outfits attacked me and tried to take my camera. One kicked me while the other started to beat me with a wooden stick, breaking one of the camera lenses I had in my bag. Luckily I was not injured. Friends and I managed to make it out of Tahrir without being caught by the police and with our cameras intact.

Another call for protests was made on Facebook for what would be known as 'The Friday of Rage' on 28 January. Protests were supposed to start after the Friday prayer. The Friday prayer at noon is a weekly communal prayer and would be a perfect way to gather others who wanted to join the protests. I made plans with friends to meet at an assembly point in my neighbourhood, 15km south of downtown Cairo, and make our way to Tahrir Square, meeting other protestors on the way. To my disbelief I woke up to a communications blackout enforced by the government – no internet, no cell phones and no SMS – only landlines were left for people to use.

We managed to regroup at the meeting point despite problems with communication. We started out as about 2,000 people and urged bystanders and even people standing on their balconies to join us. After an hour of marching our numbers had increased to more than I can guess or even see in the narrow streets of Cairo. I could see a police station in the distance – the regime's thugs and police officers stood with weapons in hand – sticks, knives and chains. When they saw our numbers, the thugs ran and hid in the police station, while the police officers pretended they were okay with us passing through. We chanted 'peaceful, peaceful' and passed through; the same thing happened an hour later when we passed another police station. On my way back both these police stations had been burnt because they'd tried to stop other protesters from joining us.

Along the way we were met by cheers from people standing on their balconies. They showered us with flowers and candy, while some took the trouble to leave their homes to offer us water and food. We reached al Qasr Al-Aini Street, only 1km from Tahrir Square, and saw about 100 anti-riot police armed with teargas, sticks, shields and rubber bullets. We marched all the way to where they held their post and shouted: 'The people don't want the regime,' and 'Tell the truth officer, are you an Egyptian or not?' for about five minutes, and then they started firing at us. The teargas was the hardest to endure: it is like taking chilli pepper and rubbing it all over your face.

We tried to push them backwards as more and more of us fell and were replaced by protesters who had just joined us. For six hours, we fought our way to Tahrir. At about 21.00, the police were ordered to leave their posts and retreat. A speeding car with diplomatic plates ran over about 20 protesters; a few live rounds were fired and some people were injured. This made things even more uncontrollable as people reacted to seeing other protesters die by burning a National Democratic Party (NDP) building nearby, trashing a nearby gas station and chasing what was left of the police force on the streets. The protesters now had total control of Tahrir Square in the middle of downtown. Military units rolled into the streets to fill the void left by the police force.

That night Mubarak talked for the first time after four days of protests. His declaration was very weak and barely met any of our requests. He dissolved the current government, appointed a vice-president for the first time, and dealt with the whole thing as if he had heard nothing that we had said. The speech went on for a few more minutes and sounded more like something he had said before on Labour Day.

Then there were two days with no police force. To understand why the police withdrew that way, you have to be aware that the people and the police in Egypt are not on good terms. You might say that the police withdrew as a vengeful act against the people of Egypt. We heard stories about policemen dressed as civilians terrorising neighbourhoods all over Cairo. We needed to be reminded why we needed them. We were shown horrible images on TV of the Egyptian museum being looted because the police had left their posts and there was a two-hour gap between them leaving and the army arriving in downtown Cairo. There were prison breaches all over Cairo for the same reason.

We spent one night in absolute terror. Everybody in the neighbourhood came down to the street with whatever weapon they could get. We stayed up all night protecting our homes. By the end of the night we were used to the gunshots and screams we could hear in the distance. As for the general atmosphere regarding the protests, some Egyptians who hadn't been to the protests wanted them to be over, as they blamed the protests for putting us in a situation where we had to protect ourselves. Most of the people who thought that way were either working for the government public sector or were serving in the police force or the military. The watch went peacefully, as we didn't talk much about politics – and the supply of freshly baked cakes and tea never stopped throughout the whole night.

It was now almost a week since the first day of the protests on the 25th. As day drew nearer, the streets became safer and better controlled by the army. A call for a more than a million Egyptians to protest was issued from Tahrir Square. Most of us had had to go back to protect our homes and the numbers in Tahrir were unsatisfactory, ranging between 20,000 and 50,000. The media and the regime were dealing with the protests as if those 50,000 people in Tahrir represented only themselves. We needed to send a stronger message to the regime: we were millions and did not want Mubarak as our president. By now, the protests, which had started spontaneously, had led to precise requests:

- Mubarak stepping down
- Dissolving the illegitimate parliament
- Taking to trial those responsible for corruption
- Changing the constitution to limit the president to two terms and having the presidential and parliament elections monitored by the justice department.

This time when we went to Tahrir the picture was totally different. There was no police presence at all, and the square was monitored by the civil committees, who made sure nobody had any sort of weapon on him and no police in civilian clothes entered the square, as it was obvious now who was doing all the looting and damage to public facilities. We were met with colourful signs, some of which were very funny; huge speakers played old Egyptian national songs and people sang along. Everybody was singing and laughing, sharing food, taking pictures and enjoying the atmosphere. The main chants of the crowds were 'leave, leave', and 'The people want the regime to step down.'

Compared to Friday this was more of a picnic. Two million people showed up at Tahrir that day. This number would have doubled had the government opened the highways for people from different parts of Egypt to join us in Cairo. Protests of the same nature took place in Alexandria and other cities – a total of three million were in the streets that day. It was clear that the protests were peaceful and that the civil committees did what the police failed to do in organising peaceful marches and protests.

Later that night, Mubarak gave another speech. This time he declared he wouldn't stand in the next presidential elections in nine months, he would make the amendments to the constitution asked for by the people and the justice department would look into the last parliamentary elections. He also stated he was willing to negotiate with the opposition. This time he seemed more flexible. His emotional speech – in which he talked a lot about himself and his accomplishments in war and peace – really had the desired effect on many of the people who were sympathetic to the protesters. They shifted their stance to be pro-Mubarak, asking that he stay until the end of his term.

As for us, the speech offered nothing new. After 30 years we were accustomed to the fake promises. As we all suspected, the next day when the numbers in Tahrir were about 50,000 again, thugs attacked the protesters trying to evacuate the square. In a surreal scene, camels and horses entered the square as the protesters were showered with rocks and Molotov cocktails. The protesters held their ground and called for help. Those of us who were not in the square rushed to help with supplies and medicine and to help keep our footing in Tahrir. We were met by thugs who stopped us from entering the square. This went on for about 12 hours and the new prime minister, who promised when he took the post that none of the protesters would be harmed, did nothing to help. The army units that were supposed to be protecting protestors didn't do anything either. We were back to the vicious cycle of fake promises. Eleven people were killed that day and 800 were injured. After one week the death toll was 300 and more than 3,500 injured. The huge number of deaths and injuries took the situation to a whole new level, as we were more determined than ever: no more negotiations before Mubarak leaves and all our demands were met.

There was no official representation of the people in Tahrir. The opposition did not represent us. When the new vice-president, Omar Suleiman, met with the leaders of the opposition, including the Muslim Brotherhood, the Wafd party and the Tagamo' party, we couldn't care less in Tahrir. For us there was really nothing to negotiate about. The demands were clear and any negotiations were in favour of the regime. When the people in Tahrir realised their revolution might be stolen by the opposition, who actually didn't participate much in Tahrir, they organised themselves and voted to elect a few of them to represent the movement in the media. Many other committees formed to talk as the voice of the people, most notably the Wisdom Circle, which included many respected Egyptian figures. Some movements were more flexible than others in their demands, but the protesters in Tahrir wanted all their demands met before any negotiations, with less emphasis on the constitutional correctness of the demands.

The Wisdom Circle was trying to reach a halfway resolution between the regime and the protesters. The opposition just ran to negotiate with the government, which made them lose credibility and any sort of support they might have had from the people. It was also important to know that before these negotiations, many key figures from the ruling National Democratic Party had resigned, including Gamal Mubarak, Hosni Mubarak's own son. Safwat Al Sharif, a politician known for his devious ways and sometimes credited as the mastermind behind all the corruption and thuggery in the streets during elections, also resigned from the party, but he still kept his seat in parliament. Ahmed Ezza, a businessman-turned-politician, who controlled 67 per cent of steel industries in Egypt and made sure the National Democratic Party monopolised the parliament, had resigned and was called in for interrogation. Still, Mubarak was the president of the party. Protesters in Tahrir were glad but not satisfied. It was not about figures. It was about a system that gave birth to those figures.

The future is uncertain. It's a psychological struggle at the moment between the regime and the people. Who has the stronger will? Mubarak is a military man who won't give up easily. Egypt is not Tunisia. The scenario of Mubarak stepping down and escaping the country feels unlikely. On the other hand, Mubarak could step down and give his responsibilities to the newly appointed vice-president. The problem with this scenario is that, according to the constitution, the vice-president cannot make amendments to the constitution or dissolve parliament, and so the people's demands wouldn't be met. But in a revolution, who cares about a constitution that was written by the regime to protect the regime? All that I was certain of at that moment was that the protests would continue as long as Mubarak was still in power.

The revolution was driven by the fury and the rage of youth against an autocratic president who has done nothing to make this country better; a government run by corrupt businessmen who are more interested in increasing the NDP than in offering better jobs and facilities; a state police that is so violent that it would lead to the deaths of 300 protesters and the injury of more than 3,000. Hosni Mubarak managed to stay in power through an authoritarian regime, backed by Western countries who don't mind all the corruption and anti-humanitarian practices as long as he kept their interests in the region safe. Now, he is trying to convince the world that the revolution is pushed by Islamic extremists and that he is the only line of defence between the Islamists and power.

If you knew him as well as we do, perhaps you would be able to see through his lies. Be aware of what is happening in Egypt because sooner or later it will affect you.

http://pambazuka.org/en/category/features/70965

This chapter first appeared in Free African Media. It is licensed under Creative Commons.

11

Egypt and the revolution in our minds

Nigel C. Gibson

17 February 2011

'What makes the lid blow off?' Fanon asks in *The Wretched of the Earth*, reflecting on the revolution against French colonialism in Algeria 50 years ago and thinking about the future 'African revolution'. In Egypt, a country where 50 per cent of the population is under 30 years old and has known no other regime than Mubarak's state of emergency, with its torture and surveillance, it was the reaction to the murder of Khaled Said, a young blogger beaten to death by the police, which was a turning point. It began with a protest of 1,000 people in Alexandria during Said's funeral and then went 'underground' onto the internet. Pictures of his crushed face are still on his Facebook page. The next spark in the North African revolution was in Sidi Bouzid, Tunisia, ignited by the self-immolation of Mohammed Bouazizi, a vegetable peddler whose cart and produce were confiscated by the police. Over the next month, despite increased repression, protests grew across Tunisia and on 14 January President Ben Ali was pushed out of the country. The date of the Egyptian revolution is 25 January but its prehistory includes years of labour struggle: the sit-ins, strikes and demonstrations of 2006; the almost daily workers' actions of early 2007; and the massive strike of textile workers in Muhalla al-Kubra in 2008, initiated by working women. These struggles led to beatings and imprisonments as well as some wage increases and bread subsidies as the regime tried to cheaply buy its way out of crisis. The mixture of economic hardship, political repression and social control indicate how deep the uprooting of the old regime had to be.

Revolution 2.0

The 25 January revolution began as a movement against the odds, despite repression and torture and violence; despite the closing down of the internet which seemed so important to its birth; despite the conservativism of the world powers – Obama especially – and at times corporate media's conformism. Despite all, the movement grew in size and grabbed the world's attention as it developed in sophistication and in articulation – expressed so brilliantly in the discussions, platforms and self-organisation (the organisation of the provision of security, food, blankets, stones and medicine is a story to be told) around and in Tahrir Square, where the once cowed and silenced people of one of the world's great cities could begin to speak and engage in seemingly endless debates and decision making in open sessions. This had all the makings of a people's revolution. There have been discussions of the revolution's similarity with the velvet revolutions of 1989, Tiananmen Square in 1989, people power against Marcos in the Philippines and Duvalier in Haiti in 1986. It is akin to Paris 1968 and its decentralised working and bottom-up democracy reflect the new beginning which began with the Hungarian revolution of 1956. Indeed, aided by social media the revolution has been dubbed Revolution 2.0, a revolution without leaders, a 'Wikipedia revolution' as Wael Ghonim (the young Google executive behind the 'We are all Khaled Said' Facebook page) put it. With everyone contributing to its content, the revolution was never simply a revolt of the middle class and as it grew it increasingly came to reflect the socio-economic composition of Africa's largest city.

The retaking of public space

The Egyptian revolution is like a Rorschach test: everyone can see something in it. And while these insights are all true, it is also a revolution of the 21st century, not simply because of the social media technology (plus Wikileaks and Al Jazeera). In this age of gated cities, of citadels, under surveillance and policed – what have been called 'global cities' – the Egyptian people opened up political space, as an ongoing public debate in the squares, outside the parliament, in the streets. Cairo, a city of 18 million

– abundant in its history and riches and also in the lived realities of the majority of its citizens who are poor – became associated throughout the world, and especially the Arab world, with liberation. The Caireans have shown the world how social media relates to social transformation and the retaking of public space. They have implicitly brought into focus the idea of the 'right to the city' as a collective project of social transformation. They were not stopped by fears about maintaining order, nor by the police and the state's paid murderers, nor by threats of a coup. Instead, they organised a continuous occupation of a city's central square by tens, then hundreds of thousands, then millions of people, defending it, feeding it, nurturing it, articulating it, developing it as their daily work. Cairo was the centre, but in other towns such as Alexandria, smaller groups – perhaps initially under the threat and reality of even more violence – continually gathered. The regime cracked. For it to remain hegemonic, Mubarak had to be sacrificed.

Towards a national revolution

For Fanon, the timing of the revolution is a moment when the militants make contact with the poor from the outskirts of towns and rural areas and realise that they have always thought in terms of a revolutionary transformation. In Egypt this is only beginning to happen. What began to amaze organisers during the last days of Mubarak's rule was the militancy of the youth from poor neighbourhoods. Before the 28 January demonstration, for example, a group of organisers 'conducted ... a field test' walking along the narrow alleys of a working-class neighbourhood to measure the level of participation: 'when we finished up the people refused to leave. They were 7,000 and they burned two police cars.'[1]

The turning point in the struggle – the point when the ruling elites decided to dump Mubarak – came not after it defeated the police and paid goons, but as workers in the port towns and across the industrial and service sectors began strikes supporting the movement and raising their own demands. With revolts also in rural areas and in smaller towns, it was the beginning of a national revolution whose first phase ended with the departure of Mubarak. Strikes have continued, indeed expanded, but what is also at stake is whether the self-organisation learnt from Tahrir Square will take on a class character and whether the public political space, the democratic space opened up by the revolution, will remain open.

Breaking the mind-forged manacles of unfreedom

Clearly things were changing during those 18 days after 25 January, and the speed of change, of development, of solidarity and fearlessness – of a new humanity experiencing freedom – took on a momentum of its own. Steve Biko, the South African Black Consciousness leader, argued that the most potent weapon in the oppressor's arsenal was the internalisation of fear in the consciousness of the oppressed. But once that mind experiences freedom – not as an abstraction but in and through collective actions – it becomes a force of revolution. 'People have changed. They were scared. They are no longer scared,' argued Ahmad Mahmoud. 'When we stopped being afraid we knew we would win. We will not again allow ourselves to be scared of a government. This is the revolution in our country, the revolution in our minds.'[2]

Once the lid is taken off a police state, it is very difficult to put back on. Mental liberation, Fanon argues, and the radical change in consciousness that accompanies revolution, entails a rethinking of everything, a questioning of everything that has been taken for granted. What had been normal for so long has been fundamentally shaken. After 30 years of life under the dictatorship, the Egyptian people had become historical protagonists. Tahrir Square, the revolution's focal point, became territorialised by those who had not counted. It became the space of a new kind of work in Fanon's sense, namely the hard but collectively joyous work of human liberation.

Mubarak's departure represents a victory for the movement but it is not the goal of liberation. Egypt remains at a crossroads, with the military as the only possible institution to renormalise it. Yet under the guise of the national interest, any return to the old norms must include suppressing freedom, strikes, demonstrations, and any other manifestation of the economic and social revolt against injustice and exploitation that has been brewing for the past decade.

The military interregnum

In 1956, four years after the 1952 Egyptian revolution and one year into the Algerian revolution, Algeria's liberation movement met in the Soummam Valley to discuss the organisation and programme of its revolution. An important principle adopted there was that rather than militarising politics, the military and any military decision had to be subservient to, and under the control of, the political struggle. It is a principle that continues to haunt Algeria and Egypt, where militarised states of emergency have been in place for decades, abrogating political rights and suppressing spaces for public discourse.

In 1959 Fanon presented his 'Pitfalls of national consciousness' (which would become a central chapter of *The Wretched of the Earth*) as lectures to the Algerian liberation army camped on the Tunisian border. Looking forward to decolonisation, he goes further than the Soummam platform, arguing that the army too often becomes the pillar of a nation, and that despite independence it does not undergo any fundamental reorganisation. The military enforces systematic pauperisation and 'the strength of the police force and the power of the army are [simply] proportionate to the stagnation in which the rest of the nation is sunk'.[3] Where there is no parliament, he continues, the army takes over – as it has done in Egypt. But this changes nothing unless the army is truly nationalised and the development of the officer class is curtailed, as it becomes a school of 'civic and political education'. Rather than a professional army, he adds, the military should become a political organisation which, as a servant of the people, needs to take the step from 'national consciousness to political and social consciousness' and become part of a genuine humanist and social national programme.[4] Too often, however, as we have seen in the 50 years since Fanon's death, the army, as he feared, takes the place of a corrupt political party, and becomes the organiser of the profiteers.[5] This certainly was the situation under Mubarak.

In Egypt the army – intimately connected to the economy and self-interested in the maintenance of the status quo – is repeating the same calls it made during the last days of Mubarak under the slogans 'return to order' and 'return to normalcy'. Yet the people are not naive. During the commune days of Tahrir Square, they understood that the tanks not only protected them but threatened them. People slept in the tank's tracks not only to stop the tanks from moving but to let everyone know that they were ready if the tanks did move; they marched around the tanks by candlelight at night to keep them in their place; and they continued to embrace the soldiers as their 'brothers', but announced further demonstrations and encouraged the soldiers to join them. Thus, after Mubarak's departure and despite the army's clearing of Tahrir Square and its threat to ban strikes and end street demonstrations, the question is: can the military put the lid back on the multidimensional revolt? How reliable are the army's young and badly paid conscripts?

Social imagination

It is the revolution happening in the minds of the people – including, perhaps, those among the army's rank and file – that is really significant. Nasser understood its importance, calling his book on the liberation of Egypt a 'philosophy of revolution'. A different philosophy of revolution came alive in the movement at Tahrir Square. As Sinan Antoon, the Iraqi-born poet, novelist and filmmaker put it, 'What distinguishes this revolution is the wonderful and sublime example it sets in terms of solidarity among protesters and citizens at large. The spontaneity and cooperation in managing their daily affairs without a hierarchy is what the state didn't expect as it deprived the people of basic services and tried to spread fear and chaos to terrorise the citizenry.' The 'commune' at Tahrir Square produced a new political form.[6] And in an attempt to decommunalise that form, it has now been deterritorialised. As youths moved to literally and symbolically clean the square, the military destroyed the shelters, banners and artworks and removed the people. Traffic now moves across the square – but traffic can also be stopped.

Whither Egypt?

There are at least two potential scenarios which Fanon also considered to be the problematic of decolonisation and the African revolution. The first is that the horizontal movement based on the inclusivity of people's power – on its ongoing support and democratic organisation – that overthrew Mubarak is understood not simply as a fragment or a moment but as something that becomes the basis for daily life. The other possible scenario is a vertical movement based on the exclusivity of an 'elite transition', controlled by professional politicians, generals and planners with their own vested interest in the status quo, which suffocates the air of freedom and the 'revolution in our minds'.

As strikes roll across the country, from industrial to service sectors, the idea of reconstituting 'Tahrir' in the factories remains a radical possibility.[7]

http://pambazuka.org/en/category/features/70972

Notes

1. David Kirkpatrick (2011) 'Wired and shrewd: young Egyptians guide revolt', *New York Times*, 9 February, http://www.nytimes.com/2011/02/10/world/middleeast/10youth.html, accessed 15 June 2011.
2. Peter Hallward (2011) 'Egypt's popular revolution will change the world', *Guardian*, 9 February, http://www.guardian.co.uk/commentisfree/2011/feb/09/egypt-north-africa-revolution, accessed 15 June 2011.
3. Frantz Fanon (1968) *The Wretched of the Earth*, New York, Grove: 172.
4. Ibid: 201–3
5. Ibid: 174
6. Nigel Gibson (2011) 'The Cairo commune', 7 February, http://libcom.org/news/cairo-commune-07022011, accessed 15 June 2011.
7. Charles Levinson, Margaret Coker and Tamer El-Ghobashy (2010) 'Strikes worry Egypt's military, youth', *Wall Street Journal*, 15 February.

12

Egypt: women of the revolution

Fatma Naib

24 February 2011

When 26-year-old Asmaa Mahfouz wrote on Facebook that she was going to Cairo's Tahrir Square and urged all those who wanted to save the country to join her, the founding member of the April 6 Youth Movement was hoping to seize the moment as Tunisians showed that it was possible for a popular uprising to defeat a dictator.

Mahfouz later explained on Egyptian television that she and three others from the movement went to the square and began shouting: 'Egyptians, four people set themselves on fire out of humiliation and poverty. Egyptians, four people set fire to themselves because they were afraid of the security agencies, not of the fire. Four people set fire to themselves in order to tell you to awaken. We are setting ourselves on fire so that you will take action. Four people set themselves on fire in order to say to the regime: Wake up. We are fed up.'

In a video she subsequently posted online, which quickly went viral, she declared: 'As long as you say there is no hope, then there will be no hope, but if you go down and take a stance, then there will be hope.'

Egyptian women, just like men, took up the call to 'hope'. Here they describe the spirit of Tahrir – the camaraderie and equality they experienced – and their hope that the model of democracy established there will be carried forward as Egyptians shape a new political and social landscape.

Mona Seif, 24, researcher

'I have never felt as at peace and as safe as I did during those days in Tahrir.'

The daughter of a political activist who was imprisoned at the time of her birth and the sister of a blogger who was jailed by the Mubarak regime, Mona Seif says nothing could have prepared her for the scale and intensity of the protests.

'I didn't think it was going to be a revolution. I thought if we could [mobilise] a couple of thousand people then that would be great.

'I was angry about the corruption in the country, [about the death of] Khaled Said and the torture of those suspected but never convicted [of being behind] the Alexandria Coptic church [bombing].

'I realised this was going to be bigger than we had anticipated when 20,000 people marched towards Tahrir Square on 25 January. That is when we saw a shift; it was not about the minimum wage or emergency law anymore. It became much bigger than this; it turned into a protest against the regime, demanding that Mubarak step down and that parliament be dissolved.

'On the night later dubbed "the battle of the camels", when pro-Mubarak thugs attacked us, I was terrified. I thought they were going to shoot us all and get it over with. The turning point for me was when I saw the number of people ready to face death for their beliefs.

'I was amazed by the peoples' determination to keep this peaceful even when we were under deadly attacks. When we caught the pro-Mubarak thugs, the guys would protect them from being beaten and say: 'Peaceful, peaceful, we are not going to beat anyone up.' That was when I started thinking: 'No matter what happens we are not going to quit until Mubarak leaves.' The spirit of the people in Tahrir kept us going.

'My friend and I had the role of ensuring that all of the videos and pictures from Tahrir were uploaded and, as the internet connection was bad in Tahrir, we would use a friend's nearby flat to make sure the images made it out so everyone could see what was happening in the square.

'I have never felt as at peace and as safe as I did during those days in Tahrir. There was a sense of coexistence that overcame all of the problems that usually happen – whether religious or gender based.

'Pre-25 January whenever we would attend protests I would always be told by the men to go to the back to avoid getting injured and that used to anger me. But since 25 January people have begun to treat me as an equal. There was this unspoken admiration for one another in the square.

'We went through many ups and downs together. It felt like it had become a different society – there was one Egypt inside Tahrir and another Egypt outside.

'The moment Tahrir opened up, we saw a lot of people that were not there before and there were reports of females being harassed.

'I know that Egypt has changed and we will transfer the spirit of the square to the rest of the country. Before Tahrir if I was [harassed] I would refrain from asking people for help, because there are a lot of people that would disappoint you by blaming you. But I think the spirit of the revolution has empowered us to spread the feeling we established wider and wider. From now on, if anything happens to me, I am going to scream, I am going to ask people to help me and I know that I will find people that will help me.

'I was in front of the TV building when the news broke about Mubarak stepping down. I found myself swept away with people screaming and cheering. It was an emotional moment that I celebrated with strangers. People were hugging me, shaking my hands, distributing sweets. At that moment we were all one.

'I no longer feel alienated from society. I now walk the streets of Cairo and smile at strangers all the time. I have gained a sense of belonging with everyone on the streets of Cairo – at least for now. Before 25 January I was tempted to leave the country. This feeling has changed now. I want to stay here. This is an extension of our role in the revolution; we have to stay here and contribute to changing our society.'

Gigi Ibrahim, 24, political activist

'In my experience women play a pivotal role in all protests and strikes.'

Political activist Gigi Ibrahim played an instrumental role in spreading the word about the protests.

'I started [my political activism] by just talking to people [who were] involved [in the labour movement]. Then I became more active and the whole thing became addictive. I went to meetings and took part in protests. I learnt very quickly that most of the strikes in the labour movement were started by women.

'In my experience women play a pivotal role in all protests and strikes. Whenever violence erupts, the women would step up and fight the police, and they would be beaten just as much as the men.

'I have seen it during the Khaled Said protests in June 2010 when many women were beaten and arrested. Muslim, Christian – all types of women protested.

'My family always had problems with me taking part in protests. They prevented me from going for my safety, because I am a girl. They were worried about the risks. I would have to lie about attending protests.

'When the police violently cleared the square on 25 January, I was shot in the back by a rubber bullet while trying to run away from the police as they tear gassed us. I returned to the square, as did many others, the following day and stayed there on and off for the next 18 days.

'As things escalated my dad got increasingly worried. On 28 January, my sister wanted to lock me in the house. They tried to stop me from leaving, but I was determined and I went out. I moved to my aunt's place that is closer to Tahrir Square and I would go there every now and again to wash and rest before returning to the square.

'At first my family was very worried, but as things escalated they started to understand and to be more supportive. My family is not politically active at all.

'The day-to-day conditions were not easy. Most of us would use the bathroom inside the nearby mosque. Others would go to nearby flats where people kindly opened their homes for people to use.

'I was in Tahrir Square on 2 February, when pro-Mubarak

thugs attacked us with petrol bombs and rocks. That was the most horrific night. I was trapped in the middle of the square. The outskirts of the square were like a war zone. The more things escalated the more determined we became not to stop. Many people were injured and many died and that pushed us to go on and not give up.

'I thought if those armed pro-Mubarak thugs came inside the square it would be the end of us. We were unarmed; we had nothing. That night I felt fear but it changed into determination.

'The women played an important role that night. Because we were outnumbered, we had to secure all the exits in the square. The exits between each end of the square would take up to 10 minutes to reach, so the women would go and alert others about where the danger was coming from and make sure that the people who were battling swapped positions with others so that they could rest before going out into the battle again.

'The women were also taking care of the wounded in makeshift clinics in the square. Some women were on the front line throwing rocks with the men. I was on the front line documenting the battle with my camera. It was like nothing that I have ever seen or experienced before.

'During the 18 days neither I nor any of my friends were harassed. I slept in Tahrir with five men around me that I didn't know and I was safe.

'But that changed on the day Mubarak stepped down. The type of people who came then were not interested in the revolution. They were there to take pictures. They came for the carnival atmosphere and that was when things started to change.

'When the announcement came we all erupted in joy. I was screaming and crying. I hugged everyone around me. I went from being happy and crying to complete shock. It took a while for it to sink in.

'The revolution is not over. All of our demands have not yet been met. We have to continue. This is where the real hard work begins, but it will take a different shape than staging sit-ins in the square. Rebuilding Egypt is going to be tough and we all have to take part in this. There are organised strikes demanding workers' rights for better pay and conditions and those are the battles to be won now.'

Salma El Tarzi, 33, filmmaker

'What kept us going was the conviction that we did not have any option – it was either freedom or go to jail.'

Having never been politically active, Salma El Tarzi was sceptical about the protesters' chances of getting their demands met until the day when she stood on her balcony and saw the crowds. She decided to join the protesters and has not looked back since.

'I was protesting on my own on the 26th and 27th, but bumped into my younger brother in the crowd by chance on the 28th. We just carried on from then onward.

'What kept us going was the conviction that we did not have any option – it was either stay and fight for freedom or go to jail.

'My dad has been very supportive. He was getting to the point where he was telling me and my brother: 'Don't run away from gun fire, run towards it.'

'While in Tahrir we were all receiving threatening calls, telling us that if we didn't vacate the square we would be hunted and killed. But we didn't care at that point. We were at the point of no return.

'Tahrir Square became our mini model of how democracy should be. Living there was not easy. We would use a nearby mosque and I would go to a friend's house every now and then to wash. But I must admit that conditions were not ideal. It was very cold; we slept on the floor. Some of us had tents and some made their own tents. Let's put it this way, due to the difficult conditions we called it the 'smell of a revolution'.

'I was one of many women, young and old, there. We were as active as the men. Some acted as nurses and looked after the wounded during the battles; others were simply helping with distributing water. But there were a great number of women that were on the front line hurling stones at the police and pro-Mubarak thugs.

'The duties in the square were divided. We were very organised. Something changed in the dynamic between men and women in Tahrir. When the men saw that women were fighting in the front line, that changed their perception of us and we were all united. We were all Egyptians now.

'The general view of women changed for many. Not a single

case of sexual harassment happened during the protests up until the last day when Mubarak stepped down. That is a big change for Egypt.

'The fear barrier was broken for all of us. When we took part in the protests it was just a protest for our basic human rights, but they [the regime] escalated it to a revolution. Their brutality and violence turned it into a revolution. What started as a day of rage turned into a revolution that later toppled the regime that had been in power for 30 years. They [the regime] empowered us through their violence; they made us hold on to the dream of freedom even more. We were all walking around with wounds, but we still kept going. We were even treating injured horses that they had used in their brutal attacks against us.

'Before 25 January I didn't have faith that my voice could be heard. I didn't feel like I was in control of my future. The metaphor used by Mubarak that he was our father and we were his children made us feel as though we lacked any motivation.

'The revolution woke us up – a collective consciousness has been awoken.'

http://pambazuka.org/en/category/features/71168

This chapter was previously published by Al Jazeera and on Radical African.

13

'The power is within us': a protest diary from Cameroon

Kah Walla

24 February 2011, revised 14 August 2011

Kah Walla, the presidential candidate for Cameroon Ô'Bosso, led peaceful protests on 23 March 2011 which were brutally quelled by the army. She produced this diary of events leading up to and during the protest.

The good news is: all who marched today are stronger morally and mentally than when we started the day. In addition, there are no broken bones, or grave injuries. Most of the people participating in the protest were doing so for their first time. In spite of the extreme and completely unnecessary brutality exhibited by the police, all of us feel stronger than ever in our resolve to bring about change in Cameroon. We are also confirmed in our strategy of non-violence in spite of having very violent forces of law and (dis)order before us.

So what happened?

Wednesday, 23 February 2011, 02.30

We left our strategy room feeling quite good. We were convinced we had a surprise itinerary which the police did not know about and we would be able to march for at least a half-hour before they fell upon us. We were also thrilled with the symbolism of our start point: Um Nyobe's house in Nkolmondo (one of Douala's poorest neighbourhoods) was full of both historic and current day symbolism and would get us off with the type of energy we needed for the day. We had met with the family and they were in full agreement. Off we went to catch a few hours of sleep before our scheduled start time of 9.00am.

08.00

The first part of our organisation team arrived at the site. Water sachets and 200 T-shirts in tow, they were busy setting up things for all to march non-violently and determinedly. The gendarmes show up, arrest six of our members and one journalist from AFP and confiscate our 200 T-shirts and our water. Our close to 300 protestors panic. The march has not even started and people are being arrested. The majority of them desist. A handful of about 20 die-hards persist. We start figuring out possible new itineraries. On the spot we decide to print 50 new T-shirts.

11.30

We get a call from our colleagues at the PURS political party. They are still willing to march and they are a good two to three dozen as well. We decide to make sure we mark this day. We set off to Feu Rouge Bessengue, new red T-shirts brandishing 'Ça Suffit' on them, in tow. We meet up with our colleagues of PURS and don the T-shirts.

About 12.15

We occupy Boulevard de la République at Feu Rouge Bessengue. No traffic can move on one of the busiest streets in Douala. Amazingly, not one single car driver or motorbike driver protests. Those who support join us in our chants. Others turn their vehicles around quietly and go. Some passers-by grab a red T, don it and join our ranks.

About 12.45

The forces of law and order show up. An armada. About 70–80 policemen, two water cannons, riot gear and shields. We remain firm and, as previously decided, sit, to show we are non-violent. These boys (and a few girls) do not have that word in their vocabulary. They use their clubs to begin seriously hitting on some of our protestors. To their grand surprise, I walk up to ask them to stop. The chiefs then realised they had Kah Walla, *l'oiseau* (bird) as one of them called me, right in front of them. For a few minutes they could not figure out what to do with me and had me walking back and forth while they decided to put me in a truck or in a car.

Finally, a big boss in civilian clothes shows up. He wants to 'teach me a lesson' as he says. He asks that I be put on the median in the middle of the street. Then he turns the entire water cannon truck on for my personal benefit. Note my two fists up in a victory symbol under the water cannon. That's the lesson I learnt: the power is within us. No amount of violence and hysteria can remove it.

The icing on the cake is that as we choked and burned from the chemicals in the water, they then asked us to climb onto their truck. As we climbed up, with our backs turned, they hit us with their clubs. The only feeling I had was one of sadness that those whom your and my taxes pay to protect us show such extreme cowardice and meanness. After climbing onto the truck they let us catch our breaths then set us free. What was the point of climbing onto the truck? Just so they could beat our backs? Sad.

13.40

The team and I head to Muna Clinic to make sure everybody is ok – a few wounds, some serious, some not too bad. Some serious welts on the backs of a few of our members, my back and eyes are still burning and I smell of hydrogen even as I write this. The amazing result though is a profound feeling of accomplishment:

- They wanted to stop us from protesting, we protested.
- We have a non-violent philosophy, which we maintained in the face of extreme violence. I could not believe it when the Cameroon Ô'Bosso guys were walking over to stop the population from throwing stones at the police. An incredible force of young Cameroonians.
- We started out almost 300 and ended up less than 50 but (being a) nugget has banished fear, for ourselves and for many other Cameroonians.
- The population did not join us in droves, but: not one person out of hundreds complained about the blocking on the road; when the violence broke out they started throwing stones at the police; they doused us with water as soon as the police let us go. They also refused water to a few policemen who had been accidentally sprayed by the water cannon.

If we ever doubted it, we now have extreme clarity on the absolute need for change and the absolute need for unwavering determination in bringing it about in our country.

Postscript: The three CPP members were released after six days in detention and without being officially charged with any crime.

http://pambazuka.org/en/category/features/71188

This chapter was first published as a blogpost by 'product of my past' (http:// postplasticpeople.wordpress.com/).

14

Uganda elections: 'an exercise in shame-faced endorsement'

J. Oloka-Onyango

3 March 2011

When the lithe, 42-year-old guerilla leader Yoweri Kaguta Museveni ('M7' or 'Ssevo' to his supporters) emerged from a five-year 'bush' war to claim the presidency of Uganda in 1986, few observers gave him much of a chance. Many questioned whether he had the credentials to lead such a fractious, decimated and demoralised population out of the doldrums.

Twenty-five years later, Museveni remains at the helm of Ugandan politics and on 18 February 2011 he received yet another endorsement in an election that extends his term until 2016. By that time, Museveni will be 72 years old, and at 30 years in power will have long since entered the record books as East Africa's longest-serving leader, outstripping both the late Julius Nyerere of Tanzania and Kenya's ex-president Daniel arap Moi.

But it will also be the time to ask whether his legacy will be that of the former Tanzanian president, who left office still revered and loved, or that of a figure of tragedy and hatred like Moi? Indeed, as North Africa witnesses the collapse of long-term dictatorships from Tunisia to Libya, it is necessary to inquire how it is that Museveni won the 18 February election, and what lessons this has for political struggle and freedom on the continent.

Drawing on Libya for comparison is particularly apt since Museveni has long been an ally of President Mu'ammar Muhammed al-Gaddafi. In one of many trips to Kampala, the eccentric and now beleaguered leader urged Museveni to stay in office for life, arguing that revolutionaries are not like company managing directors.

111

It is a lesson Museveni took to heart, removing presidential term limits from the constitution in 2005, and setting himself well on the way to a de facto life presidency.

So what explains Museveni's February victory, especially given that, while largely predicted, the margin by which he won – 68 per cent of the presidential vote and 75 per cent for his National Resistance Movement (NRM) in the parliamentary poll – stunned many? This margin should be compared with the three previous elections in 1996 (when he won with 75 per cent), 2001 (69 per cent) and 2006 (59 per cent).

According to the pundits, although he was still popular, dominant and thus likely to win, the downward trend would continue. Some even predicted that there would be a run-off because the 50.1 per cent margin would not be reached in the first round. The other issue of surprise was the relative calm and lack of violence that attended the election. Most foreign observers – from the European Union to the US government – described the vote as generally peaceful, free of bloodshed and (in the usual parlance of those who have emerged as the guardians of African electoral politics) largely a 'free and genuine' expression of the wishes of the Ugandan people.[1]

The local media described it as the most boring poll in recent Ugandan history, lacking as it did much of the drama, intrigue and confrontation that Ugandans had become accustomed to. It is thus not surprising that Museveni's rap song – 'Give Me My Stick/You Want Another Rap?' – garnered more attention than the substantive issues at stake.

To fully comprehend the outcome of Uganda's recent poll, it is necessary to understand a number of basic facts. The first is that Uganda is yet to become a functioning multiparty democracy. For the first 19 years of Museveni's rule, the country operated a 'no-party' or 'movement' system of government, which was little better than a single-party state. Under that system, government and party institutions overlapped right from the lowest level of government ('resistance' or local councils) through to parliament. Indeed, in many respects, Museveni took a leaf from Gaddafi's popular councils, creating these 'LCs' as supposedly representative of 'grassroots' democracy, but essentially a cover for single-party dominance. Today, many of the no-party structures remain intact and operative. They function as the main conduits of political mobilisation and for the channelling of state resources, buttressed by a massive local bureaucracy of government agents and spies.

Of course, the fact of incumbency guarantees Museveni unfettered access to state coffers, such that the NRM reportedly spent $350 million in the campaign, testimony to the benefits that come with office. The enduring image of the past several months has been the president handing out brown envelopes stashed with cash for various women, youth and other types of civic groupings.

The other reason for Museveni's victory lies in the highly militarised context within which politics and governance in Uganda is executed. Following five years of civil war (1981 to 1986), and 20-plus years of insurgency in the north of the country, Uganda has never been free from conflict. Unsurprisingly, the idea of peace and security looms large within the national psyche. For older Ugandans there is fear of earlier and more chaotic times, while for the younger generation who have only experienced Museveni, the claim that he has restored peace has a particular resonance. Ironically, both groups also fear that if Museveni lost an election, he would never accept the result, and instead would either return to the bush or cause such instability that it is not worth even thinking about an alternative candidate. This explains what to many is the most surprising outcome of the election: Museveni's victory in northern Uganda despite facing two 'sons-of-the-soil', ex-diplomat Olara Otunnu and the youthful Norbert Mao.

The looming presence of the military also explains why the turnout for the election at 59 per cent was much lower than any of the previous three polls, where figures were closer to 70 per cent. Many people simply stayed at home, partly out of apathy, but more on account of the fact that the streets of Kampala and other parts of the country were swamped with military personnel. More akin to the army in Libya than in Egypt, the Uganda Peoples' Defence Force (UPDF) is not reputed to exercise restraint when dealing with civilian insurrection or politically motivated opposition.

Museveni's performance in the north reflects the other side to the story, and that is the fact that Museveni is only as good as the opposition he faces. The dismal performance of the opposition is attributable to a host of factors, not least of which is the fact that there are really no opposition parties in Uganda. Rather, there are only opposition personalities – epitomised by three-time presidential contender Kizza Besigye of the Forum for Democratic Change (FDC) – who have constructed around themselves weak or non-existent party structures that only come to life in the run-up to the election.

Uganda's opposition is also bereft of firm ideological positions, and while the death of ideology is an ailment affecting the ruling NRM too, its absence among the opposition has proven particularly harmful as there is a lack of a central organising message around which the opposition can translate support and obvious disgust against Museveni into electoral victory. Thus, at the start of the election season, the opposition wavered between a united front against Museveni and a boycott, citing the bias of the Electoral Commission and the un-level playing field.

Neither option was adopted, and at the end of the day all major opposition parties decided to field candidates in both the presidential and parliamentary elections, while decrying the inequality in the contest. Nevertheless, Besigye assured his supporters of both victory and his ability to protect his vote in the event of NRM poll-rigging, a show of bravado on which he was unable to deliver.

However, Uganda Peoples' Congress (UPC) candidate Olara Otunnu took the cake by failing to show up to cast his vote on election day in a classic example of the ailments afflicting the opposition. Finally, while Museveni's victory is not much of a surprise, and in the short run ensures the continued charade of economic and political stability that has characterised the last two decades, it portends considerable apprehension for the future of the country.

While the president has dismissed comparisons with the fallen dictators of North Africa, there are indeed many parallels. The state in Uganda has assumed what can only be described as a 'Musevenist' character, such that an election like the recent one can only be an exercise in shame-faced endorsement of the incumbent. That state has also devolved to a situation in which there is little to distinguish between the personal and the political, and where it is increasingly being marked by the growth of family/ personal rule. While Museveni has only one son (in comparison to

Gaddafi's seven), Muhoozi Kainerugaba is clearly being groomed for greater things. Thus, he has taken charge of the Special Presidential Brigade, the elite force designed to guarantee his father's personal security, and he recently wrote a book about the bush war to burnish his credentials as an intellectual-cum-soldier able to fit into his father's rather large shoes.

This is clearly the same path that Ben Ali, Mubarak and Gaddafi pursued, only to find themselves thwarted by the movement of the people. While it may be true that revolutionaries don't retire, if there is no other lesson of the recent northern African upheavals, it is that revolutionaries can be forced to resign. It is all simply a matter of time.

http://pambazuka.org/en/category/features/71329

Note

1. To its credit, it was only the African Union (AU) that declined outright to describe the poll as 'free and fair'.

15

Crisis in Côte d'Ivoire: the impact on women

Massan d'Almeida

3 March 2011

On 28 November 2010, Côte d'Ivoire held a second round of presidential elections, following a first round which took place in October 2010 after several postponements. Fourteen[1] candidates participated in the first round, and Alassane Ouattara and Laurent Gbagbo, the two candidates who garnered the most votes, made it to the second round. Gbagbo is the incumbent president. After the elections, the Independent Electoral Commission declared Ouattara the winner, but these results were invalidated by the Ivorian Constitutional Court, which declared his rival, Gbagbo, the president-elect of Côte d'Ivoire.

This precipitated a crisis in the country. Gbagbo 'refused to yield to international pressure and withdraw from his position'[2] in favour of Ouattara, who was the candidate recognised by the entire international community.

Mata Coulibaly, president of SOS Exclusion, and Honorine Sadia Vehi Toure, president of Génération femmes du troisième millénaire (GFM3), are two women's rights advocates whom we interviewed. They explained how the population is experiencing this situation: 'We are going through a crisis and this is very difficult. There is tension in the country. Our days are filled with uncertainty because at any moment, a strike can be called,' said Coulibaly. Toure added: 'This is a real crisis and we are under tremendous stress. We do not know what tomorrow will bring. The social situation is deteriorating day by day. So it is highly stressful and frustrating.'

The political crisis in Côte d'Ivoire has had major diplomatic, financial, economic and social repercussions on the population, including on women and the organisations that defend their rights.

Gbagbo's refusal to step down has prompted several international organisations, including the United Nations, the European Union, the African Union and the Economic Community Of West Africa States (ECOWAS) to take punitive measures against him, his family and close friends, and the state.

The impact on daily lives

The economic cost of Côte d'Ivoire's conflict between 2002 and 2007 was severe: the gross domestic product (GDP) per person dropped by 15 per cent between 2000 and 2006 and poverty consequently increased. Before the post-electoral crisis, the economic outlook for Côte d'Ivoire seemed to have improved, with a growth of 3.8 per cent in 2009 and optimistic forecasts for an increase of revenue from cocoa and petroleum exports.

The current crisis aggravates a rather precarious situation and has accentuated the impoverishment of the population. It has had a serious impact on the daily lives of Ivorian households, causing prices of essential products to rise sharply and encouraging speculation. As Toure emphasised: 'Market prices have soared so much that some essential products such as oil, sugar, meat and onions are difficult to obtain. This is a real hardship for households. Before the crisis, many female-headed households could only afford one meal a day, so one can only imagine how much more difficult it is now for those families. Everyone is suffering.'

Coulibaly added: 'Life seems to go in slow motion. Prices have soared. For example, sometimes there is a shortage of natural gas. A quantity of coal that previously cost CFAF100 now costs CFAF200. A kilo of *oignon dur*[3] has increased from CFAF450 to CFAF1,000 while onions from Niamey have increased from CFAF600 to CFAF1,500, and a kilo of beetroot from CFAF1,900 to CFAF3,000. These examples illustrate the impact of this crisis on the shopping basket and this price increase has a tangible impact on the living conditions of Ivorians. Salaries remain the same although prices are surging. This situation forces women to economise more in order to feed their families. Regardless of whether it is a woman or man who is the head of household, everyone has similar difficulties to overcome.' Sophie (the pseudonym of an Ivorian politician who prefers to remain anonymous) confirmed that some food prices have doubled, while those of other products, such as oil, have tripled. She said that it is extremely difficult for middle-income households to feed themselves because everything has become so expensive.

The situation is no different in other cities and towns in the country. Coulibaly stated: 'The current crisis has affected the whole Ivorian territory. In Korhogo in the north, Bouaké in the centre of the country, and Man and Duokoué in the west, food prices have almost doubled. The population is tired and is growing poorer every day. In addition, the private sector is threatened with redundancies, which could lead to famine for parts of the population. We have just learnt that with the closure of the Abidjan and San Pedro ports, we will run out of gas in a few days. Côte d'Ivoire exports all its products. Another concern is that HIV/AIDS patients are no longer provided with anti-retroviral drugs and this has resulted in a proliferation of the disease and the aggravation of existing cases.'

Toure paints a similar picture of the situation, stating: 'Impoverishment is felt by everyone throughout the territory. Before the elections, the country had not yet unified and therefore in the central, northern and western areas, the living conditions were already poor. The south was not spared, but it suffered to a lesser degree. But I can assure you that now no area is better than another. Whether it be towns, villages, urban or rural areas, it is the same unbearable situation all over.'

Violence, rights and security violations

After the first, relatively peaceful round of elections at the end of October 2010, reports of violence and abuse in different regions of the country began to emerge. These incidents indicated a serious deterioration of the general human rights situation and are a reminder of the atrocities committed during the last decade. African, European and American human rights organisations, in particular Human Rights Watch (HRW) and

Amnesty International, have repeatedly sounded the alarm about the situation.

The United Nations Human Rights Council held a special session on Côte d'Ivoire in Geneva on 23 December 2010, during which the US Secretary of State Hillary Clinton made a speech and the High Commissioner on Human Rights Navi Pillay strongly condemned the human rights violations committed in Côte d'Ivoire. The Office of the Prosecutor of the International Criminal Court (ICC) has also voiced its concerns about the situation.

Most of the violence reported to date is carried out during night raids led by the security forces and other groups in the neighbourhoods of Abidjan that are considered to be predominantly populated by Ouattara's supporters. Human rights organisations have noted a series of kidnappings under similar circumstances. The victims of these kidnappings were declared missing or were found dead.[4] Coulibaly confirmed this, stating, 'Acquaintances of ours have been kidnapped.' According to Sophie, these are 'raids that are violent, ethnic-based and politically motivated, targeting individuals or groups of people whose neighbours have informed on them. The perpetrators are mercenaries who are paid to commit these murders.'

According to independent sources, human rights and women's rights activists are living in a state of constant anxiety over their safety. An experienced civil society advocate, who requested to remain anonymous, told IRIN: 'I have been in hiding ever since being threatened over two weeks ago. Sometimes, it looks as though the situation is about to calm down. This is often the impression in the daytime, but one never knows what will happen once night falls.'[5] Toure confirmed: 'We are working within a context of fear. We are truly sad about what is happening in our country. We cannot carry out our work openly for fear of reprisals. In spite of this, we are working, relying on God, and hoping that our country will rapidly overcome this situation.' Coulibaly stated: 'As a representative of the Democracy and Human Rights Fund (FDDH), I do not feel safe.'

Impact on work for women's rights

The punitive sanctions imposed on Côte d'Ivoire have had a very negative impact on non-governmental organisations that depend mainly on international funds for their survival. Toure explained that most of their financial partners in the United Nations system and the World Bank have closed their offices, which has in turn forced the NGOs to suspend most of their activities. Furthermore, due to political instability, it is increasingly difficult to operate as normal. Coulibaly stated: 'Nothing is sure. We have to tailor our plans according to how events evolve. We are afraid to go to work and sometimes we receive information or hear rumours that cause us to stay away from work.'

The widening of the division

The riots that broke out in September 2002 in Côte d'Ivoire divided the country between the south, run by the Gbagbo government, and the north, controlled by rebel forces led by Guillaume Soro, the current prime minister in the Ouattara administration. However, in 2008, after signing the Ouagadougou Agreement, the country began a reunification process, which led to the consensual organisation of the recent presidential elections.

However, some people are afraid that the alliance between Soro and Ouattara will cause a revival of the divisions and will introduce a religious dimension to the divide. Nonetheless, it should be emphasised that there are different opinions on this subject, as highlighted by Toure. 'No matter what is being said, the people in Côte d'Ivoire do not promote division,' she said. 'It is the politicians who have put us into this situation because of their personal interests. In the south, there are Christians and Muslims, and there are also people from the north, and we live together in harmony, at least those who have understood that division does not suit us, which is most of us. The same is true in the north. Therefore, there is no real division in Côte d'Ivoire, even if this is what they want you to believe. Ivorians have suffered through ten years of crisis. In the end, everyone was tired of this. Our will to leave it behind was shown by the high voter turnout in the elections: 83 per cent in the first round and over 70 per cent in the second round.' However, Coulibaly does not agree:

'The division is inevitable. The politicians accuse the people of the north of being rebels. Women are divided in the markets. Some pro-Gbagbo market women tell their pro-Ouattara counterparts to ask their leader to build them their own market.'

The current situation in Côte d'Ivoire is worrying. The Ivorian population, which underwent almost a decade of crisis, strongly desires that a peaceful outcome can be found quickly for the benefit of everyone. Human and women's rights organisations are particularly affected because funding opportunities for their work are becoming scarce. Furthermore, growing fears for their personal safety reduce their capacity to engage, and very few of them dare to openly express their analysis of the situation. Coulibaly confided to the Association for Women's Rights in Development (AWID) that, as far as she knew, no public action has been undertaken by human rights organisations and that only the Civil Society Agreement of Côte d'Ivoire (CSCI), which is a leading organisation in the country, has made proposals for a solution. Other organisations prefer not to issue statements because they do not share the same point of view or analysis of the situation. However, Toure stated that around 20 organisations and women's networks were discreetly carrying out initiatives to encourage the two protagonists to protect the lives of women and children, and to seek a peaceful outcome to the crisis.

http://pambazuka.org/en/category/features/71362

This chapter was first published by the Association for Women's Rights in Development.

Notes

1. Christophe Boisbouvier (2010) 'Côte d'Ivoire: les trois favoris passent à l'attaque', RFI, 28 October, http://www.rfi.fr/afrique/20101028-cote-ivoire-trois-favoris-passent-attaque, accessed 17 June 2011.
2. IRIN (2011) 'Côte d'Ivoire: La pression de l'économie – Compte rendu', 10 January, http://www.irinnews.org/fr/ReportFrench.aspx?ReportID=91589, accessed 17 June 2011.
3. There are two kinds of *oignons* (onions) in West Africa. The ones produced by local farmers have liquid inside them whereas the ones from Europe do not. *Oignon dur* is more expensive, but local people prefer it to the European onion.
4. IRIN (2011) 'Côte d'Ivoire: Violations des droits de l'homme – Compte rendu', 12 January, http://www.irinnews.org/fr/ReportFrench.aspx?ReportID=91604, accessed 17 June 2011.
5. Ibid.

16

Awakening protests in Morocco and Western Sahara

Konstantina Isidoros

17 March 2011, updated 21 August 2011

For international analysts closely observing Morocco's awakening uprisings, the absolute monarchy's financially draining, vice-like grip on the Western Sahara might prove to be its Achilles' heel. Unlike its fellow Gulf monarchs or the respected North African power of Algeria, Morocco has no oil wealth to lavishly soothe grievances.

Former French president Charles de Gaulle once described Morocco as a country whose revolution was still to come. The escalating discord and protests may yet see Morocco's own population speaking out against the full and detrimental magnitude of the monarchy's colossal expenditure on its 35-year war and occupation of the Western Sahara and what this means for the Moroccan people's desperate socio-economic woes.

Meanwhile, cities across the occupied Western Sahara such as El Aaiun, Boujdour and Dakhla have seen continuous, non-violent protest rallies by the indigenous Western Saharans and the now systematic pattern of violent counter-attacks by Moroccan military forces.

Morocco's Achilles' heel

The Western Sahara conflict is a hot geopolitical potato, with potent economic and political security–stability implications as the superpower dynamics between US and France engage in fierce rivalry over coveted natural resources, strategic supremacy and regional economic alliances.

Morocco's invasion and 35-year occupation of the Western Sahara threatens the fundamental tenets of our modern Western political system, which espouses the inviolable sanctity of a nation-state's own sovereignty, the basic rights of human beings and regional socio-economic stability.

As Zunes and Mundy (2010) emphasise, 'The ongoing Moroccan occupation of Western Sahara is one of the most egregious … affronts to the international system in existence today … The [United Nations] Security Council has turned a blind eye to Morocco's blatant contravention of the UN Charter (1945).' Morocco has not only flouted the International Court of Justice's original legal opinion in 1975 – and thereafter over 100 United Nations resolutions – but its Israeli-like policy of moving settlers into the Western Sahara, and thereby changing its demographics to three Moroccans for one Sahrawi, constitutes a violation of the Fourth Geneva Convention, which prohibits moving civilians into a militarily occupied territory. So too has its exploitation and plunder of Western Sahara's natural resources brought it disgrace.

Yet, although much attention goes to Morocco's international legal contraventions, it is ultimately the US and France who are violating the very legal and moral principles that they so publicly avow. For over 35 years, the US and France have been complicit in financing and morally permitting Morocco's aggressive territorial expansion, as well as tactically blocking solutions to the conflict at the UN Security Council. Without this US–French support, Morocco would never have been able to get away with, let alone sustain, such blatant violations of international law.

Western Sahara is not just the 'last colony of Africa', it is a country that has undergone incomplete decolonisation and then been re-colonised – a subtle new order of modern economic colonisation by Western powers, primarily US and France, vying for regional hegemony and economic self-interest. Playing out like re-coloured footage from the colonial past, Algeria fiercely defends its independence from France's modern economic courting, while Morocco appears, as ever, eager to be the beloved child of France. If Algeria, the slumbering lion of North Africa, were to summon the strength for a mighty warning roar, would the US and France take note? If Algeria harnessed its regionally respected courage and power to take skilful control of France's unrequited desire for its beloved North African jewel, would France drop Morocco like a hot brick?

The socio-economic impacts of the conflict

Morocco's war in and occupation of Western Sahara has done nothing for the country or its people other than drain them of vast amounts of wealth. Will Morocco's population now find the courage to voice dissent about the relentless economic burden of their regime's colossal expenditures on Western Sahara and its impact on their own socio-economic woes? How did they end up so cheated and what are the costs of war?

Morocco's national–ideological obsession with Western Sahara began during King Hassan II's reign when the monarchy faced a volatile political landscape. The concept of a 'Greater Morocco' (originally including Mauritania and parts of Algeria and Mali) was formed by nationalist elites threatening the monarchy's survival. Adopting this powerful idea enabled Hassan II to reassert royal legitimacy by portraying it as a national emergency, thus successfully distracting public attention and political dissenters from domestic problems. To this day, the illegal occupation of Western Sahara remains a central orthodoxy in Moroccan politics, with the monarchy's legitimacy said to be still dependent upon it.

Morocco's invasion of and war with Western Sahara between 1975 and 1991 increased the domestic economic-political deterioration and existing social inequities. Since the 1991 ceasefire, the costs of occupation have continued to undermine Morocco's socio-economic potential. Cited as a weak state since independence in 1956, the regime has been heavily dependent on income to sustain the hierarchical, clientelist and authoritarian 'Makhzen', which governs the country under the absolute control of its 'Alawi monarchy.

Although the occupation of Western Sahara brought opportunities to plunder natural resources, for example phosphate mining and Atlantic fishing, Morocco's colossal expenditure on propping up its war and occupation brings a bigger and economically devastating picture into focus.

Its biannual military expenditure rose rapidly from $270 million in 1972 to $367 million in 1974, $755 million in 1976 and

$770 million in 1978 (Stork and Paul 1983). By the mid-1980s, the average cost of war and occupation was estimated at $1.5 million per day (*Africa Report*, May–June 1986 as cited in Zunes and Mundy 2010: 43). In 1990, the estimated annual military expenditure – including infrastructure investment – reached $430 million (Damis 1990). Damis's 2000 study, using Moroccan-published data, estimated the cost of war at $1.17 million a day between 1976 and 1986. While this figure accounts for only 3 per cent of government spending and 9 per cent of GDP, Morocco received lavish financial war grants and arms sales from the US, France and Saudi Arabia, for example, $1 billion a year between 1979 and 1981.

Even with the foreign war grants, the statistics show that it has been phenomenally expensive for Morocco, and financially devastating. The sheer focus of the monarchy's obsession with sustaining its war has effectively drained its capacity to attend to the socio-economic development of the Moroccan population itself.

Seddon's 1989 analyses calculated Morocco's cost of war as much higher, even with foreign war grants: for example, in 1979, the war cost between $2 million and $5 million a day, and that Moroccan defence spending was 'no less than 40 per cent of the … national budget'. Tessler (1985) calculated that Morocco's total defence spending had risen from 13 per cent in 1975 to 23 per cent by 1977. Although in 1991 Saudi Arabia wrote off Morocco's debt for Moroccan participation in the first US-led war against Iraq (Economist Intelligence Unit 2003, as cited in Zunes and Mundy 2010: 45), Zoubir (1990) has shown how Morocco had to resort to additional domestic 'national solidarity taxes'.

Even after the 1991 ceasefire, Morocco's illegal occupation and military defence costs remained an expensive redirection of funds that could otherwise have benefitted the Moroccan population itself. US Department of State figures show that between 1975 and 1999, Morocco's daily military expenditure averaged $4.1 million per day. And the costs were even higher due to arms purchases – Morocco bought $529 million in arms every year between 1975 and 1991, dropping to $145 million each year between 1992 and 1999.

Morocco's implementation of the 1978 austerity plan to finance the war occurred as its debt burden increased phenomenally, triggering major labour strikes (Leveau 1997). Throughout the 1970s, Morocco's unemployment grew, while poor rainfall reduced crop yields and herd stocks, making food prices rise higher than personal incomes. With this rapidly deteriorating socio-economic situation, Morocco resorted in 1980 to an IMF economic rescue package, which at that time was the second largest of its kind across the developing world. Again, labour and student strikes hit Morocco in 1981, leading to civil unrest and army retaliation. Under pressure, Morocco succumbed to the World Bank and IMF's deeper debt and again the burden fell on Moroccan society, with yet more rises in food prices and unemployment. Yet more strikes broke out in 1984 after further food price rises and education cuts (Tessler 1985). By the late 1980s, the picture in Morocco was still of continuing social discontent. And the 1990s still showed signs of an economy in trouble: unemployment, inflation and national debt had risen, the latter going from $8.47 billion in 1980 to $20.66 billion in 1993 (Layachi 1998).

The 1991 ceasefire should have eased the burdens of the cost of war for Morocco and allowed it to stabilise its appalling domestic socio-economic position. Observers note, however, that not much has changed. The monarchy still retains unqualified power without any financial separation from the state, the biggest landowner and controller of state contracts and holding companies which remain the 'personal vehicle of the king's economic and commercial interests' (Leveau 1997).

Will these tragic statistics provide the historical opportunity for the Moroccan people to also demand an end to the billions of dollars being misappropriated to prop up their regime's Western Sahara 'distraction' instead of being spent on their own social and economic needs?

Sacred kings

With the current revolutions successfully challenging the heads of Arab republics, how safe are the Arab monarchies and does their 'divine' position leave any hope for protesters?

Taking analyses of recent events in Saudi Arabia as a reference point, Saudi author Mai Yamani has written in the *Guardian* that, 'No kingdom is an island, particularly when it sits in a sea of revolution' (27 February). Saudi prince Al-Waleed bin Talal bin Abdulaziz al-Saud conveyed in the *New York Times* (24 February) that 'Arab governments can no longer afford to take their populations for granted ... The winds of change are blowing across our region with force and it would be folly to suppose that they will soon dissipate'. Shadi Hamid, research director at the Brookings Doha Centre, suggests that the Saudi 'regime is learning all the wrong lessons from Egypt and Tunisia – the unrest in the region is not fundamentally economic, it's fundamentally about politics' (*Guardian*, 24 February). Eman al-Nafjan, a professional and mother of three who blogs as Saudiwoman, writes, 'Across the board, there's a demand for a constitutional monarchy and accountability and the end of corruption in the handling of the nation's wealth' (*Sydney Morning Herald*, 5 March).

Middle East Foreign Policy (4 March) evaluates how the Gulf states' dynastic monarchies helped them survive the last period of political upheaval in the Arab world in the 1950s and 1960s. The extended royal families' widespread presence in society provided a built-in intelligence service, keeping the families close to those they ruled. Many heads were better for monarchical survival than the single heads of rulers in Egypt, Libya, Iraq and Yemen that were lopped off, either figuratively or literally, in the Arab revolts of that earlier age. Since the first constituency of any dynastic monarch is his own family, proposing political reforms that would vastly decrease family power is likely to excite opposition not just to the reforms, but possibly to the ruler himself. Whatever reforms and promises Morocco makes to its people, they will not occur without the elite ensuring their wealthy interests remain secure.

In the *Financial Times*'s 'Arab monarchs nervously watch Morocco' (2 March), Victor Mallet's discussion suggests that Arab monarchs are far from immune to the people's revolution. In Morocco, royalists believe that traditional regal and Muslim religious credentials (the king claims to be a descendant of the Prophet Mohammed and styles himself as 'commander of the faithful') will protect Morocco's absolute monarchy from the reality of its economic injustices, the 'medieval' foundation of its current constitution and the absence of any real democracy. Despite this divine, sacrosanct untouchability, reports suggest that the 20 February protest marked the first time where pictures of the king, which normally symbolise loyalty, were not necessarily carried. Said Benjebli, a 32-year-old blogger and the chair of the Moroccan Bloggers' Association, tells Mallet that if the king does not face the populations' demands for change, '... the level of demands will increase and then people will want a republic. There is not much time to save the monarchy.'

So too does Imad Mesdoua (2011) explore the likely outcomes of Morocco's uprisings in 'The "tranquil" kingdom?'. She discusses how Morocco has sought to portray itself as the regional exception – the 'tranquil kingdom' – in the chaos of shaking republics and monarchies across the Arab world. The possibility of institutional reforms that would relegate the king to a ceremonial monarch/head of state in a constitutional model such as those of Europe's monarchies would break one of Morocco's chief taboos in a long history of Moroccan monarchs wielding sacrosanct and unchallengeable power over every institution. The current king is undoubtedly more popular than his father, bringing a 'greater leniency and modernity' to his reign alongside successfully portraying a 'model of democracy' with Western praise. However, the fundamental pillars of his father's reign – corruption, nepotism, human rights violations and the feared power of the Makhzen – have not been reformed. Wikileaks' reports suggest the current monarch institutionalised bribery and coercion at the start of his reign to ensure his family's businesses gained the upper hand over local and international competitors. Political freedom and freedom of speech only exist if they do not touch on the ultimate taboos: to criticise the monarchy or question the Western Sahara issue is a direct attack on the sacred. The vocabulary in the monarchy's official speeches gives some clue as to the gravity of it all.

Western Sahara uprisings

As Noam Chomsky pointed out in a recent interview, the brutal dawn raid by Moroccan military forces on a Sahrawi peace camp in the occupied Western Sahara in November 2010 was the start of the current waves of uprisings sweeping the Arab world.

In cities across Western Sahara such as Dakhla, El Aaiun and Smara, civil society and human rights advocates have long embarked on waves of pro-democracy protests, now seen echoing through the Moroccan population itself. It is widely believed that the Sahrawi do not want to divert attention from the Moroccan populations' own protests. But how serious the Moroccan regime takes these multidirectional campaigns can be seen in contradicting reports emerging about Moroccan military movements. In February, several sources said military troops had been moved north to prepare for the announced protests in Morocco proper. Then in March local sources reported that large army contingents were being moved back into the occupied territory. Reports on 8 March indicated that the occupied city of Boujdour was under military siege.

Although the king's two recent televised speeches announced a wide set of reforms, he nevertheless made it clear these would be carried out on his own initiative. Such reforms will prove decisive in whether the kingdom can retain its 'tranquillity'. The risk is that Arab leaders will remain 'behind closed doors in gilded palaces and well-guarded mansions, asking what can we give them and still stay in power' (Gardner, BBC, 4 March). As much as for any leader of a republic, a monarch's legitimacy depends on 'a social contract that treats the population as citizens rather than subjects, and has as its primary goal the economic and social advancement of society' (Kaplan, *Financial Times*, 2 March).

Algeria's wealth and independence on the international scene gives it much room to manoeuvre in responding to its population's demands. Morocco does not have this luxury. It remains to be seen just how much longer the monarchy can justify its archaic Western Sahara myth to the international community, while the Sahrawi live under a repressive occupation and Morocco's own population suffer socio-economic woes.

http://pambazuka.org/en/category/features/71767

The views expressed in this paper are those of the author.
Copyright © 2011 Konstantina Isidoros

Bibliography

Damis, J. (1983) *Conflict in Northwest Africa: The Western Sahara Dispute*, Stanford, CA, Hoover Institution Press

Damis, J. (1990) 'Morocco and the Western Sahara', *Current History*, 89: 165–8, 184–6

Damis, J. (2000) 'King Hassan and the Western Sahara', *Maghreb Review*, 25: 13–30

Hodges, Tony (1983) *Western Sahara: Roots of a Desert War*, Westport, CT, Lawrence Hill

International Court of Justice (1975) Judgements, Advisory Opinions and Orders: Western Sahara, http://www.icj-cij.org/docket/index.php?sum=32 3&code=sa&p1=3&p2=4&case=61&k=69&p3=5, accessed 2 October 2011

Layachi, A. (1998) *State, Society and Democracy in Morocco: The Limit of Associative Life*, Washington DC, Centre for Contemporary Arab Studies, Georgetown University

Leveau, R. (1997) 'Morocco at the crossroads', *Mediterranean Politics*, 2: 95–113

Mesdoua, Imad (2011) 'North African dispatches – Morocco: the "tranquil" kingdom?', *Ceasefire Magazine*, 2 March

Pazzanita, Anthony G. (1994) 'Morocco versus Polisario: a political interpretation', *Journal of Modern African Studies*, 32 (2): 265–78

Shelley, Toby (2004) *Endgame in the Western Sahara: What Future for Africa's Last Colony?*, New York, Zed

Stork, J. and Paul, J. (1983) *Arms Sales and the Militarisation of the Middle East*, MERIP Reports, February: 5–15

Tessler, M. (1985) 'The uses and limits of populism: the political strategy of King Hassan II of Morocco', *Middle East Review*, 17: 44–51

Zoubir, Y. (1990) 'Western Sahara conflict impedes Maghreb unity', *Middle East Report*, 163: 28–9

Zunes, Stephen and Mundy, Jacob (2010) *Western Sahara: War, Nationalism and Conflict Irresolution*, Syracuse, NY, Syracuse University Press

Useful websites

Amnesty International (www.amnesty.org)

Australia Western Sahara Association (www.awsa.org.au)

Free Western Sahara Network (http://freesahara.ning.com)

Human Rights Watch (www.hrw.org)

Illegal EU-Moroccan Fisheries Agreement (www.fishelsewhere.eu/index. php?parse_news=single&cat=140&art=1257/)

Landmine Action (www.landmineaction.org)

Norwegian Support Committee for the Western Sahara (www.vest-sahara. no)

Sandblast (www.sandblast-arts.org)

Spanish Group of pro-Sahrawi Associations (www.saharaindependiente.org)

The Western Sahara Association in California (www.calwesternsahara.org)

Western Sahara Campaign UK (www.wsahara.org.uk)

Western Sahara Resource Watch (www.wsrw.org)

17

Peoples' revolts in Burkina Faso

Lila Chouli

31 March 2011, revised 17 August 2011

Political tensions were very high and students up in arms in the West African country of Burkina Faso earlier this year after the death in police custody of a young student, Justin Zongo, on 20 February. Initially, authorities blamed the death on meningitis, sparking even more protests. Demonstrations quickly spread from Justin Zongo's native Koudougou in Centre-West province to the rest of the country and found echoes among other social groups as well. Is the Burkina unrest only an imitation of the events in the north of the continent or does it have its own specificity?

Burkina Faso has a vibrant civil society that has so far managed to resist attempts to install a one-party system or a monolithic state-controlled labour union by the different regimes that have come to power in the post-colonial period. It has always opposed abuse of power from Maurice Yameogo (first republic) to Blaise Compaore (fourth republic).

The events in Tunisia, Egypt and Libya – before the imperialist intervention – probably helped in creating a certain momentum because of the 'ruling party out' motto that underlined these movements. There were explicit references to the Tunisian and Egyptian revolutions in slogans such as 'Tunisia is in Koudougou', 'Burkina will have its Egypt moment'.[1] Some youth in Koudougou even compared Justin Zongo to Mohammed Bouazizi [2] amidst exaggerated reports about the use of Facebook. This being said, Burkina, unlike Ben Ali's Tunisia and Mubarak's

Egypt, has always had a certain amount of freedom of information and expression and the right to organise (civil society, political parties, associations) and it is much easier for young people
to meet physically to organise actions instead of needing virtual
encounters on the net.[3] The use of the internet has also evolved
with people accessing it to exchange information and analyses
of events. But the biggest similarities between North Africa and
Burkina are structural – an unequal society, the lack of opportunities, police violence, the rule of impunity, a closed political
system, a bourgeoisie in bed with a chaotic political administration, the longevity of the regime.

The authorities too have not been unaffected by developments
in North Africa, judging from their initially cautious reactions. It
was evident in the tone of their declarations, especially after the
first days of unrest when repression was at its height and caused
the deaths of six people and left 237 others wounded. The government went all out to calm public anger after the events of 22–24
February. At the end of the month, there was an official communiqué saying the governor and the head of the regional police in
the Centre-West region had been suspended. The announcement
of the arrests of police officers blamed for the violence prompted
student unions (Association nationale des étudiants du Burkina –
ANEB – and l'Union générale des étudiants burkinabè – UGEB) to
question the government's original version of the death of Justin
Zongo, the starting point of the uprising. 'You have announced
that those responsible for his death have been arrested without
clarifying how he died. Which of the guilty were arrested? Meningitis or the policemen who caused his death?'[4] The regime merely
ordered security forces back to barracks while opening investigations into the incidents in Koudougou, Kindi and Poa.[5]

The unprecedented mobilisation in North Africa should not
mask the specificities of the Burkina uprisings. This was not a case
of simple imitation – it was rooted in the objective conditions of
the country and in line with post-colonial struggles.

In fact, since the end of what was called the revolutionary
period with the assassination of Thomas Sankara on 15 October 1987, there have been several confrontations with the Blaise
Compaore regime, including some sparked by violence against
students. In May 1990, medical student and Association nationale

des Etudiants Burkinabè (ANEB) activist Dabo Boukary was tortured to death by the presidential guard. For years, authorities insisted that he had simply disappeared and it was only during the massive university strike in 1997 that the government finally hinted that he was dead. On 9 May 1995, students from Garango marched alongside their teachers fighting for better working and living conditions. Two of them, Emile Zigani and Blaise Sidiani, were killed by the police. On 6 December 2000, in Bousse, another student, this time twelve-year-old Flavien Nébié was shot in the head during a demonstration against the invalidation of the academic year at the University of Ouagadougou. The Dabo Boukary file has gone from judge to judge and authorities blame the lack of progress on the fact that the case is an old one. Flavien Nébié's death has still not been explained. The two policemen charged with the murders of Emile Zigani and Blaise Sidiani received very light sentences eight years later – one was given a 12-month suspended sentence while the other was simply set free. This submission of justice to power echoes what happened after the murders of Thomas Sankara and Oumarou Clement Ouedraogo[6] and was probably one of the reasons for public anger. The media did not escape unscathed and the director of the weekly *L'Indépendant*, Norbert Zongo, and three of his comrades were gunned down on 13 December 1998. Zongo was investigating the death of David Ouedraogo, the driver of the president's brother, Francis Compaore, when he was killed.[7] This event marked a turning point in the mobilisation against impunity, which swelled both in numbers and geographically.

Taken unawares by the mass movement, the regime began to look wobbly and the protests gathered momentum throughout the country with all social classes joining in. This was the most serious socio-political crisis in post-revolutionary Burkina. When news came of Norbert Zongo's death, thousands gathered on the streets of Ouagadougou and in the provinces. Symbols of power were attacked, including the ruling party's headquarters. Totally unprepared, authorities decided to wield the carrot and the stick simultaneously. So while it negotiated, it also came down heavily on the demonstrators – arrests, violence, setting up militias, administrative sanctions against strikers, shutting down educational institutions. Eight years later, in 2006, all charges were dismissed. The current situation in Burkina Faso, in so far as it is part of a spontaneous people's movement which includes all sections of society (school children, students, the informal sector, traders) can be seen as a direct parallel with past events. The positions have perhaps evolved in that at least some sections want the movement to go much further.

The riots that have accompanied the protests this year are not new in Burkina. For example, the 'enough is enough' movement in 1998; the traders' revolt in 2003, sparked by the blaze that destroyed the big Rood Woko market in Ouagadougou when the mayor was trying to convince them to move to other markets; in 2006, the decision to make motorcycle crash helmets compulsory in a country which lives by this mode of transport triggered huge protests; and in 2007, several 'Kunde' bars were destroyed after a series of killings were blamed on the Kunde group. In 2008 in Bobo-Dioulasso, like in many other countries, angry protests against the high cost of living started and quickly engulfed the capital. But the burning down of police stations was something completely new. As were the storming of prisons and the liberation of prisoners, acts that proclaim that the real prisoners are not locked up. Until 11 March, demonstrators had not targeted all public buildings – the focus, apart from police stations, was on town halls, which have tremendous local powers, and the offices of regional governors, that is, those seen as the face of state repression and lies. What came under attack were symbols of state, police as forces of repression, mayors who rule like semi-potentates in their localities and governors as the direct representatives of the president, as noted by the governor of the Centre-West province whose reply to demonstrators wanting to meet him was that he was in his position not because 'of the will of the people but thanks to the president of Faso who named him as his representative in Koudougou'.[8]

However, a local uprising does not always transform itself into a national insurrection, as was the case after 22 February. In July 2010, there were riots in Gaoua after the death of 21-year-old Arnaud Some, described by the police after his arrest as a delinquent. Police used real bullets to disperse the demonstrations against this crime, killing two others. The people burnt down the police station. The wave of violence, some months before the death of Justin Zongo, should have been a warning. 'It is unusual to see demonstrators showing this much anger against the symbols of state.'[9] But the regime was able to coast along until the end of 2010 – the November elections in which the opposition took part saw Blaise Compaore re-elected with more than 80 per cent of the vote after a quarter century in power.[10] The following month, the regime celebrated 50 years of independence with pomp and splendour in Bobo-Dioulasso. There was talk of making Burkina an emerging country alongside the Brics group – Brazil, Russia, India, China, and soon South Africa. All this while, Blaise Compaore continued to pile up diplomatic successes.

The protests spread

The bloody repression of the protests in Koudougou and the entire province of Boulkiemde and the appeasement attempts that followed may indicate that the regime was afraid of contagion.[11] In fact, this crisis was also part of a larger discontent – first because of Blaise Compaore's determination to modify Article 37 of the constitution, which would allow him to contest presidential elections and stay in power for the rest of his life.[12] Negotiations with the Coordination nationale de la Coalition de lutte contre la vie chère, la corruption, et pour les libertés (National Coordination Committee against the cost of living – CCVC) went nowhere while prices continued to rise, leading to comparisons with the situation in 2008. This came against a background of rising sub-regional tensions, especially in Côte d'Ivoire, and allegations of interference by the Burkinabé president. As in 1998, the issues of truth, justice and impunity were linked with social and labour issues.

The conciliatory tone of the regime in the initial stages was a sop thrown to protect its public image since it coincided with the pan-African festival of cinema in Ouagadougou (FESPACO, 26 February–5 March), a major national cultural event. This is why classes were suspended during the big student strike back in 1997, officially, to 'allow students to participate fully in the film festival', which prompted the newspaper *L'observateur Paalga* to wonder whether this was not in fact a strategy aimed at preventing student solidarity. Meanwhile, government agents infiltrated the campus. Classes were suspended throughout the country from 25 to 28 February, when it was announced that the suspension order had been extended indefinitely. Schools and universities were finally allowed to reopen only on 7 March, but were unable to do so because of the ongoing unrest.

Once the protests had spread throughout the country, the regime quickly reverted to authoritarian mode. A security blanket was thrown around the city on 11 March, the day of a protest organised by ANEB. It was only that evening that Blaise Compaore finally addressed the nation, but he mainly spoke about the material damage caused to public and private property.

The regime's response to this crisis is exactly how it responded to previous disturbances, the same carrot and stick approach while taking as a personal insult that their concessions were insufficient to calm things down. A model of the various stages in the handling of the student revolts would be as follows: demonstration, repression, arrests, court cases, disqualification (subversion), and negotiations through mediators. A mediator has been appointed after each big student crisis – in 1990 it was the human rights group Mouvement Burkinabé des Droits de l'Homme et des Peuples (MBDHP), in 1997 and 2000 the Mediator of Faso and in 2008, it was the national parliament itself along with traditional and religious leaders. A six-member special committee was set up, made up of traditional and religious leaders, both Muslim and Christian, and presided over by the Bishop of Ouagadougou. The student movement was disqualified after accusations of manipulation by the Union Nationale pour la Démocratie et le Développement (UNDD) party, alleged to be under the orders of Ivorian president Laurent Gbagbo – before 11 April 2011. It is highly improbable that UNDD leader Hermann Yameogo had enough influence to convince young people who were prepared to put their lives at risk in the fight against impunity. This opposition figure, who has on occasion been a minister of state, is an example of the turncoat mentality of some opposition personalities.

Reducing a people's protest to a student revolt

The Compaore regime did not hesitate to point fingers at the communist party (PCRV), which in Burkina Faso has always been the favourite internal enemy, enabling whichever regime in power to justify repression and consolidate power. Ever since its creation in 1978, the communist party has been a useful whipping boy, more so when it is seen as a front for groups challenging the regime, like the Collective against Impunity, the MBDHP, Confédération générale du travail du Burkina (CGT-B) or ANEB. More generally, the regime sees any social protest as being organised by official or clandestine groups determined to end the hegemony of the presidential party, and hence as a threat.

On 11 March, students were arrested without the knowledge of ANEB. The detention of ANEB activists or sympathisers has become routine for the regime and has taken place during every student protest since 1997. The government would have undoubtedly pulled out its court case card – another constant in the regime's handling of student crises. On 14 March it was announced that vacations in primary and secondary schools would be brought forward to 14–26 March 2011. Above all, it announced that state universities would close and that this included the suspension of all related services (hostels, canteens, scholarships, loans). Like their predecessors in 1990, 2000 and 2008, university students were obliged to leave the campus under very difficult circumstances. The government strategy was to paint the crisis as being based purely on student grievances on the one hand, while on the other, to put a brake on the movement. It was a failure – the mobilisation continued. This time too, militias were in evidence, like in the period after the Norbert Zongo affair. These militias generally consist of youth from the lumpen proletariat for whom such occasions could be a source of revenue, or Congrès pour la Démocratie et le Progrès (CDP) activists. In some regions militia activity was synonymous with injuries and revenge attacks.

The army enters the scene

It was against this extremely tense socio-political backdrop that a series of army mutinies took place. The country has seen other such revolts, but never on this scale (almost all regiments were affected) and with such frequency (there were eight mutinies which lasted several days and soon after a police revolt). The first mutiny on 22 March was sparked by a court ruling (on a sex scandal in Ouagadougou) which the soldiers thought was too severe. When they went on the rampage, the authorities decided to release the arrested officers and told them they could appeal against their sentence. This angered the justice department, which went on strike. Then it was the turn of the victims of the looting, mostly traders, to protest. The regime was faced with a multi-pronged protest which included the movement against impunity, the traders, the justice department and the army. But barely had the government promised to compensate the traders and the military hierarchy apologised, than another mutiny erupted on 28 March in Fada N'Gourma, where soldiers liberated one of their comrades who had been detained on charges of raping a minor.

Other demands included better wages and the departure of some senior officers. Law courts were targeted and many justice officials were forced to flee. The next day it was the turn of soldiers in Gaoua to protest, and then in Ouagadougou, mutineers attacked the mayor of the capital as well as the army chief of staff, Dominique Djindere. This led to a curfew being declared on 30 March. But social tensions were also mounting, which culminated in a general strike on 8 April called by the CCVC. And on the day educational institutions were set to reopen, school and university students declared a general strike in Koudougou and other towns. It took several army revolts to push the president to finally break his silence on 30 March, which, ironically, is the National Day of Pardon and was instituted in 2001 as part of a reconciliation attempt after the assassination of Norbert Zongo. The president pledged to meet all sections of society and to listen to their concerns and announced that the crisis was over. There followed a series of meetings, starting with traditional and religious leaders, who were much in demand as the president and his government talked to them before anyone else. But their mediation was totally rejected, sometimes aggressively by the youth involved in the movement for justice for Justin Zongo. The government, however, continued to depend on the mediation of traditional and religious leaders despite their loss in credibility. However, they also talked to the traders, the justice department employees, rank and file soldiers, and school and university students.

The 8 April general strike was a big success and demonstrators included all ages, social categories and political persuasions. The participation of traders was a first, since they are an important electoral base for the CDP, as was that of the hitherto clandestine PCRV, which came out publicly for the first time. The 'Get out' slogan was also very much in evidence. The protest actions by the justice department trade union, angered that on the day they had gone on strike the Appeals Court of Ouagadougou agreed to grant bail to the five accused soldiers, were also unprecedented. They called on all justice department workers 'to respect the principle of equality before the law and consider the generous court ruling in other cases as a precedent', in other words, to not hand down prison sentences and instead grant bail to whoever asks for it on the basis on Article 1 of the constitution, which says all citizens are equal before the law.

On 14 April, tensions ratcheted up further with a revolt in the Regiment of Presidential Security (RSP), officially to press for overdue housing and food allowances. The threat of a military coup seemed real. While there have been revolts in the army before, it had never touched the elite presidential guard, which is described as the army within the army (there are many who wonder why an entire battalion has to be dedicated solely to the president's security: the Committee of Elders set up after the Norbert Zongo affair had also recommended that this battalion be disbanded). When they revolted, the president left the capital in the night and took refuge in his native village of Ziniare, though other sources suggest he sought protection in the French embassy.[13] The mutiny quickly spread and there was gunfire and looting in the city. Many senior officers went into hiding. The residence of the army chief of staff, General Gilbert Diendere, was burnt down. The same evening, another first in the fourth republic, the government was dissolved and a major reshuffle carried out in the army.

Nonetheless, more mutinies erupted during the night. The following day, hundreds of traders who had suffered during the army rampage, came out angrily and began attacking symbols of state (the governor's office, the town hall, parliament, the CDP headquarters). That night, there was a revolt in the Po garrison, a symbol for Blaise Compaore, who was once the commanding officer of these soldiers and with whose support he deposed Jean-Baptiste Ouedraogo to install Thomas Sankara in power on 4 August 1983. Further mutinies occurred in Tenkodogo and Kaya, where the residences of senior military personnel were destroyed.

Different explanations were given for these mutinies – impoverishment, embezzlement of allowances by senior officers, their lack of respect, the establishment of a new French military base allegedly to fight against Al Qaeda in the Islamic Maghreb. On 18 April, the RSP reaffirmed their 'loyalty' to President Compaore and called on their comrades to return to barracks, while the country acquired a new prime minister, the country's ambassador to France, Luc-Adolphe Tia.

The new government was roundly criticised for retaining party loyalists. Meanwhile the president named himself the minister for defence and army veterans. Instead of making structural changes, the regime decided to merely change its communication strategy. The targets of the mutineers and demonstrators clearly showed that the real cause of the discontent was the system itself, but the minister of security nonetheless blithely announced that the crisis had nothing to do with the leadership. On 27 April, the Republican Security Guard revolted, and this was followed by mutinies in several other towns (Bobo-Dioulasso, Dédougou, Banfora, Fada N'Gourma, Gaoua and others). Unlike the military, the police did not resort to any looting, but the reasons for their disgruntlement were the same as their army counterparts. Consultations began with paramilitary troops in case they were needed.

On 28 April, the prime minister announced a series of measures aimed at reducing the cost of living in the country, including scrapping the development tax, reducing the IUTS (salary tax) by 10 per cent, promotions in the public sector, and the suspension of housing development schemes[14] pending an expert review of the situation and of fines on electricity bills. The measures were insufficient to have a real impact on the majority of the population. Even if some of them also benefitted the agricultural sector, they were essentially aimed at the urban population. But the majority of people (cotton farmers, miners) live in rural areas in conditions of misery and over-exploitation.

With the acceleration of land grabbing and the predatory tactics of agribusiness and mining giants, the land question has become a central issue. In a country where 80 per cent of the population live from agriculture, the scrapping of the TDC, a tax on two- and four-wheelers aimed at financing local development, hardly affects people who cannot afford a vehicle. A salary hike, which has yet to be decided, would be salutary, but this too would concern only a tiny minority. In this sense, the demands, not to mention the response, are very limited. However, they do show the clout of social movements because up until now all such demands were either rejected because of 'budgetary constraints' or simply ignored. The prime minister also promised to guarantee the independence of the judiciary – he ended the ten-year mandate of *directeurs généraux* (many were replaced), announced a revision of the criteria for the nomination to senior positions and fairer access to promotions. He warned that senior personnel accused of mismanagement or corruption would be relieved of their duties pending their trial – two mayors were suspended and charges brought against them.

Reactions to the mutinies

Opposition parties in Burkina Faso, like the Sankarist l'Union pour la renaissance/parti sankariste (UNIR/PS), also tried to jump onto the bandwagon of popular protests for their own benefit. Opposition demands that Blaise Compaore leave office were based on the assumption that the army revolts were an ideal opportunity to capitalise on general discontent. But like the UNDD, the UNIR/PS, even though it appropriated the 'Blaise get out' slogan, was more a follower than a leader. It was also reported that the Chef de file de l'opposition politique (CFOP) hesitated between demanding Compaore's resignation and guarantees that he would not stand for re-election. Whatever the details, it was clear that Benewende Sankara cruelly lacked political vision and had overestimated the official opposition and underestimated the power of the people. Incredibly, given the local socio-political context, the opposition took initiatives without securing the backing of trade unions, civil society organisations and the informal sector. The CFOP invited union leaders to only one meeting and then after decisions were taken. Not surprisingly, the protest was a failure and though it was called by 34 parties, it was only able to mobilise a maximum of 400 people. It was also counterproductive, as the regime did not hesitate to use the poor turnout as proof that the leadership of the country was not under attack.

There is no doubt that the mutinies had an impact on social movements and especially on labour unions. On 1 May, they gathered not for a demonstration but a meeting, citing security concerns and possible infiltration as the reason. It also appeared that they had agreed to give the prime minister a grace period and there were many who were confused about why the traditional Labour Day march had been cancelled. The only plausible explanation, albeit without proof, is that the labour movement was worried that the insurrectional atmosphere in the country would spark a *coup d'état*. Perhaps they were worried that if the demonstration got out of hand, the army would move in. Postcolonial history shows that labour unions are always the first victims of *coups d'état* and emergency powers and Burkina in the post-revolutionary period was no exception.

Things calmed down from this point on in the capital but spontaneous protests continued elsewhere in the country. Mobilisation was more corporatist, but all sectors were affected – bakers, miners (tools were downed in several mines), administrative staff, teachers, finance ministry staff, hospital employees, workers in banks, telecommunications and the sugar industry, fishermen and artisans – all took part in the protests. Their demands were not new but their tactics consisted of peaceful marches and open letters. Even cotton producers joined the movement by calling for a boycott of production if they did not get higher prices. This 'peasant revolt', a rare occurrence even outside Burkina, turned violent in some regions and clashes with security forces or fights between strikers and scabs left several people dead.

Restoring state authority

While social tensions calmed down in May, there was still much anger in the armed forces and the mutinies continued – on 14 May in Po and on 23 May it was the turn of the National Guard (used to perform military honours for top officials and dignitaries) to protest. The army appeared out of control and even the new defence minister was powerless. Meanwhile the new government once again embarked on marathon negotiations with all social groups and professions, turning as before to religious and traditional authorities for support. As *L'Indépendant*[15] noted, 'one has to go back to the commando style tactics of the revolution to find a parallel to the current situation'. The intensity of the unrest was almost comical with the people demanding concrete actions. Five more regiments revolted on the night of 29 May in Kaya, Dori, Tenkodogo, Dedougou and Koupela in the hope that the authorities would give in to their demands as they had previously. But the response was different to what was expected.

Shortly after a visit by the army chief of staff, soldiers in the Bobo-Dioulasso regiment, the second biggest army camp, which until then had been unaffected by the unrest, revolted and terrorised the population with looting, shooting and rape. From 31 May to 2 June the economic capital of the country resembled the Far West. On 3 June, the government sent in troops to put down the rebellion – these included members of the régiment paratrooper commando (RPC) of Dedougou, the mobile gendarmerie and the RSP, some of whom had taken part in previous mutinies. They were greeted by one section of the people as saviours while for others, mere mention of RSP put them in a cold sweat. Officially, the intervention left six soldiers dead along with a young girl, reportedly 'caught in the crossfire'. A veritable hunt for mutineers began. The government promised tough sanctions and announced that 566 soldiers had been sacked and that court cases would be brought against 217 of them. The Bobo-Dioulasso intervention marked a turning point in the three-month-old crisis. The formation of a new government and the major changes announced in the army had failed to put an end to the revolts, which since 22 March had progressed at the rate of one regiment joining the mutiny every ten days. This at least should have made the authorities cautious. However, they managed to stamp out the unrest and soon returned to their usual tactics – the big strike called by finance ministry workers on 13 June was put down ruthlessly.

It was in the context of this unprecedented socio-political crisis that the regime set up a consultative council for political reforms (CCRP), made up of various social groups – political parties, associations, religious and traditional authorities. The CCRP was tasked with coming up with proposals for political reform by 14 July. Such committees are routinely set up during each period of extreme social tension and many Burkinabé dismissed the latest avatar as a ploy.

The majority of opposition and civil society groups stayed away from the committee, which was clearly in the hands of the president and his minister for political reforms. Since the system itself could not be questioned, the debates only revolved around tweaking a few things here and there so that the status quo continued. Yet, the committee was patently illegal given the unclear status of many opposition members.[16] For their part, the official opposition and civil society groups, while heaping scorn on the committee, continued to take part in the debate through declarations and press releases. Once again, the regime had managed to set the political agenda and the terms of debate. Institutionalisation has begun to creep in and the regime has not abandoned the idea of modifying Article 37, an underlying aspect of the various revolts. Perhaps it will learn the lessons from Senegal and the extraordinary mobilisation against President Wade's plans to modify the constitution.

Despite some common grievances, the revolts of the people and those of the army could not find common ground – in fact the civilian population was the first victim of the mutineers (deaths, injuries, rape). But one similarity still stands out – the blindness of the military hierarchy and of the regime to the precariousness of the socio-economic conditions of the people, army or civilian – so a common platform could still be forged.

The disarming of the Bobo-Dioulasso mutineers, just before the school vacations, was a turning point and after three extremely febrile months which brought the ruling oligarchy close to panic, military and political authorities once again gained the upper hand. It was business as usual to such an extent that some wondered whether 'all this hadn't been staged to prove how powerful the regime was and send a warning to potential protestors'.[17] Nonetheless, it would be premature for the regime to cry victory – maybe they can win over or at least control civil society groups but it is an entirely different ballgame with the bulk of protestors, who came out spontaneously and whose anger and determination was such that they were prepared to put their lives on the line. Sporadic unrest continues and the countryside is explosive. The prices of basic necessities have not come down sufficiently and many victims of the repression are still waiting for justice. As the newspaper headlines put it – the country is sitting on a volcano. The waves of rebellion that hammered the country have not died down; they have only retreated to the oceans of despair, waiting for the smallest storm to unleash them again.[18]

A shorter version of this chapter was published in Pambazuka News at http://pambazuka.org/en/category/features/72114

Translated from French by Sputnik Kilambi

Notes

1. *L'Observateur Paalga*, n° 7826, 23 February 2011.
2. *San Finna*, n° 605, 28 February–5 March 2011.
3. Interestingly there have been unverified reports that on the eve of the ANEB march and every other demonstration the SMS services were cut. The new security minister, Jerome Bougouma, admitted on 30 April that telephone operators had suspended the service because they 'were being used to foment panic and unrest'.
4. Letter from ANEB Koudougou to the governor, 28 February 2011.
5. Council of Ministers, 2 March 2011.
6. He was a key political figure and was alongside Blaise Compaore and Thomas Sankara right from the start of the 'revolution'. After the 15 October 1987 *coup d'état*, he backed the new head of state. On 9 December 1991 he was assassinated in a highly secure zone in the city.
7. He was wrongly accused of stealing a vast amount of money and handed over to the presidential guard. He died on 18 January 1998 in the sick-room of the presidency. The chief medical officer wrote on his death certificate: 'succumbed to his illness on 18 January 1998.
8. *San Finna*, n° 605, 28 February–5 March 2011.
9. *Le Pays*, n° 4824, 16 March 2011.
10. Only 1.7 million of a potential 7 million electors actually voted.
11. Koudougou is known to be a rebel town. Security forces posted there are reported to have said they were deployed to subjugate the population. See *Eveil education*, 173, 7 March 2011.
12. The article, which restricts the presidential mandate to two terms, was first modified in 1997 and then reactivated in 2000 after the protests that followed Norbert Zongo's death. In 2005, the Constitutional Council ruled that the law was not retroactive, paving the way for Blaise Compaore to stand for re-election twice.
13. *L'Evènement*, n° 208, 25 April 2011.
14. A housing development scheme where land is cleared and infrastructure laid (electricity, waste, water) and plots are sold for residential and commercial purposes. But 'since "decentralisation", there have been lots of corruption scandals in the allocation of plots by local authorities', Club du Sahel et de l'Afrique de l'Ouest (CSAO/OCDE), *Pression sur les terres ouest-africaines : concilier développement et politiques d'investissement*, 9 December 2009.

15. *L'Indépendant*, n° 922, 17 May 2011.
16. Under the law, for an opposition party to be legal, it has to submit an official declaration to the CFOP, which most members of the CCRP have not done.
17. *L'Indépendant*, n° 929, 5 July 2011.
18. *Le Reporter*, n° 74, 15–31 July 2011.

18

North African dispatches: why Algeria is different

Imad Mesdoua

7 April 2011

He's gone! Pharaoh finally understood he was the problem. Better yet, Hosni Mubarak finally managed to find a safe exit through which he, his family and, most importantly, his finances could make a run for it!

With his departure, Egypt breathes again. In fact, the Arab street as a whole celebrated the success of the Egyptian revolution. For weeks, the entire region was there to witness history unfold as millions of Egyptians took to the streets and in a truly heroic movement deposed the seemingly unshakable autocrat. In the euphoria which followed Mubarak's departure, the army seized power and promised to go ahead with reforms demanded by the protestors. Mubarak had done the same following Sadat's assassination, and one cannot help but fear the possibility of a regime perpetuating itself through the sacrifice of its figurehead.

Throughout the revolt, the army's lukewarm support for the revolution and its tardy rally to the cause are greater causes for concern than celebration. Surely the end of Mubarak is not the end of the system nor is it the start of the democracy which the movement's founders probably envision. Revolutions are often confiscated by those who join them last. Egyptians, like the Tunisians before them, should not stop at this success and make the fight for democracy a daily struggle.

Whilst Egypt rejoiced, nearby Algeria stood in anticipation at the call for pro-democracy protests on 12 February. A coalition made up of several members from civil society and political

parties called for a rally on Algiers's 1 May Square and throughout the nation, hoping to emulate the wind of change blowing
through the region. Despite the coalition's high ambitions, only a
few thousand people showed up.

Why was this case? Algeria has always been a land of rebels,
the 'Mecca for revolutions and revolutionaries'. In the 1960s, it
emerged as an independent nation following an atrocious war
with the French coloniser, which gained it a sobriquet as the
land of the '1.5 million martyrs'. In 1988, a recession-hit Algeria
witnessed events comparable to those which recently took place
in Egypt and Tunisia. Millions of Algerians took to the streets in
nationwide riots and protests to demand the end of the FLN's
(National Liberation Front) one-party rule and reclaim their
political and socio-economic rights.

In this respect, Algeria is the unrecognised antecedent to
much of the revolts we are now witnessing. The rise of an Islamist tsunami and the coming to power of the army, as a result of
cancelled democratic elections, would sadly put an end to an
unparalleled – and short-lived – period of democracy. The North
African nation quickly plunged into a tragic decade of violence,
and Algerians were left profoundly scarred from a civil war of
unmatched brutality, widespread terror and complete paranoia.

Today, the country's problems remain multiple and complex,
but stem from a reality easily observed: Algeria is rich, Algerians
are not. Whilst macroeconomic indicators are green, social and
human development indicators show bright red. Home to considerable oil and gas reserves, Algeria has yet to rid itself of an exclusive reliance on primary sector exports to generate growth. This
has simultaneously created a dangerously heavy dependency
on importation. In 12 years, Algeria has made a whopping $600
billion in benefits from its oil industry, with not much to show for
it. Salaries are low, unemployment is high and inequality continues to grow, despite figures which state otherwise.

Despite efforts to restore state investment aimed at infrastructure and education, money is often poorly spent or squandered.
The plague of corruption and nepotism recently materialised
in the eyes of the public when the country's economic pillar,
SONATRACH (a petroleum company), was found to be riddled
with handouts and shady dealings among officials.

Finally, the bureaucracy continues to be a burdensome, oner-ous and tedious labyrinth, stifling the formation of capital and the encouragement of innovation. Start-ups that do flourish do so under the state's watchful eye, which inevitably hinders the chance for job creation. Doctors, teachers and the civil service rely on very low wages compared to other economies where capital is created as opposed to simply distributed.

Finally, no real diversification to other resource-generating sectors was ever undertaken and the country's shy industri-alisation has always been subjected to petty ideological battles and superfluous regional favouritism. In this climate, Algeria's economy and stability continue to be influenced by international oil and gas prices, as well as those of basic foodstuffs.

As recently as December 2010, countrywide riots broke out in response to sharp increases in the prices of cooking oil and sugar. In a country where many struggle to make ends meet, slight increases in basic food prices easily provoke the ire of the underprivileged. The Algerian press often mentions that in the single year 2010, 10,000 riots and protests took place throughout the country. More than anything, there is the imperative for hous-ing. Riots also regularly break out over unjustly distributed public housing as it has become a fundamental frustration in the day-to-day lives of many families.

Why, then, did Algerians, in this apparently negative environ-ment, not march in the hundreds of thousands? One factor was the fear of violence breaking out. The government mobilised for the occasion a daunting arsenal of helicopters and around 30,000 anti-riot police in the capital, a sign that nothing was being left to chance by the higher echelons of the country's polity.

Despite a recent promise to lift the country's 19-year state of emergency, protestors were coldly reminded that protests were not authorised in the capital Algiers. With trains suspended and all major access routes carefully monitored, any sort of move-ment from neighbouring counties was rendered impossible. All of these measures obliviously made for a particularly tense build up, which evidently left many wondering whether it was worth putting their own security at risk.

The tragic reality for Algerians today is that no political party or figure seems able to rally people and aptly voice their grievances around one truly coherent set of political objectives (in this case, change). This problem originates primarily in the political elite's inability or unwillingness to rejuvenate itself. Both the opposition and government boast figures from an older generation. With a population among the world's youngest – the average Algerian being 24 – any political figure over the age of 50 talking of 'change we can believe in' is bound to seem out of touch or irrelevant.

All of these observations bring me to the final possible reason behind Saturday's meagre showing. This movement for change does not yet resonate for a majority because, with the inclusion of certain political parties and/or figures, it can look like another venture through which these individuals and groups can gain greater exposure. Though intense grievances exist in the country, Algerians continue to be highly sceptical of political parties – whether they are of the opposition or not. They are seen as self-serving or in league with the powers that be, thereby rendering their actions legitimate to audiences already supporting their beliefs.

Young Algerians remain desperate for change, thirsty for a better life and disenchanted with their overall situation. Politics and ideology aside, they aspire to nothing more than dignity and a visionary project for their society. For some it can come through economic accomplishment and personal stability. For others it is a sense of belonging and a renewed trust in the country's politics. Over the past weeks, the attempts by over a dozen people to immolate themselves publicly served as a bleak reminder to all of the profound malaise felt throughout vast sections of the nation. In this context, while many will continue to debate the success or failure of Saturday's march; what is certain is that the march broke the long-standing taboo against challenging the status quo.

http://pambazuka.org/en/category/features/72294

19

Libya: behind the politics of humanitarian intervention

Mahmood Mamdani

7 April 2011

Iraq and Afghanistan teach us that humanitarian intervention does not end with the removal of the danger it purports to target. It only begins with it.

Having removed the target, the intervention grows and turns into the real problem. This is why to limit the discussion of the Libyan intervention to its stated rationale – saving civilian lives – is barely scratching the political surface.

The short life of the Libyan intervention suggests that we distinguish between justification and execution in writing its biography. Justification was a process internal to the United Nations Security Council, but execution is not.

In addition to authorising a 'no-fly zone' and tightening sanctions against 'the Gaddafi regime and its supporters', Resolution 1973 called for 'all necessary measures to protect civilians under threat of attack in the country, including Benghazi'. At the same time, it expressly 'excluded a foreign occupation force of any form' or in 'any part of Libyan territory'.

UN conflicts

The UN process is notable for two reasons. First, the resolution was passed with a vote of 10 in favour and five abstaining. The abstaining governments – Russia, China, India, Brazil, Germany – represent the vast majority of humanity.

Even though the African Union had resolved against an external intervention and called for a political resolution to the conflict,

151

the two African governments in the Security Council – South Africa and Nigeria – voted in favour of the resolution. They have since echoed the sentiments of the governments that abstained, saying that they did not have in mind the scale of the intervention that has actually occurred.

The second notable thing about the UN process is that though the Security Council is central to the process of justification, it is peripheral to the process of execution.

The Russian and Chinese representatives complained that the resolution left vague 'how and by whom the measures would be enforced and what the limits of the engagement would be'.

Having authorised the intervention, the Security Council left its implementation to any and all. It 'authorised Member States, acting nationally or through regional organisations or arrangements'.

As with every right, this free-for-all was only in theory; in practice, the right could only be exercised by those who possessed the means to do so. As the baton passed from the UN Security Council to the US and NATO, its politics became clearer.

Money trail

When it came to the assets freeze and arms embargo, the resolution called on the secretary general to create an eight-member panel of experts to assist the Security Council committee in monitoring the sanctions.

Libyan assets are mainly in the US and Europe, and they amount to hundreds of billions of dollars: the US Treasury froze $30 billion of liquid assets, and US banks $18 billion. What is to happen to interest on these assets?

In the absence of any specific arrangement assets are turned into booty, an interest-free loan, in this instance, to US Treasury and US banks. Like the military intervention, there is nothing international about implementing the sanctions regime. From its point of view, the international process is no more than a legitimating exercise.

If the legitimating is international, implementation is privatised, passing the initiative to the strongest of member states. The end result is a self-constituted coalition of the willing. War furthers many interests. Each war is a laboratory for testing the next generation of weapons. It is well known that the Iraq war led to more civilian than military victims.

The debate then was over whether or not these casualties were intended. In Libya, the debate is over facts. It points to the fact that the US and NATO are perfecting a new generation of weapons, weapons meant for urban warfare, weapons designed to minimise collateral damage.

The objective is to destroy physical assets with minimum cost in human lives. The cost to the people of Libya will be of another type. The more physical assets are destroyed, the less sovereign will be the next government in Libya.

Libya's opposition

The full political cost will become clear in the period of transition. The anti-Gaddafi coalition comprises four different political trends: radical Islamists, royalists, tribalists and secular middle-class activists produced by a Western-oriented educational system.

Of these, only the radical Islamists, especially those linked organisationally to Al Qaeda, have battle experience. They – like NATO – have the most to gain in the short term from a process that is more military than political. This is why the most likely outcome of a military resolution in Libya will be an Afghanistan-type civil war.

One would think that this would be clear to the powers waging the current war on Libya, because they were the same powers waging war in Afghanistan. Yet, they have so far showed little interest in a political resolution. Several facts point to this.

The African Union delegation sent to Libya to begin discussions with Gaddafi in pursuit of a political resolution to the conflict was denied permission to fly over Libya – and thus land in Tripoli – by the NATO powers.

The *New York Times* reported that Libyan tanks on the road to Benghazi were bombed from the air, Iraq war-style, when they were retreating and not when they were advancing.

The two pilots of the US fighter jet F15-E that crashed near Benghazi were rescued by US forces on the ground, now admitted to be CIA operatives in a clear violation of Resolution 1973 and that points to an early introduction of ground forces.

The logic of a political resolution was made clear by Hillary Clinton, the US secretary of state, in a different context: 'We have made clear that security alone cannot resolve the challenges facing Bahrain. Violence is not the answer, a political process is.'

That Clinton has been deaf to this logic when it comes to Libya is testimony that, so far, the pursuit of interest has defied learning the political lessons of past wars, most importantly Afghanistan.

Marx once wrote that important events in history occur, as it were, twice – the first time as tragedy, the second time as farce. He should have added, that for its victims, farce is a tragedy compounded.

http://pambazuka.org/en/category/features/72300

20

Swaziland: uprising in the slipstream of North Africa

Peter Kenworthy

30 June 2011

A new, well-educated generation of Swazis have been inspired by the uprisings in North Africa, as well as compelled by their own increasingly desperate mass unemployment and poverty, to try and replace the undemocratic and corrupt absolute monarchy that is Swaziland with a democratic and fair system.

The know-how and tactics of these youths combined with the mass mobilisation for democracy and socio-economic justice has been ongoing for decades in Swaziland. Together they comprised the campaign or uprising on 12–15 April, which appears to be a significant breakthrough. It may not have brought about immediate democratisation but it is surely 'the beginning of the end', as a poster held by a demonstrator on 12 April proclaimed.

There are several common factors between the Swazi uprising in April and the North African uprisings that preceded and influenced the one in Swaziland. These are that no one had expected them and that they happened because of a combination of financial turmoil, youth unemployment and a year-long, democratic mobilisation. The use of online media tools such as Facebook and Twitter meant that the demonstrators could bypass the highly censored national media. And the uprisings were dependent not on one or a few leaders, but on many, meaning that the regimes could not simply shut the uprisings down by arresting a few key people.

One of the main differences between Swaziland and North Africa in building a successful protest movement is that the technology available to the masses in North Africa, which was crucial in keeping the masses informed, is simply not yet there in Swaziland. Only about 5 per cent of the Swazi population have an internet connection, although mobile phones with internet connections are becoming increasingly available.

An absolute monarchy

Swaziland is a small land-locked country in southern Africa, bordering South Africa and Mozambique. It is nominally a middle-income country, but this disguises the fact that a few Swazis live in luxury while the majority languish in poverty. Swaziland has the highest Aids rate in the world, one of the lowest life expectancies, and two-thirds of the population survive on less than one dollar a day. Hundreds of thousands are on food aid from the World Food Programme.

Human and political rights are routinely disregarded in Swaziland, even though Swaziland has signed the African Charter on Human Rights. According to Amnesty International's 2010 international report, Swazi 'police and other security officials, including informal policing groups, continued to use excessive force against criminal suspects, political activists and unarmed demonstrators. Incidents of torture and other ill-treatment were also reported.'[1]And Freedom House gave Swaziland a political rights score of seven – the lowest there is – in 2010, concluding that: 'Swaziland is not an electoral democracy.'

Since independence from Great Britain in 1968, Swaziland has been run by an absolute monarch. King Sobhuza II, the father of the present monarch Mswati III, suspended the constitution, banned all political parties, and proclaimed a state of emergency (which has yet to be lifted) on 12 April 1973. The king appoints and dismisses the government and prime minister at will, and in effect runs the country as a landlord would his farm in medieval Europe, deciding over everything from land allocation to the budget through a traditional system of chiefs and headmen.

The Swazi monarchy thereby crushed the ambitions of all Swazis, apart from those of a small parasitic elite based within the monarchy. The ambitions of the middle classes were curtailed by banning political parties and those of the working classes by suppressing the labour movement. The monarchy also enhanced its power grip over society in general by controlling mineral royalties, business and land administration.

Media criticism of the regime and monarchy has been muted by the fact that the king owns one of the country's two large newspapers and the other is mainly funded by advertisements, of which the government is the biggest provider. Consequently, all the official media in Swaziland employ a great deal of self-censorship.

'I found that during the three years I have lived in Swaziland that if I want to really know what's going on in the kingdom, I should not bother with the Swazi media,'[2] said former associate professor at the University of Swaziland Richard Rooney recently; he edits the widely read, foreign-based, Swazi Media Commentary.

According to the Media Institute of Southern Africa, the unfortunate tendency of the Swazi media to refrain from criticising the regime was particularly obvious in the days leading up to 12 April 2011. 'The only independent newspaper in the country, the *Times of Swaziland*, has managed to give government almost free reign to spread their propaganda ... In all the protest coverage, the protestors were not given an opportunity to respond to the many accusations from the government/traditionalists.'[3]

And public criticism has also been muted by the fact that anyone expressing a remotely nonconformist view about the current regime is seen as a terrorist, and either left to languish in jail on trumped-up charges, or simply beaten up by the police.

Any genuine information or analysis about the regime and the potential of democracy in Swaziland has therefore had to come from other sources, such as the independent magazine, *The Nation*, foreign-based online websites such as the Swazi Media Commentary, debate forums such as that of the Swaziland Solidarity Network, new social media tools such as Facebook and Twitter, and the sharing or photocopying of foreign, mainly South African, newspaper clips about Swaziland.

The problem for Swazis who want change, and want to read online analyses about how this change will come and be implemented, is that so few of them have an internet connection. A magazine like *The Nation* is not widely read, perhaps because it is too expensive or highbrow for the average Swazi, and even copying newspaper articles can be seen as a criminal offence, as happened with a young man who was taken to court for copying and distributing an article from a South African newspaper that was unfavourable towards the regime.

Many Swazis, especially in the rural areas where three-quarters of the population live, therefore get their political information and analysis from a combination of word of mouth, political party and union activities, and civic education.

The important role of civil society

Civil society in Swaziland works for democracy from all angles, including though consciousness building at the political level, through the labour movement, by coordination of the democratic forces, by campaign work and by cooperation with like-minded organisations in South Africa.

The unions and the Swaziland United Democratic Front (SUDF) in particular were an important part of the 12–15 April campaign or uprising, as they played an integral part in its planning. But the Foundation for Socio-Economic Justice, the Swaziland Democracy Campaign and The People's United Democratic Movement were also fully behind the campaign, the latter issuing a press statement that saluted 'the workers and the people of Swaziland for standing up to the hostile regime and press[ing] through with their demands'.

The Foundation for Socio-Economic Justice (FSEJ), formed in 2003, has built a mass-based democratic force of conscious individuals and organisations through civic education about democracy and rights, especially in the rural areas that are traditionally conservative and comparatively loyal to the monarchy. The organisation has played a vital role in making the uprising possible by enabling those who receive civic education to link their poverty and lack of freedom to the policies of the present regime and vent their anger at the root cause of their troubles: the regime. The consciousness building of FSEJ and others is also vital if Swaziland is not to become yet another African democracy ruled by the political and financial elites.

The People's United Democratic Movement (PUDEMO) has been the main political movement for democratic change since it was founded in 1983 and will probably form or be part of a future multiparty democratic government. PUDEMO's manifesto, written in 1985, is clearly in opposition to the present regime in stating that the movement is 'fully dedicated to creating a democratic Swaziland', that 'the country's wealth shall be enjoyed by all citizens and shall be shared equally', that 'the land shall be given to all those who work it', that there shall be 'free, compulsory, universal and equal [education] for all children' and that 'human rights shall be observed and respected'.

Regardless of its peaceful and democratic nature, however, PUDEMO's leadership and members have repeatedly been charged with anything from wearing a PUDEMO T-shirt to high treason for alleged 'terrorism', beaten up, tortured and even, on rare occasions, killed by the Swazi state and police. This has more or less neutralised the movement and forced its members to advocate democratic change in one of the democratic movement's other organisations.

The SUDF was formed in 2008 by a number of civil society organisations, trade unions and political movements, including PUDEMO. The founding of the SUDF resulted from a belief that to create a strong civil society that could work actively for democratisation and poverty eradication, there would have to be political education, mass mobilisation and more unity and coordination among the pro-democracy forces in Swaziland. 'Unity for democracy is ultimately what triggers change. The secret lies in mass mobilisation,' as Sikelela Dlamini of the SUDF puts it (in correspondence with the author).

'But the SUDF has assumed a more underground role than when it was established in February 2008,' says Dlamini. 'It has had to "delegate" its leadership of the overall push for democratisation to its labour federation affiliates, including the Swaziland Federation of Trade Unions (SFTU), the Swaziland Federation of Labour (SFL) and the Swaziland National Association of Teachers (SNAT). Any other way has prompted the state to swiftly use its courts of law or security apparatus to declare workers' demonstrations and protests illegal and stop them on the basis that they are of a political nature. The SUDF therefore played a subtle yet central role in the organisation and actual carrying out of the 12–15 April demonstrations.'

The unions have played a leading role in the struggle for democracy and socio-political rights; both in the recent spate of demonstrations and historically, not least because they are the only organisations legally allowed to hold demonstrations through the Industrial Act. Swaziland has ratified all International Labour Organisation conventions, giving Swazi workers the right to union membership and strike action, although strikes are more or less impossible to organise legally in practice, and employers discriminate against union members. The two main union federations, the SFTU, the SFL, with a combined membership of over 85,000, have, together with the SNAT, recently formed a new common labour federation, the so-called Trade Union Congress of Swaziland (TUCOSWA).

The unions are not officially politically affiliated to any party or movement, although the SFTU, SFL, SNAT, and now TUCOSWA, are part of the SUDF and openly advocate democratisation and socio-economic justice.

The Swaziland Democracy Campaign (SDC) was formed in 2010 and is 'a broad coalition of progressive organisations inside Swaziland and in South Africa united around the demand for multiparty democracy in Swaziland', aiming to focus international attention on Swaziland. The connection with South Africa has been forged as a 'common cause against oppression', according to the founding document of the SDC, and is important because of the concurrent campaign in South Africa, Swaziland's neighbour and main trade partner, by the SDC.

One of the important things that these organisations, not least the more party-political PUDEMO, need to have in place is a clear, concrete and coherent set of policies, both so that they can 'sell' the idea to the masses as a superior alternative to the present system, and so that they will succeed after such a system has been realised.

This also means that the democratic movement must focus on both the overarching political goals of democracy and the more limited, but tangible, daily goals of improving the conditions for the many poverty-stricken Swazis, and that they must ensure that any reforms are won from below by the efforts of the masses, not given from above.

'The views of the movement need to be based on a concrete set of policies that relate to concrete issues such as land policy or educational policy, and that people can therefore relate to,' says Morten Nielsen (in conversation with the author) from Africa Contact, one of the few foreign NGOs to work with and support the Swazi democratic movement. 'And this set of policies for a future democratic Swaziland is not really there at present.'

Another important matter is that of democratic inclusivity. Unless the masses play a major part in the democratisation of Swaziland, the democracy that will result from this process will be but an empty shell. True democratisation cannot be a top-down process. This is why civic education and increasing the internal democratic nature of the membership organisations (to serve as a concrete lesson in democracy and a framework for a future democratic society for members) is so important. And the importance of the year-long consciousness building from below could be seen in the way the 12 April uprising was led, not by the few but by the many, and how it continued even after the entire leadership of the democratic movement was detained.

The 12–15 April uprising

Clearly worried about the scope and potential of the 12 April campaign and demonstrations, the regime and its police and security forces took many precautions. Its preparations started well before the actual event. The Swazi army was sent for training in Pakistan and huge quantities of military hardware were bought (the military budget now being equivalent in size to the health budget). 'We are spending a lot on the army but we are not anticipating what is happening in North Africa. The army is there to avoid such situations', Finance Minister Majozi Sithole told French news agency, AFP.[4]

The Swazi senate had also mandated the minister of labour and social security to try and prevent the demonstrations from happening. The Swazi media, perhaps pressurised by the regime, only quoted government sources and generally discredited the campaigners in what the Facebook campaigners called a 'smear campaign', and security forces were searching high and low for anyone suspected of being involved in the campaign.

The regime clearly also tried to intimidate Swazis into not participating in the demonstrations. Swaziland's prime minister,

Barnabas Dlamini, had warned anyone considering doing so that his security forces would 'crush the protests', and police commissioner Isaac Magagula stated, 'everyone is a suspect until proven otherwise'.

The regime is known for arresting people who are suspected of having any relation whatsoever to the democratic movement. That the Swazi police forces and armed forces do this with impunity is in no small part due to the 2006 constitution, which in effect declares all political parties to be terrorist organisations, and the Suppression of Terrorism Act, which defines terrorism in very sweeping terms. Swazi legislation thus gave the police and security forces almost unlimited powers to clamp down heavily on peaceful demonstrations on 12 April – powers that were widely employed.

The regime pre-emptively detained student leader Maxwell Dlamini and other key figures in the movement before 12 April. Many others were detained between 12 April and 15 April, the regime detaining the entire leadership of the unions, PUDEMO, the SUDF and the SDC, as well as anyone else they suspected of taking any part in the demonstrations in an attempt to bring the uprising to a standstill. Many people were arrested for simply going about their daily business, driven to far-away forests and left there to find their own way back.

'The security forces are literally grabbing everyone they can lay their hands on from the streets and detaining them,' said an SDC press statement from 12 April. That the demonstrations therefore continued after the arrest of the entire leadership of the democratic movement is testament to the success of the democratic movement's strategy of mass leadership and that the Swazi population are well and truly fed up with the regime.

The protests continued unabated perhaps because the demands of the protestors were democracy and socio-economic justice, as opposed to the demands of previous demonstrations in Swaziland for more specific and mundane matters such as higher salaries and against redundancies. This time round the protestors dared to acknowledge and proclaim that all their previous and existing grievances have been caused by Mswati's undemocratic and corrupt regime, says Sikelela Dlamini (in correspondence with the author). 'It was pointless to continue to mount piecemeal one-day protests for shortage of hospital drugs, unreasonable electricity tariffs, withdrawal of government scholarships, wasteful public spending, and latterly mandatory pay cuts, etc., when all of these ills emanated from mismanagement inherent in the undemocratic Tinkhundla system of governance.'

That Swazis want democracy seems beyond doubt, although determining anything in a country that does not allow free and fair elections or a free press is obviously difficult. The increasing willingness to demonstrate for democratic change, regardless of the brutal response of the police and the decreasing numbers of voters in the present non-party election system where the king effectively decides everything, more or less proves this point.

A Facebook uprising?

Much has been made of the use of these modern sources of communication in the campaign. It has even been claimed that announcing the Swazi uprising on Facebook weeks before it took place was a strategic ploy to reveal the true, brutal nature of the Swazi regime because the Facebook campaigners knew that the world's press would be following Swaziland closely on 12 April, and knew that the revolutionary language of the Facebook campaign would provoke a violent response from the Swazi regime. The brutal nature of the regime would thus become obvious for all to see, internationally and in Swaziland.

This strategy turned out to be something of a double-edged sword, however. 'While Swaziland remains predominantly rural with limited internet connectivity, the hype around an uprising managed to filter throughout the country,' says Dlamini (in correspondence with the author). 'It generated unrealistic excitement and anticipation on the part of a general citizenry, who became spectators while the bulk of those who generated the Facebook hype also resided outside the country and could not coordinate activities on the ground to actuate their cyber aspirations.'

It also allowed the regime to be much better prepared for the demonstrators than it had been for the last large-scale demonstration in Swaziland, on 18 March 2011. Here the regime had seemed surprised at the numbers of demonstrators. Between 8,000 and 10,000 marched on 18 March, making it one of the biggest political demonstrations in the history of the country.

And as people in the mass movement pushing for multiparty democracy in Swaziland have retorted, uprisings do not just spring up because they are announced on Facebook. They might be lit by a spark, as was literally the case in Tunisia, but they are fuelled and sustained by the years of groundwork undertaken by civil society organisations and political movements such as the FSEJ, the SUDF, PUDEMO and the trade unions. These organisations have organised, conscientised and prepared the masses for the moment the spark was lit.

'The years of hard work, dedication and sacrifice by cadres of the progressive movement, civil society and all social forces are what have made people aware of their problems,' says COSATU's international relations secretary, and former Swaziland Solidarity Network general secretary, Bongani Masuku (in correspondence with the author).

These organisations were probably also responsible for putting the bulk of the people on the streets – people that actually managed to bypass and brave the police roadblocks, random arrests and general intimidation and participate in the demonstrations.

They had called for demonstrations demanding socio-economic justice and democracy between 12 April and 15 April, whereas the Facebook campaigners had a 'more radical and broad approach that seeks to topple the government,' says Thamsance Tsabedze from FSEJ (in correspondence with the author).

'The king must vacate office immediately,' the Facebook campaign stated on their website.[5] 'Our aim is to remove the king and make sure there's multiparty democracy,' one of the instigators of the Facebook campaign, Pius Vilakati, a former Swazi student leader who is now exiled in South Africa, told the *Mail & Guardian*.[6]

Was 12 April a success?

Judged by the numbers attending the protests or by the concrete results, the 12 April uprising was not as successful as the North African uprisings (although none of these countries have actually democratised yet either). Only a few thousand managed to evade the many police roadblocks and mass arrests on 12 April and the following days of protest, and the king and his undemocratic regime is still in power. And this is despite the Facebook campaign promising that 'a hundred thousand men' (and presumably women) would 'march into the country's city centres to declare a 2011 democratic Swaziland free of all royal dominance' and the SUDF's Dlamini stating (that 'we are looking to put at least 20,000 disgruntled Swazis out on the streets'.

But perhaps we should judge the Swazi uprising not as a failed end result. Perhaps we should instead see it as a manifestation of a growing resoluteness amongst the people of Swaziland. PUDEMO certainly seemed to see it this way, saluting 'the workers and the people of Swaziland for standing up to the hostile regime and pressing through their demands,' as a press statement put it.

The uprising was also an important step away from political apathy in Swaziland, an important step in bringing the sometimes fragmented Swazi democratic movement together in demanding democratisation and socio-economic justice for all Swazis, and an important step in informing the world of the misdeeds of the Swazi regime.

Before 12 April most people outside Swaziland, after all, thought they knew the kingdom as a peaceful tourist destination, if they knew of the country at all. After the brutality of the Swazi regime on 12 April and the following days had been publicised in newspapers around the world, and condemned by countries such as the US, EU member states and South Africa, it will be very difficult for anyone to cling to this image of Swaziland.

Viewed in this light, 12 April was a success that will hopefully prove to be the beginning of the end for Africa's last absolute monarchy. As Rooney, the editor of Swazi Media Commentary, said, 'It might still be the day that led to something else.' Swazis will certainly be far less likely to accept reformist changes from the regime now. 'The event sent a clear message to the regime that their end is nigh,' as Tsabedze of FSEJ put it (in correspondence with the author).

Having said this, the democratic movement will perhaps have to reconsider its tactics for the future demonstrations to ensure that those demonstrating are not put in any needless danger and for these demonstrations to succeed in overthrowing the regime and bringing about a true democracy in Swaziland. 'I think in the future the democratic movement will have to ensure that the information machinery is well oiled and that people are well mobilised and ready for any challenge,' Tsabedze concludes (in correspondence with the author).

The future

What the eventual outcome will be of the Swazi uprising is perhaps too early to predict, as it is with the other uprisings in North Africa, the Middle East, and in occupied Western Sahara (which was, unbeknown to most people, the first country to experience an uprising, in October 2010, when a peaceful protest camp was attacked by Moroccan security forces).

What we can already say, however, is that the 12 April demonstrations, along with the mass demonstrations on 18 March, have seemingly galvanised and incited not only those in the democratic movement in Swaziland, but also ordinary people, who turned out in droves for the two occasions.

And what we can hear is that the unions have said that they will continue the uprising with monthly demonstrations against the Swazi regime, that the campaign to make the international community act continues unabated, and that there have been rumours that King Mswati is considering a controlled unbanning of political parties and a transitional system of democratic, multiparty elections in a desperate attempt to cling on to power.

The internal financial turmoil, where the IMF reported in January 2011 that 'the debt dynamic [in Swaziland] is becoming unsustainable', where the Swazi government has revealed that it will not be able to pay the salaries of its over 30,000 civil servants as of June 2011, should certainly ensure an increasing dissatisfaction with the regime and a good turnout for these demonstrations.

That Swaziland will have a system change seems inevitable at this point. 'April 12–15 may have come and gone; but its impact in shaping the socio-political direction of Swaziland will be felt for many generations to come,' says Dlamini (in correspondence with the author). 'It is very clear to every Swazi now that a return to multiparty democracy is not just inevitable, but also an imminent alternative. King Mswati III faces the unenviable choice to further resist and risk being pushed aside, or make hasty concessions and lose significant ground but save the institution of the monarchy from extinction.'

The only questions that remain are whether change will come sooner or later, peacefully or not, whether such a new system will be truly participatory or not, and whether it will ensure socio-economic justice for the many poverty-stricken Swazis. If there is no change of system and government soon, the IMF is waiting in the wings, ready to demand the structural adjustments that demand financial, but not democratic, openness and reform (cutbacks and layoffs) that have been detrimental to the poor and middle classes in so many other African countries.

Whether the international community of governments, organisations and individuals that, according to Dlamini (in correspondence with the author), 'sacrifices the Swazi people on the altar of silence and shameless indifference' will follow the lead of the democratic movement and finally start to exert some pressure on the Swazi regime for its crimes before, during and after 12 April is another matter, however.

This external pressure could be by way of smart sanctions, as PUDEMO and others including the SFTU have demanded for some time now, or by other measures. What is clear is that external pressure would probably ensure a more swift and peaceful democratisation, whereas the regime will probably respond with more violence towards the democratic movement if it feels it can get away with it internationally.

The US, the EU and South Africa could shut the regime down in a matter of days if they really wanted to. Over 90 per cent of Swaziland's imports and 60 per cent of its exports are with South Africa, and the US and EU are also significant trading partners. The same goes for multinational companies such as Coca-Cola in particular, who have a huge concentration plant in Swaziland because of the kingdom's substantial sugar cane production. 'Coca-Cola presently contributes about 40 per cent of the kingdom's gross domestic product,' according to Rooney's Swazi Media Commentary.

But since these countries and companies have chosen until now not to pressurise the regime on its human rights record and lack of democratisation, and only look like taking small steps towards any public criticism of the Swazi regime after 12 April, it will probably take public and civil society pressure from both inside and outside Swaziland to make them change their minds.

There are already voices within South Africa, North America and the EU that have been calling for democratisation and socio-economic justice in Swaziland for some time now, such as ACTSA (the successor organisation to the Anti-Apartheid Movement) in Great Britain, Africa Contact in Denmark, and COSATU, the SDC and the Swaziland Solidarity Network in South Africa.

Those who truly and selflessly wish to help Swaziland achieve these goals must be cautious, however. 'International support' and 'partnership' are concepts that have often been distorted and misused to serve the purposes of more or less disguised neo-imperialist agendas over the years – not least in Africa. The foreign governments, NGOs and others outside Swaziland must understand that struggle for inclusive democratisation and socio-economic justice in Swaziland cannot be dictated from New York, London, Beijing or Pretoria. For what is the use of all the talk of democracy and human rights if it really means that Swaziland, and other countries in Africa, are to be steered from afar yet again?

http://pambazuka.org/en/category/features/74436

Notes

1. Amnesty International (2010) *Annual Report: Swaziland 2010*, 28 April, http://www.amnestyusa.org/research/reports/annual-report-swaziland-2010, accessed 8 September 2011.

2. Peter Kenworthy (2011) 'Swazi media commentary: telling the truth about Swaziland', Pambazuka News, 2 February, http://www.pambazuka.org/en/category/features/70617, accessed 8 September 2011.

3. Media Institute of Southern Africa – MISA Swaziland (2011)'Times disappoints with protest coverage', 12 April, http://www.sz.misa.org/index.php?option=com_content&view=article&id=120:times-disappoints-with-protest-coverage, accessed 8 September 2011.

4. IOL News (2011) 'Swazi group calls for April 12 revolt', 26 February, http://www.iol.co.za/news/africa/swazi-group-calls-for-april-12-revolt-1.1032761, accessed 8 September 2011.

5. swaziapril12zing (2011) http://swaziapril12zing.wordpress.com/, accessed 8 September 2011.

6. Louise Redvers (2011) 'Policy of peaceful protest divides Swazi activists', Mail & Guardian Online, 21 April, http://mg.co.za/article/2011-04-21-policy-of-peaceful-protest-divides-swazi-activists, accessed 8 September 2011.

Further reading

ACTSA's Swaziland campaign: http://www.actsa.org/page-1223-Swaziland.
    html

Africa Contact's Swaziland campaign: http://afrika.dk/frit-swaziland

About COSATU's Swaziland campaign: http://www.cosatu.org.za/show.
    php?ID=1722&cat=Campaigns

PUDEMO: http://www.pudemo.org/

Stiff Kitten's Blog: http://stiffkitten.wordpress.com/

Swaziland Democracy Campaign: http://www.swazidemocracy.org/home.
    htm

Swazi Media Commentary: http://swazimedia.blogspot.com/

Swaziland Solidarity Network: http://www.ssnonline.net/

Swaziland United Democratic Front: http://sudfinfo.wordpress.com/

Visit Swaziland unofficial tourist site: http://visitswaziland.wordpress.com/

21

The lies behind the West's war on Libya

Jean-Paul Pougala

14 April 2011

It was Gaddafi's Libya that offered all of Africa its first revolution in modern times – connecting the entire continent by telephone, television, radio broadcasting and several other technological applications such as telemedicine and distance teaching. And thanks to the WMAX radio bridge, a low-cost connection was made available across the continent, including in rural areas.

It began in 1992, when 45 African nations established RASCOM (the Regional African Satellite Communication Organisation) so that Africa would have its own satellite and slash communication costs in the continent. This was a time when phone calls to and from Africa were the most expensive in the world because of the annual $500 million fee pocketed by Europe for the use of its satellites for phone conversations, including those within the same country.

An African satellite only costs a one-time payment of $400 million and the continent would no longer have to pay a $500 million annual lease. Which banker would not finance such a project? But the problem remained – how can slaves, seeking to free themselves from their master's exploitation, ask the master's help to achieve that freedom? Not surprisingly, the World Bank, the International Monetary Fund, the US and Europe made only vague promises for 14 years. Gaddafi put an end to these futile pleas to Western 'benefactors' with their exorbitant interest rates. The Libyans put $300 million on the table; the African Development Bank added $50 million more and the West African

Development Bank a further $27 million – and that is how Africa got its first communications satellite on 26 December 2007.

China and Russia followed suit and shared their technology and helped launch satellites for South Africa, Nigeria, Angola, Algeria, while a second African satellite was launched in July 2010. The first totally indigenously built satellite, manufactured on African soil in Algeria, is set for 2020. This satellite is aimed at competing with the best in the world, but at ten times less the cost – a real challenge.

This is how a symbolic gesture of a mere $300 million changed the life of an entire continent. Gaddafi's Libya cost the West, not just depriving it of $500 million per year but the billions of dollars in debt and interest that the initial loan would generate for years to come and in an exponential manner, thereby helping maintain an 'occult' system in order to plunder the continent.

The African Monetary Fund, African Central Bank and African Investment Bank

The $30 billion frozen by Mr Obama belongs to the Libyan Central Bank and had been earmarked as the Libyan contribution to three key projects which would add the finishing touches to the African federation – the African Investment Bank in Syrte, Libya, the establishment in 2011 of the African Monetary Fund to be based in Yaounde with a $42 billion capital fund and the Abuja-based African Central Bank in Nigeria which, when it starts printing African money, will ring the death knell for the CFA franc through which Paris has been able to maintain its hold on some African countries for the last 50 years. It is easy to understand the French wrath against Gaddafi.

The African Monetary Fund is expected to totally supplant the African activities of the International Monetary Fund, which, with only $25 billion, was able to bring an entire continent to its knees and make it swallow questionable privatisation, for example forcing African countries to move from public to private monopolies. No surprise then that in December 2010, the Africans unanimously rejected attempts by Western countries to join the African Monetary Fund, saying it was open only to African nations.

It is increasingly obvious that after Libya, the Western coalition will go after Algeria because, apart from its huge energy resources, the country has cash reserves of around €150 billion. This is what lures the countries that are bombing Libya and they all have one thing in common – they are practically bankrupt. The US alone has a staggering debt of $14,000 billion; France, Great Britain and Italy each have a $2,000 billion public deficit compared to less than $400 billion in public debt for 46 African countries combined.

Inciting spurious wars in Africa in the hope that this will revitalise their economies, which are sinking ever more into the doldrums, will ultimately hasten the Western decline, which actually began in 1884 during the notorious Berlin Conference. As the American economist Adam Smith predicted in 1865 when he publicly backed Abraham Lincoln over the abolition of slavery, 'the economy of any country which relies on the slavery of blacks is destined to descend into hell the day those countries awaken'.

Regional unity as an obstacle to the creation of a United States of Africa

To destabilise and destroy the African Union (AU), which was veering dangerously (for the West) towards a United States of Africa under the guiding hand of Gaddafi, the European Union first tried, unsuccessfully, to create the Union for the Mediterranean (UPM). North Africa somehow had to be cut off from the rest of Africa, using the old tired racist clichés of the 18th and 19th centuries, which claimed that Africans of Arab origin were more evolved and civilised than the rest of the continent. This failed because Gaddafi refused to buy into it. He soon understood what game was being played when only a handful of African countries were invited to join the Mediterranean grouping without the AU being informing, although all 27 members of the European Union were invited.

Without the driving force behind the African federation, the UPM failed even before it began, stillborn with Sarkozy as president and Mubarak as vice-president. The French foreign minister, Alain Juppé is now attempting to re-launch the idea, banking no doubt on the fall of Gaddafi. What African leaders fail to understand is that as long as the European Union continues to finance the AU, the status quo will remain, because there is no real independence. This is why the European Union has encouraged and financed regional groupings in Africa.

It is obvious that the West African Economic Community (ECOWAS), which has an embassy in Brussels and depends for the bulk of its funding on the European Union, is a vociferous opponent to the African federation. That is why Lincoln fought in the US war of secession, because the moment a group of countries come together in a regional political organisation, it weakens the main group. That is what Europe wanted and the Africans have never understood the game plan, creating a plethora of regional groupings, COMESA, UDEAC, SADC, and the Great Maghreb, which never saw the light of day thanks to Gaddafi, who understood what was happening.

Gaddafi, the opponent of apartheid

For most Africans, Gaddafi is a generous man, a humanist, known for his unselfish support for the struggle against the racist regime in South Africa. If he had been an egotist, he would not have risked the wrath of the West to help the African National Congress (ANC) both militarily and financially in the fight against apartheid. This was why Mandela, soon after his release from 27 years in jail, decided to break the UN embargo and travel to Libya on 23 October 1997. For five long years, no plane could touch down in Libya because of the embargo. One needed to take a plane to the Tunisian city of Jerba and continue by road for five hours to reach Ben Gardane, cross the border and continue on a desert road for three hours before reaching Tripoli. The other solution was to go through Malta, and take a night ferry on ill-maintained boats to the Libyan coast. A hellish journey for a whole people, simply to punish one man.

Mandela did not mince his words when the former US president Bill Clinton said the visit was an 'unwelcome' one: 'No country can claim to be the policeman of the world and no state can dictate to another what it should do.' He added: 'Those that yesterday were friends of our enemies have the gall today to tell me not to visit my brother Gaddafi; they are advising us to be ungrateful and forget our friends of the past.'

Indeed, the West still considered the South African racists to be their brothers who needed to be protected. That is why the members of the ANC, including Nelson Mandela, were considered to be dangerous terrorists. It was only on 2 July 2008, that the US Congress finally approved a law to remove the name of Nelson Mandela and his ANC comrades from their black list, not because they realised how stupid that list was but because they wanted to mark Mandela's 90th birthday. If the West was truly sorry for its past support for Mandela's enemies and really sincere when they name streets and places after him, how can they continue to wage war against a man who helped Mandela and his people to be victorious?

Are those who want to export democracy themselves democrats?

And what if Gaddafi's Libya were more democratic than the US, France, Britain and other countries waging war to export democracy to Libya? On 19 March 2003, President George Bush began bombing Iraq under the pretext of bringing democracy. On 19 March 2011, exactly eight years later to the day, it was the French president's turn to rain down bombs over Libya, once again claiming it was to bring democracy. Nobel peace prizewinner and US President Obama says unleashing cruise missiles from submarines is to oust the dictator and introduce democracy.

The question that anyone with even minimum intelligence cannot help asking is this: are countries like France, England, the US, Italy, Norway, Denmark and Poland, who defend their right to bomb Libya on the strength of their self-proclaimed democratic status, really democratic? If yes, are they more democratic than Gaddafi's Libya? The answer in fact is a resounding NO, for the plain and simple reason that democracy doesn't exist. This isn't a personal opinion, but a quote from someone whose native town, Geneva, hosts the bulk of UN institutions. The quote is from Jean-Jacques Rousseau, born in Geneva in 1712, who writes in the third book of the famous *Social Contract* that 'there never was a true democracy and there never will be'.

Rousseau sets out the following four conditions for a country to be labelled a democracy and according to these, Gaddafi's Libya is far more democratic than the US, France and the others claiming to export democracy:

1) **The state** The bigger a country, the less democratic it can be. According to Rousseau, the state has to be extremely small so that people can come together and know each other. Before asking people to vote, one must ensure that everybody knows everyone else, otherwise voting will be an act without any democratic basis, a simulacrum of democracy to elect a dictator.

The Libyan state is based on a system of tribal allegiances, which by definition groups people together in small entities. The democratic spirit is much more present in a tribe, a village, than in a big country simply because people know each other, share a common life rhythm which involves a kind of self-regulation or even self-censorship in that the reactions and counter reactions of other members impact on the group.

From this perspective, it would appear that Libya fits Rousseau's conditions better than the US, France and Great Britain, all highly urbanised societies where most neighbours do not even say hello to each other and therefore do not know each other even if they have lived side by side for 20 years. These countries leaped to the next stage – 'the vote' – which has been cleverly sanctified to obfuscate the fact that voting on the future of the country is useless if the voter does not know the other citizens. This has been pushed to ridiculous limits, with voting rights being given to people living abroad. Communicating with and among each other is a precondition for any democratic debate before an election.

2) **Simplicity in customs** and behavioural patterns are also essential if one is to avoid spending the bulk of the time debating legal and judicial procedures in order to deal with the multitude of conflicts of interest inevitable in a large and complex society. Western countries define themselves as civilised nations with a more complex social structure whereas Libya is described as a primitive country with a simple set of customs. This aspect too indicates that Libya responds better to Rousseau's democratic criteria than all those trying to give lessons in democracy. Conflicts in complex societies are most often won by those with more power, which is why the rich manage to avoid prison because they can afford to hire top lawyers and instead arrange for state repression to be directed against someone who stole a banana in a supermarket rather than a financial criminal who

ruined a bank. In the city of New York, for example, where 75 per cent of the population is white, 80 per cent of management posts are occupied by whites, who make up only 20 per cent of incarcerated people.

3) **Equality in status and wealth** A look at the Forbes 2010 list shows who the richest people in each of the countries currently bombing Libya are and the difference between them and those who earn the lowest salaries in those nations; a similar exercise for Libya will reveal that in terms of wealth distribution, Libya has much more to teach than those now fighting it. So here too, using Rousseau's criteria, Libya is more democratic than the nations pompously pretending to bring democracy. In the US, 5 per cent of the population owns 60 per cent of the national wealth, making it the most unequal and unbalanced society in the world.

4) **No luxuries** According to Rousseau there cannot be any luxury if there is to be democracy. Luxury, he says, makes wealth a necessity, which then becomes a virtue in itself; wealth, and not the welfare of the people, becomes the goal to be reached at all cost, 'Luxury corrupts both the rich and the poor, the one through possession and the other through envy; it makes the nation soft and prey to vanity; it distances people from the State and enslaves them, making them a slave to opinion.'

Is there more luxury in France than in Libya? The reports on employees committing suicide because of stressful working conditions, even in public or semi-public companies, all in the name of maximising profit for a minority and keeping them in luxury, happen in the West, not in Libya.

The American sociologist C. Wright Mills wrote in 1956 that American democracy was a 'dictatorship of the elite'. According to Mills, the US is not a democracy, because it is money that talks during elections and not the people. The results of each election are the expression of the voice of money and not the voice of the people. After Bush senior and Bush junior, they are already talking about a younger Bush for the 2012 Republican primaries. Moreover, as Max Weber pointed out, since political power is dependent on the bureaucracy, the US has 43 million bureaucrats and military personnel who effectively rule the country, but they are not elected and are not accountable to the people for their actions. One person (a rich one) is elected, but the real power lies with the caste of the wealthy, who are then nominated to be ambassadors, generals, etc.

How many people in these self-proclaimed democracies know that Peru's constitution prohibits an outgoing president from seeking a second consecutive mandate? How many know that in Guatemala, not only can an outgoing president not seek re-election to the same post, no one from that person's family can aspire to the top job either? Or that Rwanda is the only country in the world that has 56 per cent female parliamentarians? How many people know that in the 2007 CIA index, four of the world's best-governed countries are African? That the top prize goes to Equatorial Guinea whose public debt represents only 1.14 per cent of GDP?

Rousseau maintains that civil wars, revolts and rebellions are the ingredients of the beginning of democracy. Democracy is not an end, but a permanent process of the reaffirmation of the natural rights of human beings, which, in countries all over the world (without exception), are trampled upon by a handful of men and women who have hijacked the power of the people to perpetuate their supremacy. There are, here and there, groups of people who have usurped the term 'democracy' – instead of it being an ideal towards which one strives it has become a label to be appropriated, or a slogan which is used by people who can shout louder than others. If a country is calm, like France or the US, that is to say without any rebellions, it only means, from Rousseau's perspective, that the dictatorial system is sufficiently repressive to pre-empt any revolt.

It would not be a bad thing if the Libyans revolted. What is bad is to affirm that people stoically accept a system that represses them all over the world without reacting. And Rousseau concludes: '*Malo periculosam libertatem quam quietum servitium* – if gods were people, they would govern themselves democratically. Such a perfect government is not applicable to human beings.' To claim that one is killing Libyans for their own good is a hoax.

What lessons for Africa?

After 500 years of a profoundly unequal relationship with the West, it is clear that we do not have the same criteria about what is good and bad. We have deeply divergent interests. How can one not deplore the 'yes' votes from three sub-Saharan countries (Nigeria, South Africa and Gabon) for resolution 1973, which inaugurated the latest form of colonisation, baptised 'the protection of peoples'? The resolution legitimises the racist theories that have informed Europeans since the 18th century, according to which North Africa has nothing to do with sub-Saharan Africa, and is more evolved, cultivated and civilised than the rest of Africa.

It is as if Tunisia, Egypt, Libya and Algeria were not part of Africa. Even the United Nations seems to ignore the role of the African Union in the affairs of member states. The aim is to isolate sub-Saharan African countries to better control them. Indeed, Algeria ($16 billion) and Libya ($10 billion) together contribute 62 per cent of the $42 billion which constitute the capital of the African Monetary Fund (AMF). The biggest and most populous country in sub-Saharan Africa, Nigeria, and then South Africa are far behind with only $3 billion each.

It is disconcerting to say the least that for the first time in the history of the United Nations, war has been declared against a people without having explored the slightest possibility of a peaceful solution to the crisis. Does Africa really belong any more to this organisation? Nigeria and South Africa are prepared to vote yes to everything the West asks because they naively believe the vague promises of a permanent seat at the Security Council with similar veto rights. They both forget that France has no power to offer anything.

Reform of the United Nations is not on the agenda. The only way to make a point is to use the Chinese method – all 50 African nations should quit the United Nations and only return if their long-standing demand is finally met: a seat for the entire African federation or nothing. This non-violent method is the only weapon of justice available to the poor and weak that we are. We should simply quit the United Nations because this organisation, by its very structure and hierarchy, is at the service of the most powerful.

We should leave the United Nations to register our rejection of a world view based on the annihilation of those who are weaker.

They are free to continue as before, but at least we will not be party to it and say we agree when we were never asked for our opinion. And even when we expressed our point of view, like we did on Saturday 19 March in Nouakchott, when we opposed the military action, our opinion was simply ignored and the bombs started falling on the African people.

Today's events are reminiscent of what has happened with China in the past. Today, the Ouattara government, the rebel government in Libya, is recognised in the same way that at the end of the Second World War China the so-called international community chose Taiwan to be the sole representative of the Chinese people instead of Mao's China. It took 26 years, until 25 October 1971, for the UN to pass resolution 2758, which all Africans should read to put an end to human folly. China was admitted to the UN on its terms – it refused to be a member if it did not have a veto right. When the demand was met and the resolution tabled, it still took a year for the Chinese foreign minister to respond in writing to the UN secretary general, in a letter which did not say yes or thank you, but spelt out the guarantees that China required so that its dignity would be respected.

What does Africa hope to achieve from the United Nations unless it plays hard ball? We saw how in Côte d'Ivoire a UN bureaucrat considers himself to be above the constitution of the country. We entered this organisation by agreeing to be slaves; to believe that we will be invited to dine at the same table and eat from plates we ourselves washed is not just credulous, it is stupid.

When the AU endorsed Ouattara's victory and glossed over contrary reports from its own electoral observers simply to please our former masters, how can we expect to be respected? When South African president Zuma declares that Ouattara has not won the elections and then says the exact opposite during a trip to Paris, one is entitled to question the credibility of these leaders who claim to represent and speak on behalf of a billion Africans.

Africa's strength and real freedom will only come if it can take properly thought-out actions and assume the consequences. Dignity and respect come with a price tag. Are we prepared to pay it? Otherwise, our place is in the kitchen and in the toilets in order to make others comfortable.

http://pambazuka.org/en/category/features/72575

22

South Africa: on the murder of Andries Tatane

Richard Pithouse

21 April 2011

There are moments when a society has to step back from the ordinary thrum of day-to-day life and ask itself how it has become what it has become. There are times when a society has to acknowledge that it cannot go on as it is and ask itself what must be done to set things on a new and better course.

The historians of our children and grandchildren's generation will write the history of our failure to redeem the promise of our democracy and the struggles that brought it into being. They will debate the significance of the various moments that have marked the plunge from the soaring language of the Freedom Charter and the constitution to the stupid, ugly, strutting fascist camp of Bheki Cele and Julius Malema.

We can be sure that they will agree that when we confronted, for the first time, the sickening spectacle of an unarmed man being murdered by the police on the television news, a decisive point was reached. When the police murdered Andries Tatane in Ficksburg on Wednesday they murdered a man who had, with thousands of others, taken to the streets in protest at the unconscionable contempt with which the poor are treated in this country.

All these years after the end of apartheid, abundant rivers of Johnny Walker Blue have been drunk while millions live in shacks without water, electricity or toilets. We still have a two-tier education system that condemns most of us to a precarious, dangerous and difficult life. More than 50 per cent of young black men and 60 per cent of young black women are unemployed.

This is an entirely unviable and unjust situation. The protest in Ficksburg, and the ongoing national rebellion of the poor of which it is part, are an entirely legitimate response to the sheer contempt with which the ANC treats the people in whose name its leading members grow richer as their language and the public performance of their power becomes more infused with violence.

Andries Tatane's sister, Seipati, told reporters that he was 'forever reading books' and that he volunteered to help the matrics with maths and science at the local school. He helped, we are told, the Boitumelo High School to improve its pass rate from 38 per cent to 52 per cent. A witness said that he was singled out by the police after asking them why they were targeting an elderly protestor with their water cannon. He had planned, as is his unquestionable right in a democracy, to stand as a candidate in the local government elections next month.

The officers who murdered Tatane were still on duty in Ficksburg on Friday. The day after Tatane was killed, Elizabeth Mtshali, due to give birth in a month's time, was shot in the neck by the police with a rubber bullet while carrying a plastic drum to fetch water. At times like this you'd be forgiven for thinking that the shack settlements of South Africa were in occupied Palestine.

Of course Andries Tatane is not the first unarmed person to have been murdered by the police during a protest after apartheid. In fact he's not even the first person from Ficksburg to be killed in this way.

More than ten years have passed since Michael Makhabane, a student from Ficksburg, was murdered by the police on the campus of the former University of Durban-Westville during a protest against the exclusion of poor students from the university. He was shot in the chest at point black range and from above with a shotgun.

In August 2004 around four and half thousand young people, many of them school pupils from Intabazwe in Harrismith, occupied the N2 in protest. On the first day of the protest 24 children were injured, 38 were arrested and a 17-year-old boy, Teboho Mkhonza, was shot dead.

But 2004 was the year in which the rebellion of the poor was just beginning. By 2009 the number of protests was ten times higher than it had been in 2004 and it was still higher last year.

There is no record of the number of people that have been killed as this rebellion has spiralled around the country. The Independent Complaints Directorate (ICD) is, plainly, neither a trustworthy nor effective organisation. It has often been deliberately obstructive and has failed to investigate many clear instances of serious police repression, including torture. But its 2010 report confirms that, despite its obvious failings, it investigated 1,769 cases of people dying in police custody or as a result of police action that year. Let us be clear. The state, cheered on by Bheki Cele's swaggering machismo, is waging some kind of war on its people.

We are just under a month away from the local government elections and things may well get worse in the coming weeks. Elections are generally a dangerous time for grassroots activists and poor people's movements, but local government elections are invariably the most dangerous time.

On election day in 2004, Landless People's Movement activists were tortured in the Protea South police station in Soweto. The day after the 2006 local government elections, the police shot Monica Ngcobo dead and seriously wounded S'busiso Mthethwa in Umlazi in Durban. They claimed that Ngcobo had been shot in the stomach with a rubber bullet. They lied, as their spokespeople habitually do. She was shot in the back with live ammunition.

The elections next month will be bitterly contested in many areas with various parties running credible candidates, popular independent candidates entering the fray and boycotts being organised. If decisive action is not taken to persuade the police that their job is to facilitate rather than repress the right to protest, we may have to add more names to those of Solomon Madonsela, murdered by the police in Ermelo in February, and Andries Tatane, murdered by the police in Ficksburg last week.

In 1976 Sam Nzima's photograph of a dying Hector Pieterson being carried away from the police by Mbuyisa Makhubo planted in the global imagination a clear image of the brutality of apartheid. Events without enduring public images are often only private traumas. But an event with a public image, like the murder of Hector Pieterson, can divide a society into a collective awareness of a time before and after a public trauma.

In October 2005 two teenage boys, Zyed Benna and Bouna Traoré, were killed by electrocution while fleeing the police in

Paris. France was wracked with riotous protest for the next two months. In December 2008 Alexandros Grigoropoulos, a 15-year-old boy, was killed by the police in Athens leading to a month-long insurrection across Greece. In December last year Mohammed Bouazizi set himself alight in Sidi Bouzid in Tunisia after enduring one humiliation too many at the hands of the police. The consequences of the reaction to his death are still playing out in Bahrain, Egypt, Libya and Swaziland.

In the past it has been possible for much of South African society to deny the increasing brutality with which our police repress grassroots dissent. The police have generally had a vastly better capacity for public relations than any poor people's organisation and so the average newspaper reader is usually confronted with the police spin on events or, at best, two very different versions of what has happened when a body is left battered or broken after a protest. But the video footage of the murder of Andries Tatane leaves no room for doubt about what kind of society we have become.

The ANC likes to pretend to itself that it is a revolutionary organisation that, alone, can claim fidelity to the struggles against apartheid. It likes to pretend to itself that all opposition is motivated by malicious reactionary schemers. It is time that those of us in and out of the party face up to the plainly evident fact that the most dangerous reactionaries are the ones leading the country. The new struggles to ensure that every woman and man in our country is treated with the dignity which every human being deserves are entirely legitimate.

http://pambazuka.org/en/category/features/72753

This chapter first appeared on The South African Civil Society Information Service (www.sacsis.org.za).

23

Unrest in Algeria: the window is closing fast

Lakhdar Ghettas

21 April 2011

'Algeria is "sitting on a volcano". We will continue to sift for opportunities to support reform, and should be prepared to offer our frank but private opinion of Algeria's progress along the way.' This was how David Pearce, the former US ambassador to Algiers, concluded his report to the State Department four days after the April 2009 presidential elections, an election which paved the way for a third term for Abdelaziz Bouteflika, following an amendment of the constitution in November 2008 which removed the restriction on only two consecutive mandates. Algerians and close observers of Algerian affairs did not, of course, need Wikileaks cables to know that Algeria was sitting on a volcano. Algeria has been in a state of paralysis since plans for the third term went ahead two years ago. It was a moment when the Algerian ruling establishment crossed the Rubicon.

A general state of government dysfunction manifests itself in every aspect of Algerian affairs, not least the scandal in Algeria's state-owned energy giant, Sonatrach and several other corruption affairs in various key sectors. As the ruling establishment struggled to reconcile their entrenched disagreements, a state of paralysis gripped the already blocked channels of communication between state and society. This meant that violent protests and riots have become the only medium of exchange between the top and bottom structures of the state. Genuine civil society in Algeria has been decimated and replaced, over the last two decades or so, by a facade, a weak and discredited structure of rent distribution and cooptation. Algeria's return to the World Cup, after 20 years, galvanised the national spirit and delayed the inevitable explosion of frustration fuelled by the lack of opportunity for the youth in a country which has struggled to take off economically, despite the unprecedented public investment programmes ($200 billion for 1999–2008 and $286 billion for 2009–2014) and $150 billion in reserves. As soon as the World Cup anaesthesia was over, Algerians woke up to the same bitter reality, and as the Tunisian uprising rolled into its third week, Algerian youth were rioting in the streets in early January, protesting at exclusion and demanding social justice. Those riots were very violent in over 20 provinces and resulted in five killed, several hundreds wounded and over 1,000 arrested. The destruction of public property and damage to private businesses was significant. But because this was Algeria, a country that is no stranger to violent protest, the riots were overshadowed by the uprising next door in Tunisia, whose last revolt dated to the early 1980s. By 10 January calm was re-established while the government rushed to pass an emergency economic incentive package in order to cap tariffs and grant tax breaks on imports of basic foodstuffs. The government blamed the riots on lobbies challenging new commercial regulations, and opted to believe that the problem was merely fuelled by hikes in foodstuffs. Witnessing the uprising in one of the neighbourhoods of Algiers from its eruption to the return of calm, I warned at the time that the issue was primarily political.

The spectacular way in which Ben Ali fled and Mubarak resigned increased panic within the ruling establishment in Algiers. A more comprehensive economic package targeting the youth was deployed, which included almost interest-free loans and subsidies for housing. The news of the uprising coming from neighbouring Libya added to the distress of the establishment, while timid but growing calls for genuine reform started to open the debate on an issue which had until then been ignored. Panic was at its peak. The tragic turn of events in Libya was a golden opportunity for the regime: it could play on the Algerian peoples' fear of returning to the bloody civil conflict of the 1990s should they press further demands for radical reforms. Nevertheless, what remained of genuine civil society managed to form a broad coalition, headed by the respected human rights militant Ali Yahia Abdennour, aged 90, intellectual Dr Fodil Boumala and

185

columnist Kamel Daoud, to name a few. The National Coordination for Change and Democracy (CNCD), led by Dr Mustapha Bouchachi, the president of the Algerian League for the Defence of Human Rights, succeeded in breaking the barrier of fear when it managed to stage a march in Algiers, despite the unprecedented and disproportionately heavy riot-police blockade. The 19-year-long state of emergency was lifted de jure soon thereafter, but it remains in force de facto in that marches are still banned and a new legal framework of security measures has been substituted for the state of emergency.

The escalation of violence in Libya suited the regime's rhetoric in deterring any peaceful mass mobilisation for fear the country might default back to the instability of the 1990s. The regular Saturday marches organised by the CNCD lost momentum and the regime's bet on the collective tragic memory and fear seemed to be winning. The government then geared up its campaign to claim that Bouteflika had been in office for only 12 years (unlike Ben Ali, Mubarak, Gaddafi and Abdullah Salah) and that, in comparison, the government had delivered. In other words, Algeria is not Tunisia, nor for that matter Egypt or Libya.

On those two accounts my counter-argument has been the following: the regime would be making a big mistake to exaggerate the impact of the memory of the 1990s on the 20 and 30-year-olds. If fear of returning to the violent and tragic 1990s is so deeply instilled among Algerians, then how does the regime explain that Algerians have been protesting violently almost non-stop, especially over the last two years? How does it explain the 11,000 riots in 2010 and the 70 protests registered last March alone? There is no denying the presence of fear but it is not as profound among this disfranchised young generation as it is among its elders. The lack of opportunity has offset fear below the deterrence threshold. On the argument that the government has delivered, I would say the riots themselves over jobs, public services and housing undermine those claims and anything achieved is dwarfed by what could have been achieved given the financial means available to the government ($150 billion in reserves) and the regime's duration (two terms and half). The humiliating way in which the constitution was amended to allow a third term tarnished the meagre achievements of Bouteflika's rule.

Meanwhile, calls for genuine reform emerged from within the ranks of the regime. Key historic figures like Abdelhamid Mehri and Hocine Ait Ahmed have both addressed open letters to Bouteflika, urging him to execute profound political reforms so as to coincide with Algeria's 50th anniversary of independence next year. There have been similar calls from within the ranks of the military, as well as the intelligence services Département du Renseignement et de la Sécurité (DRS) in the form of articles in *Le Monde diplomatique* (and the Algerian daily *El Watan*). The latter's 15 March dossier on the DRS was historic in that for the first time public debate has been opened on the security intelligence services and their role within the affairs of the state. It is clear something is in the making. Now even the coalition parties forming the ruling government have called for profound reforms, including amendments to reinstate into the constitution the two-term restriction and dissolving the whole facade of a democratic structure (parliament, local assemblies, call for anticipated elections, etc).

This has created the perception that the regime is on the defensive and compelled to buy social peace in order to quell any sign of unrest. It is what I call 'the now-or-never moment'. Over the last two weeks several sectors have staged sit-ins in Algiers, despite the heavy security presence. The list is long but four need be examined to elicit the trend. First, the students went on strike and camped outside the Ministry of Higher Education, as well as the presidential palace, for over a month. Second, paramilitary communal guards, formed in the 1990s to help combat terrorism alongside the regular military and police forces, managed to march in Algiers, in uniform, to protest against plans to disband the corps. Third, teachers on temporary contracts for many years maintained a sit-in outside the presidential palace for 10 years despite police harassment aimed at breaking up the protest. Fourth, Sonatrach workers in the gas-rich field Hassi R'mel went on hunger strike for a few days over socio-economic grievances, following which the company's top management has come to meet their demands this week. All four protests managed to have most of their demands satisfied after two weeks of arm-wrestling with the regime. This has had an instant domino effect on the other sectors, and right now resident doctors (7,500 doctors) and the powerful independent civil servants union, which comprises the personnel of Algeria's 1,541 municipalities, have all gone on strike. Meanwhile, protests of neighbourhoods and the jobless have been flaring up here and there more often. This week 19-year-old Mohamed Slmani set himself alight and succumbed to his burns several hours later. Over 30 have now gone down that path, among whom six have died.

The regime might have perfected tactics of all sorts (media campaigns, heavy security policing, etc) in order to abort the revived civil society mobilisation in the aftermath of the Tunisian uprising, and one might argue that it has succeeded in that effort. What we are observing now, however, is that the mass mobilisation the regime feared has gone sector-based, making it impossible to discredit it as Islamist, ethnic or subversive. The regime was caught off-guard by the impressive march of 3,000 paramilitary guards, the persistence of palace sit-ins by the students, the resilient teachers and the disarming hunger strike of the Sonatrach workers. Each threatened a nightmare scenario: confrontation with elements that fought terrorism, disenfranchising the students and risking pushing them into the arms of the opposition movement, a prolonged strike as the high school baccalaureate exam loomed and, finally, paralysing the most sensitive energy sector which generates the country's hard currency.

Having witnessed the results obtained by their fellow active countryfolk in the space of two weeks or so, the 'now-or-never' spirit has been spreading like wildfire, reaching every sector; even the journalists of the state's mouthpiece *El Moudjahid* and the national radio have staged sit-ins. The state apparatus is chronically dysfunctional but now it is being rapidly paralysed. The regime will not be able to satisfy all of the 'now-or-never' protests. The only way out from this deadlock is for the regime to break this cycle by declaring a roadmap for real reform. A few viable projects have been devised by credible figures, for example Dr Ahmed Benbitour's initiative. It is also 'now-or-never' for timely change, in that the regime might not have another chance to effect significant reforms in the future should it miss this opportunity.

Should the regime fail to seize this opportunity and introduce profound changes that address the real political problems in Algeria then I am afraid the following scenario will come into play: the fact that some sectors driven by the 'now-or-never' spirit will inevitably be disappointed and not see their demands met – in that the government will arguably not be able to satisfy the socio-economic grievances of protesting workers – could mean they forge tacit and ad hoc alliances with those outside the active segment of the society, i.e., the jobless and disfranchised youth who rioted last January. In other words, the disappointed workers who are on strike now would march behind and support the jobless and marginalised youth who have been in the streets for several years now. This possible scenario would give momentum to another widespread uprising, which would in turn focus the minds within the ruling establishment on the urgency of change.

Should things come to this scenario, then I am confident a fraction of the January uprising in terms of intensity would force the way for real change, probably in a more peaceful and less costly way than the Tunisian and Egyptian experiences. There is still time for the regime to end the 'now-or-never' domino effect and go ahead with genuine reforms, but the clock is ticking. Over the next few months new factors will come into play as well: the end-of year exams in high schools and the spectre of a missed year should universities not regain normalcy, followed by summer with Ramadan in the hottest month this year (August, when domestic demand for electricity reaches its peak because of increased use of air conditioning not only in the south but also in the north). Either of these factors might become the trigger, especially electricity supply shortages (judging by last summer's experience, where riots flared up in many towns and villages of the south-east over the issue). There was a region-wide violent precedent to this in the mid-1970s. Let us hope that the ultimate national interest of Algeria focuses minds, above all because time is of the essence and the window of opportunity is closing fast. The regime would be making a costly mistake to believe that the chaotic situation in Libya and the fragile one in Tunisia and Egypt would make the West favour stability in Algeria, for the simple reason that Algeria cannot escape the ripple effects of the geopolitical earthquakes in the region, two of which are on its eastern borders. History is on the march.

http://pambazuka.org/en/category/features/72762

This chapter was first published on the website of the London School of Economics IDEAS Centre for Diplomacy and Strategy.

24

Whose dictator is Gaddafi?

Yash Tandon

12 May 2011

To put the West's case bluntly and simply, it has apparently inter-vened in Libya to 'protect the people' from the 'dictator' Gaddafi. This begs the question: whose dictator is Gaddafi?

If there is one third-world leader in the whole galaxy of the empire's neocolonial dictators who best exemplifies the contradic-tion between the empire and a neocolony, it is Gaddafi. Libya is a neocolony in the sense that Kwame Nkrumah used the term, and Gaddafi, like Robert Mugabe, is objectively a neocolonial dictator, though subjectively anti-imperialist.

To understand this apparent contradiction, one needs to appreciate the vital difference between a colony and neocolony. A neocolony is ruled by the empire not directly, but indirectly – through its agents in the countries concerned. On the other hand, a neocolonial economy, and hence the neocolonial state, is, in the ultimate analysis, controlled by the empire – on behalf of global finance capital. There is a government in the seat of governance, and this government, or regime, is often in open defiance of the empire. When the empire talks of regime change, it means change in government without losing its control over the neocolony.

To put the matter from the other side, a neocolony is not, as the term might imply, a docile, submissive, community. It is a community, or a people, still in struggle against the empire for its full liberation. The people occasionally rebel against the government if they are oppressed or economically marginalised, as has happened in Egypt, Tunisia, Libya and Zimbabwe, among others. In rebelling against a neocolonial government, however, the people also rebel, objectively, against the empire, against the neocolonial economic and political order. These are two sides of the same coin; they are the same phenomenon. On one side of the coin you see the face of Gaddafi; flip the other side and you see the face of the empire. The challenge facing neocolonial upstarts like Gaddafi and Mugabe is how to ensure the face of the empire remains visible on the coin. Of course, the empire has the reverse challenge. In the case of both Zimbabwe and Libya, the empire has been better than its rebellious neocolonial dictators in keeping the coin with the dictator's face visible at the top.

How has the empire managed to do this? It has done so by using three weapons: one, by exploiting the divisions among the people; two, by using the humanitarian card; and three, by exploiting its bigger control over the world media. In both Libya and Zimbabwe, the empire has been able to portray itself as a saviour of the people, an ally to help them remove the government and put in place one that is more democratic. This is what is currently happening in the Arab world and many parts of Africa, where the people have taken to the streets to protest against a system that is oppressing and exploiting them.

Each neocolony is different. Each has its own history, culture, economic links with the global economy, and ethnic, religious and class configuration. To understand the specific character of Libya and Gaddafi, a bit of history is necessary. It is important to bear in mind that Libya is part of an ancient civilisation going back to the Phoenicians in the 5th century BC, well before the birth of Western civilisation. In more recent times, after the collapse of the Ottoman empire, Libya fell into the hands of Italy. In October 1911, Italian battleships attacked Tripoli, bombing the city for three days. Resistance followed under Omar Mukhtar's mujahideen guerrilla forces. Thousands of Libyans were forced to leave their land and live in concentration camps. Thousands died of hunger and illness and some of them were hanged or shot because they were believed to be helping the mujahideen. The Libyan historian Mahmoud Ali At-Taeb said in an interview with the Libyan magazine *Ash-Shoura* (October 1979) that in November 1930 there were at least 17 funerals a day in the camps due to hunger, illness and depression. Mukhtar's nearly 20-year struggle came to an end when he was captured in battle and on 16 September 1931 hanged in front of his followers in the concentration camp of Sollouq by the orders of the Italian court. He was about 83 years old, but he kept on fighting until death. Today Mukhtar's face is shown on the Libyan 10-dinar bill. His final years were immortalised in the movie *The Lion of the Desert* (1981). This history, and the heroic resistance put up by Libya's national hero, Omar Mukhtar, go some way to explaining the arrogance of Gaddafi towards Western civilisation and colonisation.

This is the legacy that inspires Gaddafi, just as in Zimbabwe it is Kaguvi's spirit (his *mudzimu*) that inspired Mugabe and the people to fight the second Chimurenga against the British empire. Coming to modern times, on 1 September 1969, Colonel Gaddafi overthrew King Idris in a bloodless military coup. The British tried to dislodge him (the so-called Hilton assignment) but failed. Gaddafi has been in power ever since. In 1977, he renamed the Libyan Arab Republic the Great Socialist People's Libyan Arab Jamahiriya. Gaddafi created a system of Islamic socialism which blended Arab nationalism: direct, popular democracy; aspects of the welfare state; and Islamic morals (among them, outlawing alcohol and gambling), on all of which he elaborated in his *The Green Book*. He closed down American and British military bases and partly nationalised foreign oil and commercial interests in Libya. In June 1972 he announced that any Arab wishing to volunteer for the Palestinian struggle for liberation could register at any Libyan embassy and would be given training on armed combat. In the hope of persuading the West to end support for Israel, he promoted oil embargoes as a political weapon. On 7 October 1972, he praised the Lod airport massacre, carried out by the Japanese Red Army. In 1976 after a series of attacks by the Irish Provisional IRA, he claimed that he had been supplying arms to the IRA.

Notwithstanding all this, and despite Gaddafi being a thorn in the flesh of the empire, Libya (like Zimbabwe) has remained a neocolony of the empire. A few facts attest to this reality. Libya is OPEC's 8th largest oil producer. It depends primarily upon revenues from the petroleum sector, which contributes practically all export earnings and over half of GDP. According to the International Energy Agency, more than 70 per cent of its oil is exported to European countries, especially Italy, France, Germany and Spain, many of whom have invested heavily in Libyan oil. For example, by the end of October 2010, the number of French companies in Libya had nearly doubled since 2008 – most of them in the energy sector. It is no wonder that President Sarkozy is so nervous about the outcome of the current civil war in Libya. Italy alone buys a quarter of Libya's oil and 15 per cent of its natural gas. In all these years, Italian companies continued to retain a strong presence in Libya, which owned significant shares in Italy's Eni oil corporation, Fiat, Unicredit bank and Finmeccanica. In January 2002, Gaddafi purchased a 7.5 per cent share of Italian football club Juventus for $21 million, through a long-standing association with Italian industrialist Gianni Agnelli. In addition, several other European and British compa-nies have maintained strong commercial interests in Libya. This is at the national level, but at the personal level, the Gaddafi family became extremely wealthy as a result of his continu-ing links with the empire. The $70 billion Libyan Investment Authority (LIA) is a state institution, but it would be a safe bet that Gaddafi has full control over it (or had, until it was recently frozen). While he financed many groups fighting the empire, he and his sons, known to live in opulent luxury in the West, often donated money to liberal causes, such as the London School of Economics Centre for the Study of Global Governance; indeed, the former director of the LSE, Anthony Giddens (Prime Minis-ter Tony Blair's political mentor), visited Gaddafi in 2007 to give him some lectures on democracy.

However, Gaddafi has his idiosyncrasies. He is trusted neither by the empire nor by his fellow heads of state in the Arab League and the African Union. President Museveni, in praising Gaddafi as a nationalist, criticised him for his mistakes, among others: backing Idi Amin in Uganda; pushing for a United States of Africa; proclaiming himself king of kings; ignoring the plight of Southern Sudan; and promoting terrorism. For the empire, Gaddafi had become an unreliable, indeed dangerous, neocolo-nial dictator. The empire had to bring him to book.

Here is a brief account of how the empire disciplined Gaddafi and finally succeeded. For most of the 1980s and 90s, Libya was under the empire's economic and diplomatic sanctions. In April 1986, a joint US air force, navy and marine corps force attacked Libya. In 1993 the UN imposed sanctions against it. As the sanctions began to bite, President Nelson Mandela made a media-hyped visit to Gaddafi in 1997, followed by the UN Secretary General Kofi Annan. As a result of these overtures, Gaddafi agreed in 1999 to hand over two Libyans accused of planting a bomb on Pan Am Flight 103, which came down over Lockerbie, Scotland. Gaddafi paid compensation to victims of Lockerbie – $2.7 billion to the families of the 270 victims, that is up to $10 million each. The UN sanctions were thereupon suspended, but US sanctions against Libya remained in force. Gaddafi went on to cooperate with investigations into previous Libyan acts of state-sponsored terrorism and agreed to end his nuclear weapons programme. On 15 May 2006, the US State Department announced that it would restore full diplomatic relations with Libya, and that it would be removed from the list of nations supporting terrorism. Libya was thus restored to its *ancien regime* status as a neocolony.

Following Gaddafi's rehabilitation, several imperial heads of state, most flamboyantly British Prime Minister Tony Blair, French President Sarkozy and Italian Prime Minister Silvio Berlusconi, rushed to Tripoli to shower the dictator with kisses and hugs in photo opportunities and to secure from him investment opportunities as well as access to oil. In March 2004, Blair went to Libya and praised Gaddafi for his cooperation. In July 2007, Sarkozy signed a number of bilateral and multilateral (European Union) agreements in Libya. In August 2008, Berlusconi signed a landmark cooperation treaty in Benghazi, under which Italy agreed to pay $5 billion to Libya as compensation for its former military occupation, in exchange for Libya agreeing to stop illegal immigration to Italy, and investments in Italian companies. As the diplomatic editor of the *Daily Telegraph*, David Blair, said, Libya's 'Brother Leader', had gone from being 'the epitome of revolutionary chic' to 'an eccentric statesman with entirely benign relations with the West' (*Daily Telegraph*, 13 August 2009). Britain's current prime minister, David Cameron, not to miss his turn, went to Libya to sell arms to the empire's neocolonial dictator, even as the people were marching against him in Tripoli.

But soon the imperial dictators were to regret their sudden passion for Gaddafi. The Tunisian and Egyptian people's revolutions took them by surprise. When the contagion spread to Libya, the empire could no longer defend the recently rehabilitated Gaddafi. It jumped on the democratic bandwagon, making a quick U-turn, and ditched Gaddafi as quickly as it had dashed to hug him. That Gaddafi had run a tight-fisted autocratic regime in Libya for decades was a well-known fact. His autocracy was never a matter of much concern to the empire. There were other equally harsh regimes in the service of the empire in other parts of the Arab world, such as Bahrain and Yemen, as well as in many pro-imperial neocolonies in Africa. What tipped the scale against Gaddafi was his unreliability and not the fact that he was a dictator. The challenge the empire had faced since his turnaround in 1999 had been how to turn Gaddafi from a dictator who served revolutionary causes to one who would serve imperial interests without creating problems for them. When this did not happen, he had to go, as indeed did Tunisia's Ben Ali and Egypt's Mubarak, long-time allies (read, neocolonial dictators) of the empire.

But getting rid of Gaddafi became a bigger problem for the empire than getting rid of Ben Ali and Mubarak. Earlier, I explained two vital differences between a colony and neocolony. There is a third difference between the two. Unlike colonies, neocolonies are sovereign states and members of the UN. They have rights as independent nations, rights to self-determination and rights to development. The empire cannot just bomb a sovereign member of the UN, for example, without the UN's sanction, especially of its Security Council, which is the organ in the UN that deals with matters of international peace and security. This creates hurdles for the empire. In the UN context, for example, the empire has to get Russia and China (the two other permanent members of the Security Council that hold the power of veto) on board, and at least a majority of the remaining non-permanent members before it can attack a neocolony. The empire could not just attack Libya and take out Gaddafi. A proper rationale had to be engineered – one that could be sold to the empire's own sceptical publics, to allies in the other neocolonies and to allies in non-imperial Europe and the rest of the third world. The critical support needed here was that of the other neocolonies in the Arab world, best of all if it could be expressed institutionally by the Arab League. After much neocolonial persuasion and carrot dangling, this was achieved. For years the league has been belittled, even ridiculed, by the empire for its flabbiness and foibles. Suddenly, when the league supported the no-fly zone against

195

Libya, it became 'the voice of the Arab people'. In the event, Russia and China abstained, as did India and Brazil, for reasons that we cannot go into here. For good measure, the African neocolonies – South Africa, Nigeria and Gabon – voted in favour of the resolution.

Once these enabling conditions of a new diplomatic reality were created, the empire was quickly able to get the Security Council to pass a consensus resolution. Resolution 1973 (2011) demanded 'an immediate ceasefire in Libya, including an end to the current attacks against civilians', which it said might constitute crimes against humanity; it imposed a ban on all flights in the country's airspace – a no-fly zone; and tightened sanctions on the Gaddafi regime and its supporters. It authorised member states, 'acting nationally or through regional organisations or arrangements, to take all necessary measures to protect civilians under threat of attack in the country, including Benghazi, while excluding a foreign occupation force of any form on any part of Libyan territory' – requesting them to immediately inform the secretary general of such measures.

However, even before the ink was dry, France had begun to bomb Libya. Soon France was joined by Britain and the United States, until the authority of the UN was effectively transferred from it to NATO. International lawyers will no doubt write copious papers on the legality of the actions that followed in terms of both the resolution and international law. For example, in an 'open letter to President Barack Obama on the crisis in Libya', the National Conference of Black Lawyers argued that there was 'no lawful basis for commencing a military campaign' in Libya. But in the world of diplomatic reality, this is just a lot of noise after the fact. And in any case, there are always several contending views on the legality or otherwise of such actions. Above all, there is no equivalent of the Nuremburg Tribunal or the International Criminal Court that dare put on trial the imperial dictators – Obama, Clinton, Sarkozy or Cameron. The ICC is essentially a neocolonial tool of the empire, meant to be used only against third world or former east and central European dictators and violators of human rights.

Libya is a neocolonial state; it is imperial finance capital which, despite contradictions, is in effective control of the state and its economy. Gaddafi has been an unwilling neocolonial dictator for finance capital, with a rather utopian vision to liberate himself and Libya from the empire – utopian because he wanted to fight the empire while still keeping the country's and his own wealth within the imperial industrial, financial and banking system. The empire might have accommodated him, and indeed did rehabilitate him after his turnaround in 1999, but the Arab spring upset the programme of the empire, and it had to quickly make a U-turn and ditch Gaddafi just as it had Ben Ali and Mubarak. How things might move forward in Libya is a big issue.

http://pambazuka.org/en/category/features/73153

25

An African reflection on Tahrir Square

Mahmood Mamdani

12 May 2011

The discussion on justice in this conference [on social justice, Cairo, May 2011] focused on two of its forms: criminal and social. There has been little discussion of political justice. My object in this talk will be to look at the events identified with Tahrir Square through the lens of political justice.

I want to begin with giving you a taste of how Tahrir Square has resonated with official Africa. Not only has this new way of doing politics, politics without recourse to arms, bewildered officialdom; it has also sent a chill down many an official spine.

I will give an example from Uganda.

In Uganda, it has provided the lens through which all participants have made sense of a new form of protest that we call 'Walk to Work'. The immediate background to it was government's refusal to permit any form of peaceful assembly to protest any aspect of its policy. The one exception was a permit the government granted the Pan-African Movement, an organisation that had been set up under the auspices of Presidents Museveni and Gaddafi a couple of decades ago, to march in solidarity with Colonel Gaddafi and the Libyan people and in opposition to NATO's (North Atlantic Treaty Organisation) bombardment of Libya. The march was to end up as a rally to be addressed by an army commander. But the government changed its mind at the last minute, most think because it realised the demo could be joined by opposition supporters, or for that matter anyone disgruntled with government policy, and so the government decided to tear-gas and disperse its own demonstration.

Soon after that, the opposition announced that it would resort to a new form of protest: it would walk to work in response to rising fuel and commodity prices. Walk to Work, the opposition said, was not an assembly and so required no police permit. The result was a true theatre of the absurd as police arrested opposition politicians walking to work and then looked for reasons to justify it. Let me give you a few instances from press accounts of the events that followed.

Salaamu Musumba, a high opposition official, was walking with one other person, and was stopped by a policeman. 'Have you no car?' asked the policeman.

Musumba answered, 'Yes I have.'

'Then why are you walking?'[1]

Musumba was arrested.

Asked what was wrong with walking, the information minister suggested that the opposition must have a hidden agenda; if not, why would it not 'come up with proposals on how to handle the challenges ... instead of going to the streets'.[2]

The minister of internal affairs said the problem was more sinister. The motive behind Walk to Work was really political, which is why the organisers should have sought police guidance. But the organisers did not follow official guidelines: 'Police was not notified, the organisers did not identify themselves, the routes were not agreed to,' he said. Asked why the police had sprayed schools and health centres with teargas, he said the fault really lay with those walking: '[S]ome of them, when engaged by the police, decided to run into schools and health centres to use children and patients as human shields.'[3]

The chief political commissar of the police insisted that since the Walk to Work demo was bound to turn into a procession, the organisers were law-bound to notify the police. 'I have no quarrel with anybody who wants to walk but it must be in accordance with the law by notifying the police and agreeing on the routes and maintenance of order.' Realising the absurdity of calling on people to get a police permit specifying when and where to walk, he added: 'Many people walk but this has turned into a political matter.'[4]

Inspector General of Police Major General Kale Kaihura tied himself in knots, seeking to explain the distinction between ordinary walking and political walking. Referring to the leading opposition leader, Kizza Besigye, he said, 'Besigye can walk. There is no problem and he does not have to notify the police. However, when he wants to use walking or running as a demonstration, then he has to notify us.'[5] Pressed to explain what was wrong with political walking, the inspector general of police said the opposition's real intention was to create a Ugandan version of Egypt's Tahrir Square.[6]

When the uprising we identify with Tahrir Square first happened, media commentators dismissed the very possibility of something similar happening in East Africa. In their view, local society was too ethnically divided to rise up as one. But events have shown that unity does not precede political praxis; it is produced through political struggle. This is why the memory of Tahrir Square today feeds opposition hopes and fuels government fears in many an African polity. To paraphrase a 19th-century political philosopher, the spectre of Tahrir Square is coming to haunt Africa's rulers.

Observers of Europe have seen in Tahrir Square the spread of colour revolutions said to have begun in Eastern Europe with the fall of the Soviet Union. I want to place Tahrir Square in a different context. I propose to look back more than a quarter of a century, really three and a half decades, to an event that occurred on the southern tip of this continent, Soweto. Soweto 1976 signified a turning point in South African struggle. Soweto was identified with the onset of community-based organisation. Three years earlier, in 1973, spontaneous strikes in the city of Durban had sparked initiatives that led to the formation of independent trade unions. Together, Soweto and Durban, community-based organisations and independent trade unions, changed the face of anti-apartheid politics in South Africa.

Soweto 1976 was a youthful uprising. It marked a generational shift. In an era when adult political activists had come to accept as a truism that meaningful change could only come through armed struggle, Soweto pioneered an alternative imagination and an alternative mode of struggle. Soweto changed the conventional understanding of struggle from armed to popular struggle. Ordinary people stopped thinking of struggle as something waged by professional fighters, armed guerrillas, with the people cheering from the stands, but as a popular movement with ordinary people as key participants. The potential of popular struggle lay in sheer numbers, guided by a new imagination and new methods of struggle. Finally, this new imagination laid the basis for a wider unity.

To understand the efficacy of this new imagination, we need to begin with an understanding of the mode of governance, the mode of rule, to which it was a response. Apartheid rule had split South African society into so many races (whites, Indians, coloureds) and so many tribes (Zulu, Xhosa, Pedi, Venda and so on), by governing races and tribes, and even each tribe, through a separate set of laws, so that even when they organised to remove or reform the law in question, those opposed to apartheid organised and acted separately: the whites as Congress of Democrats, coloureds as the Coloured People's Congress, Indians as the South African Indian Congress and Africans as the African National Congress (ANC). Each of these qualifiers – coloureds, Indians and Africans – mirrored how the official census named each population groups.

In this context came a new person, a visionary leader, Steve Biko, at the helm of a new movement, the Black Consciousness Movement. Biko's message undermined apartheid statecraft. Black is not a colour, said Biko, black is an experience. If you are oppressed, you are black. In the South African context, this was indeed a revolutionary message. The ANC had spoken of non-racialism as early as the Freedom Charter in 1955. But the ANC's non-racialism only touched the political elite. Whereas individual white and Indian and coloured members of the political elite joined the ANC as individuals, ordinary people continued to be trapped by a political perspective that still reflected the same old narrow racial and tribal boundaries. The point about Biko was that he forged a popular vision with the potential to cut through these boundaries.

Ten years later, in 1987, occurred another event reminiscent of Soweto. This was the Palestinian intifada. The first intifada had a Soweto-like potential. Like the children of Soweto, the youth of Palestine too shed the romance of armed struggle. They dared to face bullets with no more than stones. Faced with feuding liberation movements, each claiming to be a sole representative of the oppressed people, the youth of the intifada called for a wider unity. I am suggesting that we see Soweto and the first intifada as political antecedents of Tahrir Square.

The Egyptian revolution

Even though Tahrir Square has come more than three decades after Soweto, it evokes the memory of Soweto in a powerful way. This is so for a number of reasons. One, like Soweto 1976, Tahrir Square in 2011 too shed a generation's romance with violence. The generation of Nasser and after had embraced violence as key to fundamental political and social change. This tendency was secular at the outset. But the more Nasser turned to justifying suppressing the opposition in the language of secular nationalism, the more the opposition began to speak in a religious idiom. The most important political tendency calling for a surgical break with the past spoke the language of radical political Islam. Its main representative in Egypt was Sayyid Qutb. I would like briefly to look at Qutb as the standard bearer of radical political Islam.

I became interested in radical political Islam after 9/11, which is when I read Sayyid Qutb's most important political book, *Signposts*. It reminded me of the grammar of radical politics at the University of Dar es Salaam in the 1970s, when I was a young lecturer there. Sayyid Qutb says in the introduction to *Signposts* that he wrote the book for an Islamic vanguard; I thought I was reading a version of Lenin's *What is to be Done?* Sayyid Qutb's main argument in the text is that you must make a distinction between friends and enemies, because with friends you use persuasion and with enemies you use force. I thought I was reading Mao Zedong on the correct handling of contradictions amongst the people. Later, at Columbia, I realised that I could also have been reading the German philosopher Karl Schmidt. In all these cases, the point of politics is to identify, isolate and eliminate the enemy, which is also why violence as a method of struggle is central to politics.

I asked myself: how should I understand Sayyid Qutb? In the context of 9/11, the question had a triple significance. The first concerned the relationship between culture and politics. Official public intellectuals in post-9/11 US insisted that one's politics reflects one's culture. Second was a claim that civilisations develop in separate containers – one Muslim, the other Christian, a third Hindu and so on, each closeted from the other, so that democracy and Islam belong to separate containers. Democracy in the public sphere requires that you leave Islam at home. Only secular Muslims could be worthy citizens of a democratic republic.

Third, underlying their claim was the assumption that there are two kinds of culture – modern and pre-modern – in the contemporary world. Modern culture changes. It is capable of reflexivity and internal debate. Able to identify and remove its weaknesses and build on its strengths, it is historically progressive. In contrast, pre-modern culture is traditional and static. It functions not only as an inheritance at birth but as a sort of life sentence. The bearer of this culture suffers as if from a twitch, so that culture is like an unthinking response to external events. I was familiar with a version of this literature in my reading of African politics. But I sensed something new in the post-9/11 literature. Africans were said to be pre-modern, and so would need to be tutored. Arabs, unlike Africans, were said to be anti-modern, the real other of modernity. They would have to be contained rather than tutored, quarantined and watched carefully. The violence of 9/11 was said to be a prime example of this anti-modern culture.

I was critical of this perspective, this kind of understanding of the development of discourses through history. Is the history of thought best understood inside separate civilisational containers? Should I understand Sayyid Qutb's thought inside a linear tradition called political Islam? Or do I also need to understand it as part of a wider debate that cut across discursive traditions and defined his times? Was not Sayyid Qutb's embrace of political violence in line with a growing embrace of armed struggle in movements of national liberation in the 1950s and 1960s – most accepting the claim that armed struggle was not only the most effective form of struggle but also the only genuine mode of struggle?

I had little doubt that Sayyid Qutb was involved in multiple conversations. He was involved in multiple debates, not only with Islamic intellectuals, whether contemporary or belonging to previous generations, but also with contending intellectuals from other modes of political thought. And the main competition then was Marxism–Leninism, a militantly secular ideology which seemed to influence both his language and his understanding of organisation and struggle.

I would like to explore further what it means to shed the romance with revolutionary violence. It means to move away from a reified notion of friend and enemy, of good and evil, where the enemy was evil and had to be eliminated. The language of evil comes from a particular religious tradition, one that has been secularised over time: you cannot live with evil, you cannot convert it, you must eliminate it. The struggle against evil is necessarily a violent struggle. I first came across this tradition when I read Tomaz Mastenak's history of the Crusades, and when I read it, I understood the difference between modern notions of pre-modern and anti-modern culture: pre-modern primitive was open to conversion, but the anti-modern was not; it would have to be eliminated.

The second resemblance between Soweto and Tahrir Square was on the question of unity. Just as the anti-apartheid struggle in South Africa had uncritically reproduced the division between races and tribes as institutionalised in state practices, so it seemed to me that mainstream politics in Egypt had politicised religious difference. Tahrir Square, I thought, innovated a new politics. It shed the language of religion as central to politics but it did so without embracing a militant secularism that would outlaw religion in the public sphere. Instead, it seemed to call for a broad tolerance of cultural identities in the public sphere, one that would include both secular and religious tendencies. The new contract seemed based not on exclusion but inclusion – those who seek to participate in the public sphere must practise an inclusive politics with respect to others. The violence against the Coptic Christian minority in the weeks before Tahrir Square suggested that sectarian violence was often initiated by those in power, but without an effective antidote, it tended to rip through the social fabric.

Tahrir Square shared a third significance with Soweto. Soweto forced many people around the world to rethink their notions of Africa and the African. Before Soweto, the convention was to assume that violence was second nature with Africans, who were incapable of living together peacefully. Before Tahrir Square, and particularly after 9/11, official discourse and media representations, particularly in the West, were driven by the assumption that Arabs were genetically predisposed not only to violence, but also to discrimination against anyone different.

The question of the political

I think of the common political history of the Middle East as defined by Ottoman rule. The millet system that defined Ottoman governance was in many ways similar to British indirect rule, which it preceded. If the millet system politicised religious identity, British indirect rule politicised ethnicity as tribal identity. The millet system created a religiously sanctioned form of political authority inside the community, just as British indirect rule created an ethnically sanctioned form of political authority inside the community it politicised. If the millet system politicised religious identity, British indirect rule politicised ethnic or tribal identity. The African experience suggests that the key question faced by post-colonial societies is political: what are the boundaries of the political community? Who is a South African? Who is a Ugandan? Who an Egyptian? Is the Egyptian identity Islamic, or Arab, or territorial, so that we may say, as a paraphrase of the 1955 Freedom Charter of South Africa, that Egypt belongs to all those who live in it? What is at stake?

At stake is citizenship – who belongs and who does not, who has a right to rights and who does not. I would like to illustrate the argument with the example of Sudan. I want to focus on two official attempts to define the basis of nationhood and thus citizenship in Sudan, the first a claim that the nation is Muslim, and the second that the nation is Arab. Following these claims came two critiques of these nation-building and citizenship projects, one internal and the other external, but each claiming to formulate a critique from the vantage point of those disenfranchised by these projects.

I should like to begin with Ustad Mahmoud Mohamed Taha's critique of the Islamist political project. The interesting point is that Ustad Mahmoud did not dismiss the possibility of a democratic Islamic political project; in fact he posed it as an alternative to the official Islamist project identified with Hassan Turabi. Ustad Mahmoud's critique was an internal critique. Calling for an alternative project, he formed an alternative organisation to the Muslim Brothers, called Republican Brothers. I am not sure why he called it that for, in spite of its name, Republican Brothers included both brothers and sisters. Ustad Mahmoud's alternative was based on two claims.

Ustad Mahmoud distinguished between the Qu'ran as a holy text and every reading of it as human and earthly. This distinguished the sacred text from its reading, which was seen as a human interpretation. Taha's interpretation was provided in his book *The Second Message of Islam*. The argument is not unfamiliar to Egyptian ears or to students of *tafsir*. The Qu'ran contains two messages, each a response to a different context – Mecca and Medina. The prophet preached in Mecca and formulated legislation in Medina. The Meccan message focused on morality – and was thus transhistorical. In contrast, the message in Medina was bound to the specific needs of the society. This body of legislation, known as the Sharia, was more time-bound than any other part of the Qu'ran. The challenge, claimed Ustad Mahmoud, was to rethink the legislation in Medina in light of the moral vision of Mecca, that all are equal before God, man and woman, nation and nation, tribe and tribe. Taha identified two key challenges in an Islamic polity: the rights of non-Muslims, and the rights of women.

I want to locate the debate on Islam and politics in a wider context. That context is the wider debate of culture and politics in the post-colonial world. What is the relationship of culture, whether its cutting edge be religion or ethnicity, to politics?

It seems to me that two contrasting views have been formulated over the colonial and post-colonial view. The first is the modernist view that tradition – and religion or ethnicity as an integral part of it – must be banished to the private sphere to create the space for a democratic public sphere. We may call the second view nativist. It calls for a return to origins, to the period before colonialism, to the genuine and authentic history and culture of the colonised as the anchor from which to fashion a response to the modern world. It seems to me that just as the first view, militant modernism, is unable to make sense of pre-colonial history, militant nativism, the second view, is unable to come to grips with the colonial experience, especially the experience of the millet system and indirect rule which, from the domain of the culture of the colonised, fashioned resources for the colonial project. It thus created a single and authoritative authority said to be culturally legitimate with the right to define and enforce the official version of culture, whether as religious or ethnic.

Here then is the challenge for us: just as colonial powers found inside Islam and other religions and ethnic cultures the resources for an authoritarian colonial political project, we too must return to that same history of culture and find inside it resources necessary for a democratic political project. Neither a demonising of that history, as militant modernism is apt to do, nor its romanticisation, as is the case with militant nativism, will do. The response will have to be a more analytic and critical embrace of that history.

I want to move on to John Garang's critique of Arabism as a political project. Garang is the foundational thinker of the Southern Sudanese struggle of both Islamism and Arabism as political projects in Sudan. Garang wrote against a backdrop where the dominant critique of Arabism highlighted either the question of geography or that of race. The first claimed that, as a fact of geography, Sudan is an African, and not an Arab, country. The second found the identity of Sudan better identified by race. Sudan, it said, is an African country, a country for Africans, where Arabs can only be welcomed as guests. If you are an Arab, you are not an African and, vice versa, if you are an African, you cannot be an Arab. It went on to conclude that the problem with most northern Sudanese is that they fail to accept that they are Arabised Africans, really Africans and not Arabs. This failure to understand the true nature of their selves – their self-identity, this false consciousness – is really a sign of self-hatred. Those who claim to be Sudanese Arabs are really self-hating Africans.

Only against this prevailing mode of thought can we understand the truly subversive, and liberating, character of Garang's thought. Garang began by identifying how the failure to address the problem of political identity directly led to refuge in notions of culture and race. I will quote from his historic speech to the conference of Sudanese oppositional movements at Koka Dam:

I present to this historic conference that our major problem is that the Sudan has been looking for its soul, for its true identity. Failing to find it … some take refuge in Arabism, and failing to find this, they find refuge in Islam as a uniting factor. Others get frustrated as they fail to discover how they can become Arabs when their creator thought otherwise. And they take refuge in separation.

He then goes on to distinguish culture from politics: the cultural is not territorial, but the political is. The problem with cultural nationalism is that it confuses the two: culture and territory.

> We are a product of historical development. Arabic (though I am poor in it – I should learn it fast) must be the national language in a new Sudan, and therefore we must learn it. Arabic cannot be said to be the language of the Arabs. No, it is the language of the Sudan. English is the language of the Americans, but that country is America, not England. Spanish is the language of Argentina, Bolivia, Cuba, and they're those countries, not Spain … We are serious about the formation of a new Sudan, a new civilisation that will contribute to the Arab world and to the African world and to the human civilisation. Cross fertilisation of civilisation has happened historically and we are not going to separate whose civilisation this and this is, it may be inseparable.

Here was a clear alternative to the political project called 'The clash of civilisations'.

What can we learn from this?

New ideas create the basis of new unities and new methods of struggle. Modern power seeks to politicise cultural differences in society and, having done so, turns around and claims that these divisions are inevitable for they are natural. To be successful, a new politics must offer an antidote, being an alternative practice that unites those divided by prevailing modes of governance. Before and after Soweto, Steve Biko insisted that, more than just biology, blackness was a political experience. This point of view created the ideological basis of a new anti-racist unity. I do not know of a counterpart to Steve Biko in Tahrir Square – maybe there was not one Biko but many Bikos in Egypt. But I do believe that Tahrir Square has come to symbolise the basis for a new unity, one that consciously seeks to undermine the practice of religious sectarianism.

Consider one remarkable fact. No major event in contemporary history has been forecast, either by researchers or consultants, whether based in universities or in think tanks. This was true of Soweto in 1976. It was true of the fall of the Soviet Union in 1989 and it was true of the Egyptian revolution in 2011. What does it say about the state of our knowledge that we can foretell a natural catastrophe – an earthquake, even a tsunami – but not a political shift of similar dimensions? The rule would seem to be: the bigger the shift, the less likely is the chance of it being foretold. This is for one reason. Big shifts in social and political life require an act of the imagination – a break from routine, a departure from convention – why social science, which is focused on the study of routine, of institutional and repetitive behaviour, is unable to forecast big events.

It took nearly two decades for the Soweto uprising to deliver a democratic fruit in South Africa. The democratic revolution in Egypt has just begun – it seems to me that Tahrir Square has not led to a revolution, but to a reform. And that is not a bad thing. The significance of Egypt, unlike that of Libya next door, is three-fold. First is the moral force of non-violence, of the many rather than just the few. Second, non-violence of the multitude makes possible a new politics of inclusion. And finally, it makes possible a radically different sense of the worth of self. Unlike violence, non-violence does not just resist and exclude. It also embraces and includes, thereby opening up new possibilities of reform, possibilities that seemed unimaginable only yesterday.

Key to the period after Tahrir is the political challenge that lies in the days, months and years ahead. That challenge is to reform the Egyptian state, to shape through a political process the answer to the question: who is an Egyptian? Who has a right to citizenship, to equal treatment under the law?

http://pambazuka.org/en/category/features/73187

The chapter is the text of a keynote speech at the Annual Research Conference on 'Social justice: theory, research and practice', at the American University of Cairo, Cairo, 5 May 2011.

Notes

1. John Nagenda (2011) 'To walk or not to walk', *Saturday Vision*, 16 April: 8.
2. *Saturday Vision* (2011) 16 April: 2.
3. *New Vision* (2011) 15 April: 3.
4. *Daily Monitor* (2011) 14 April: 2.
5. *New Vision* (2011) 14 April: 14. When the opposition insisted on

continuing to Walk to Work, every Monday and Thursday, the official Communication Commission (UCC) sent verbal instructions directing radio and television stations to stop running live coverage of the events. *Daily Monitor* (2011) 15 April: 3.

6. (2011) 'MPs plot hunger strike', *The Observer*, 14–17 April: 3.

2b

How might things move forward in Libya?

Yash Tandon

26 May 2011

Before I deal with the question of how things might move forward in Libya it is important to remind ourselves that Libya is a neocolonial state, and Gaddafi has objectively been a neocolonial dictator for global finance capital, even though subjectively he was and is anti-imperialist. The imperial powers, 'the empire', might have accommodated him, and indeed did rehabilitate him after his turnaround in 1999, over a decade ago, but the so-called Arab spring upset the programme of the empire, and it had to quickly take a U-turn and ditch Gaddafi.

So what now? The empire, with the connivance of sections of the Libyan population, had hoped to get rid of Gaddafi quickly. The limited 'United Nations' no-fly zone operation has metamorphosed into a 'NATO' (North Atlantic Treaty Organisation) military operation, which is now in violation of its original mandate. The empire, in its hubris and delusion, had imagined for a while that the UN might extend its authority to allow 'boots on the ground'. But this failed. Russia and China, who have veto power in the Security Council, argue that the NATO countries have gone far beyond their mandate. Gaddafi, the empire's erstwhile dictator in Libya, whom they cuddled and kissed after his 1999 turn around, has proven to be more resilient than expected. He is back on his anti-imperialist nationalist trail. The imperial war machine has failed to dislodge him.

As I write, NATO has since March 2011 flown over 6,000 sorties into Libya, 2,400 involving bombing strikes. This is a staggering number by any measure. Faced with a protracted war, the empire is now using subterfuge, deceit and doublespeak to illegally extend its military operation in Libya. It kills individuals targeted from the air but nonetheless denies doing so and continues to play the myth that it is only 'protecting the civilians'. This is a blatant lie. It brazenly bombed Gaddafi's personal compound in Tripoli on 22 March, hoping to kill him. Like in the case of Osama bin Laden, the empire has an awesomely simplistic and gruesome military strategy – cut off the head of the snake and the rest of the body will slither or wither away. During the 22 March bombing, however, the empire succeeded only in killing some of Gaddafi's children, in what can without fear of contradiction be described as a criminal act. This ought to motivate Luis Moreno-Ocampo, the prosecutor of the International Criminal Court, to investigate and charge NATO leaders for criminal acts. Of course, we know this will not happen. In the international arena impunity has only one face, the imperial face.

So back to the question: what now for Libya?

Although it sounds like a cliché, it is true that the future of Libya lies in the hands of the people of Libya. Even the empire hypocritically endorses the principle – it has to, or else it will have no legitimacy, no excuse, for its action in Libya. But the fact of the matter is that the empire cannot allow self-determination to its neocolonies. That, by definition, would be the end of the neocolonies, and hence the death of the empire. The empire must divide and rule.

In Libya it has actively encouraged a section of the people to fight a proxy war for the empire. To put it starkly, Benghazi (a province) is fighting a war against Tripoli (the centre) on behalf of the empire. The French were active in Benghazi even before the UN Security Council resolution, and were the first imperial country to recognise the National Transitional Council (NTC) at Benghazi. But few countries have followed suit, and so, technically, the Gaddafi regime remains the only legally constituted actor in the conduct of Libya's diplomatic relations. Against him, the empire uses 'the people' as an ideological metaphor to describe the entire 'nation' that is supposed to have revolted against Gaddafi. This is another myth. The media story, for example, that 'the pro-democracy fighters in Misrata are engaged in trench warfare against

Gaddafi' is loaded. It is aimed at conveying the message that the 'pro-democracy' forces are holding out against the dictator. It is also aimed to prepare the psychological and political ground to justify the empire's open and clandestine military support to the people. The question to then ask is, 'Which people?' Who among the NTC at Benghazi represent the people? The 'people' is a simplified presentation of a complex reality, because there must be people even in Benghazi who must have realised by now that they are hostages of the empire, that they cannot run the show on their own without the empire. But these 'rebels among the rebels' (if this is what they may be called) are probably marginalised by the coalition of political forces around the NTC at Benghazi. It is a complex issue; not as simple as the empire and its media make it out to be.

The hard reality is that as long as the empire dictates the terms and means of engagement with Gaddafi, the people will never determine their future. It is as simple as that. When a nation has surrendered its sovereignty to the empire, it can recover it only when it liberates itself from the empire. When the streets revolted against the regime of Gaddafi, it was also revolting against the imperial order. But now the situation is out of the people's control. The empire has taken over the task of removing Gaddafi from power and, apparently, is helping the people to put in power a more democratic regime. This new regime, the empire will make sure, is bound so tightly to the apron strings of the empire that it continues to service the empire's economic and strategic interests in the region – including access to oil, stopping the inflow of boatloads of refugees to Europe and, above all, the protection of Israel, the empire's outpost in the region against threats posed by, for example, Hamas, Syria and Iran.

So, then, back to the question: what is the possible way forward for the nation of Libya? Here, it might be helpful for the nation (a better term than 'people') to take a leaf from the experience of the nation of Palestine to move forward in their struggle for national self-determination. Palestine is an occupied nation. The people of Palestine cannot negotiate with Israel as long as their lands are occupied. And yet, this is what the empire has been encouraging the Palestinians to do for the last 60 years. It is an impossible situation. How can Palestine negotiate as an equal when it is occupied? The empire has come in to 'mediate' but it is not a neutral mediator. It is not an honest broker. Countries like Norway that have brokered negotiations between Palestine and Israel act as surrogates of the empire, in fact, as an integral part of the imperial system. The so-called Oslo Accord mediated by Norway, for example, was a partisan process on behalf of collective imperialism.

As Ziyad Clot, one-time adviser to the PLO (Palestine Liberation Organisation), says:

> The 'peace negotiations' were a deceptive farce whereby biased terms were unilaterally imposed by Israel and systematically endorsed by the US and EU. Far from enabling a negotiated and fair end to the conflict, the pursuit of the Oslo process deepened Israeli segregationist policies and justified the tightening of the security control imposed on the Palestinian population, as well as its geographical fragmentation. Far from preserving the land on which to build a state, it has tolerated the intensification of the colonisation of the Palestinian territory. Far from maintaining a national cohesion, the process I participated in, albeit briefly, was instrumental in creating and aggravating divisions among Palestinians. In its most recent developments, it became a cruel enterprise from which the Palestinians of Gaza have suffered the most. Last but not least, these negotiations excluded for the most part the great majority of the Palestinian people: the seven million Palestinian refugees. My experience over those 11 months in Ramallah confirmed that the PLO, given its structure, was not in a position to represent all Palestinian rights and interests. (Clot 2011)

Of course, nothing remains the same forever. Even after 60 years of sustained efforts by the empire to divide the nation of Palestine, to compel them to negotiate peace terms with Israel with aid funds and graft, and to force it accept its apartheid existence, the people of Palestine are finally united (at least for now, for the empire and Israel will continue their efforts to divide them). Hamas and Al Fatah have buried their hatchets and, as I write, are presenting a common front to Israel and the empire – what the Israeli Prime Minister Netanyahu disingenuously described as 'a victory for terrorism' and a 'mortal blow to peace'.

A further word of advice from Ziyad Clot on Palestine applies to Libya too:

Finally, I feel reassured that the people of Palestine over-whelmingly realise that the reconciliation between all their constituents must be the first step towards national liberation. The Palestinians from the West Bank and the Gaza Strip, the Palestinians in Israel and the Palestinians living in exile have a common future. The path to Palestinian self-determination will require the participation of all in a renewed political platform. (Clot 2011)

The people of Libya will eventually also realise that the contradiction between Tripoli and Benghazi is a secondary contradiction between the peoples, fuelled by the empire in the name of humanitarian intervention, which is selectively applied in the case of Libya, but not, for instance, in the case of Bahrain or Yemen. They will realise that their principal and immediate contradiction is with the empire. In the case of Palestine, the new regime in Egypt played a catalytic role in bringing Hamas and Fatah together. Perhaps they can play a similar role in Libya. Egypt can also play a role in mobilising the Arab League against NATO's illegal bombing of Libya. Following the bombing of Tripoli, Secretary General Amr Moussa said that the league's approval of a no-fly zone on 12 March was based on a desire to prevent Gaddafi's air force from attacking civilians and not designed to endorse the intense bombing and missile attacks — including on Tripoli and on Libyan ground forces.

The people of Libya must apply their own historical wisdom in resolving differences among themselves. Patience is especially valued in the desert. It takes a long time to reach your destination on camels, and you must prepare your journey properly and with care. Also, the desert is the arena for wars and fierce battles. But an oasis is different. An oasis is not only a break with the desert but also a neutral place of sanctity and peace, inhabited mostly by women and children. Visitors never enter the life of the oasis; they leave the people in the oasis alone. It is taboo for visitors to interfere with the hospitality of the inhabitants of the oasis. This is not so with the Western empire. This is an empire historically born out of pillage and plunder. It is an empire of globalisation of interference; in this empire there is no room for an oasis of decency. The empire believes, wrongly, that it can bomb Afghanistan and Libya to force submission. The Western empire is an uncivilised culture. It displays its crass culture when it rejoices at the killing of Gaddafi's children in their homes. The empire does not understand that though you can hold a grain of sand in the palm of hand and puff it away, it has taken millions of years to make the sand. Eastern civilisation is still young, but it has been there a long time, longer than the Western civilisation; you cannot just puff it away like a grain of sand. The empire is oblivious to the finer aspects of civilisation; it does not realise that though it may win in the short run, it might lose in the long run.

And so back to Libya again. The Libyans must get back to their 'oasis culture', find a place where they can leave their guns and camels outside the tents and sort out their differences and unite against the empire – like in Palestine.

The next question is whether there is a role for the larger international community in this sordid war. By the international community I do not mean the empire's coalition of the willing but the community outside the war coalition. How can the leaders of the third world help, for example? After the initial UN Security Council resolution, these countries have unfortunately allowed the United Nations to be used by the empire, with the blatant complicity of the current Secretary General Ban Ki-moon. They must take control of the political and diplomatic processes of the UN.

How might they do so? First, they must bring the Libya issue back to the council for a review of the original mandate. Failing that, they could bring the matter before the General Assembly under the 'Uniting for Peace' resolution, which the Americans first used in 1950 to get the UN's endorsement for action in Korea. This resolution states that in cases where the UN Security Council fails to act because of disagreement between its five permanent members, the matter will be addressed by the General Assembly, using the mechanism of the emergency special session. Second, the leaders of the third world must also review Security Council resolution 1674 of 28 April 2006. This resolution reaffirms paragraphs 138 and 139 of the 2005 World Summit Outcome Document containing, among other things, the concept of the 'responsibility to protect', or R2P, which has been seriously abused by the empire in the case of Libya.

The concepts of the responsibility to protect and of humanitarian intervention are matters that I take up in Chapter 29 of this book. The imperial dictators are inflicting carnage on Libya with complete impunity. What we are witnessing in Libya is not 'audacity of hope' but audacity of madness. This carnage and madness must stop.

http://pambazuka.org/en/category/features/73566

Copyright © 2011 Yash Tandon

Reference

Clot, Ziyad (2011) 'Why I blew the whistle about Palestine', *Guardian*, 14 May

27

The Tunisian revolution did not come out of nowhere

Sadri Khiari speaks to Béatrice Hibou

26 May 2011

The Tunisian revolution has been the detonator of the wave of protests and uprisings which have spread across North Africa and the Middle East since January 2011. Sparked by the self-immolation of Mohammed Bouazizi on 17 December 2010, the Tunisian revolution quickly spread from the towns in the central mining and agricultural regions of the country to the coastal cities, including the capital Tunis. Mass demonstrations, riots and strikes compelled President Ben Ali to flee the country on 14 January. The ultimate outcome of the still fluid revolutionary process remains undetermined. So far popular mobilisation and the forces activated by them – a series of parties, associations, unions, and intellectuals now organised in a loose coordinating committee (Le comité de salut public la tunisienne) have succeeded in forcing the retreat and partial dissolution of the networks of repression of the Ben Ali regime, changing the composition of the interim government a number of times and implementing their demand for a constituent assembly, from which Ben Ali's old ruling party, Le Rassemblement constitutionnel démocratique (RCD) will be excluded for ten years. Governed by a new electoral law passed on 11 April, elections for this assembly are scheduled for 24 July.

Béatrice Hibou: What is your interpretation of the Tunisian events?
Sadri Khiari: One can explain a popular revolution as little as one can anticipate its beginning. It appears as a break in the normal course of things, an abrupt acceleration of political temporality, a

historical rupture that expresses itself by the surging crowds that insert themselves into the centres of power in order to brutally push aside those who are supposed to lead and represent them. The popular revolution can thus be identified in the exceptional moment when politics dispenses with its mediations; direct democracy becomes reality, raw, tumultuous and alive. On the occasion of recent developments in Tunisia, numerous commentators remembered Lenin's famous formula: 'a revolutionary period is characterised by the inability of those at the top to rule and govern in the old way and the stubborn refusal of those below to be governed in the old way.' From this point of view, the revolution is the instant when the conflict between those 'at the top' and those 'below' reaches a boiling point.

The Tunisian revolution is no exception in this regard. Mohammed Bouazizi's tragic suicide represented this breaking point. But the strategist of Russia's October Revolution spoke of a 'revolutionary period,' not of revolution. He recalled the period of uncertainty when the conflict rages on but is not yet settled, when the relations of force are unstable and open up a horizon of multiple possibilities without guarantees. In Tunisia, the powerful popular mobilisation that forced Ben Ali to take to his heels is a revolution, a moment in a revolutionary period which is obviously not yet over. In 'the land of Jasmin', the pot was about to boil over.

BH: Why did we not see that the revolution was imminent?
SK: If there was one country in the Arab world that appeared sheltered from revolutionary influence, it was Tunisia. Saturated with publicity about the peaceful tranquillity of a Tunisia destined to produce sand and parasols, and a few golden-skinned waiters as well, European public opinion could not possibly imagine this country as the site of dramatic political conflicts. Tunisia seemed to be a country without a history. This tourist imagery did not necessarily dominate all the political, intellectual and media spheres, in which there was general confidence in the 'stability' of Tunisia, but the blindness of these spheres undoubtedly grew out of a measure of self-delusion. One only sees what one wants to see and what one wants to show to others. Determined to support the regime of President Ben Ali, the big powers (US, France, the EU) and the international financial institutions never stopped

promoting a discourse of Tunisian 'stability': proper levels of growth and satisfactory macroeconomic equilibrium; slow but sure integration into the world market; the formation of a middle class destined to play the role of social shock absorber; a reasonable and peace-loving foreign policy; and, finally, a democratic transition, albeit one slowed by a lack of transparency in governance and hampered by the imperative of maintaining security against the 'threat of Islam'. In other words, the only potential of political destabilisation was detected where it did not exist: in Islamic fundamentalism.

This type of discourse was carried widely by the big international media outlets and a good number of commentators and social scientists. It was not only a result of self-interested complacency about the Tunisian regime. It was also helped along by elitist, bureaucratic and state-centred ways of understanding society. There was little interest in observing the real development of public opinion among the disadvantaged strata of the Tunisian population; their (occasionally spectacular) forms of resistance garnered no, or very little, attention. All that analysts took into account were the attempts of organised oppositional forces to act in the rational sphere of politics, even as they were either not officially recognised or severely repressed.

But no matter how active they were, political organisations and resistance groups represented an extremely small fringe of the population. In part because of repression, their marginality was frequently but wrongly interpreted as indicating the absence of effective opposition against Ben Ali's regime. I could also point to the suspect ideological representation of Tunisians as docile and peaceful, with a penchant for reform and negotiation. This form of culturalism is congruent with the tourist imagery that confuses the professional servility of the elevator attendant with an almost natural tendency to prefer reconciliation to conflict. I would like to finish by pointing to the tendency of numerous researchers to focus only on structures, institutions and other mechanisms of power without taking into account the forms of resistance they provoke. Politics, understood as relations of force, is thus emptied of its content and Tunisian history appears condemned to eternal inertia.

BH: Did this appearance of stability only exist in the eyes of foreigners? Why did the domestic opposition not see the revolts coming?

SK: Indeed, even in Tunisia, the explosive political situation was hardly recognised by observers, even those engaged in one resistance movement or another. Or, to be more precise, if a large-scale spontaneous revolt similar to the bread riot of 1984 was considered possible, this revolt was not expected to take on an explicitly political dimension, let alone lead to the downfall of the president of the republic. Outside a few far left groups like the Communist Workers' Party of Tunisia (Parti communiste des ouvriers tunisiens – PCOT), directed by Hamma Hammami, or a personality like the former leader of the Tunisian human rights league, Moncef Marzouki, the prospect of large popular mobilisation did not figure prominently in the strategic vision of oppositional forces. In this light, it is significant that in 2008, during the revolt in the mining basin of the Gafsa region – a decisive moment I will come back to later – most opposition forces stayed quiet for a number of weeks before demonstrating timid support. This support was meant to underline the severity of the social situation and the urgent need to pass reforms rather than to widen the realm of popular contestation.

One could develop a sociological analysis of the parties and associations in question and note the degree to which their cadres belonged to relatively privileged sectors of Tunisian society, but such an approach, while not without pertinence, would ignore other equally important factors such as the long history of political militancy of many of these cadres. For example, a number of Tunisian opposition leaders began their long trajectory in political groups whose revolutionary ambitions and attempts to appeal to the people had been systematically dashed. Also, the models of radical rupture to which they subscribed in the past collapsed or turned out to be ineffective when the myth of a soft democratic transition based on negotiations between certain factions of power and 'reasonable' currents of the opposition started to spread.

I also need to underline that the Tunisian opposition, isolated and persecuted, was forced to seek support outside the country in the hope of exercising pressure on the regime. One of the perverse effects of this political choice was that lobbying for human rights was substituted for attempts to change the relations of force in Tunisia. These are only a few dimensions of the problem but, in any event, it is clear that just as the signs of a political crisis were difficult to miss even for those without a sociological microscope, spontaneous or organised forms of mobilising the disadvantaged strata of the population were not part of the political equation for most Tunisian opposition forces.

BH: Despite these signs of mobilisation, the regime appeared solidly in place...

SK: It is true that this may seem paradoxical. Allow me to use this opportunity to remind you of the fragile foundations that allowed Ben Ali to stay in power during a considerable 23 years. The success of the *coup d'état* on 7 November 1987 can be explained above all by the profound decomposition of the top layers of power within Habib Bourguiba's state. This was a crisis of succession, prolonged and intensified by another crisis: the growing inadequacy of the socio-political pact put in place after independence in 1956 and the emergence of new social realities. Widely contested, the hegemony of the Destour movement was transformed into simple authority, resting much more on coercion and clientelistic mechanisms than on consent, to use a Gramscian concept. Examples of this transformation were the alignment with power of the Union générale tunisienne du travail (UGTT) in 1985 and the ferocious repression of the Ennahda party (political Islam) in the months preceding Ben Ali's coup. Ben Ali moved into the Palais de Carthage, the presidential residence, while those at the top appeared incapable of governing as before and those at the bottom, who had been in ascendancy since the 1970s, suffered a grave defeat with the repression of their two principal forms of expression, the UGTT and Ennahda.

Thin as a sheet of paper, Ben Ali's legitimacy rested for a few months on the illusion that he was going to annul Bourguiba's last years and reform the regime by incorporating the different social and political forces. An apparent trade union reconciliation, a democratic opening administered in homeopathic doses and tolerance of the activities of the Ennahda movement allowed him to neutralise opposition. The latter became more virulent toward the end of 1989, and then the Gulf War started. Ben Ali refused to participate in the anti-Iraqi military coalition and thus won momentary popularity; he managed to garner the support of certain elements of the democratic opposition while the leadership of Ennahda was divided between pro- and anti-Saddam factions. The police apparatus was then set in motion, benefitting from the crisis of Ennahda. Already begun before the Gulf War, the dismantling of the party accelerated and took a rare form of violence, particularly between 1991 and 1994. The slogan 'no freedom for the enemies of freedom' allowed Ben Ali to benefit from a decade of passive complicity on the part of the overwhelming majority of the Tunisian democratic movement and, until his downfall, the major Western powers. In lockstep with the repression of Ennahda, the most combative trade union tendencies as well as all forms of democratic protest were brutally silenced.

This brief reminder of the first years of the Ben Ali regime is important, it seems to me, in order to understand some of the underlying reasons why Ben Ali was able to install authoritarian rule despite his notable incapacity to build a new moral legitimacy and a renewed social compromise. I will refrain from describing the mechanisms of repression, restriction, and control put in place in the 1990s to compensate for the lack of legitimacy of the regime. I must, however, add that the mafia-like practices at the highest levels of power – arbitrary police and administrative rule, generalised clientelism and corruption – contributed to a sense, widely shared among all social strata, that power was an incarnation of authority without moral standing. Ben Ali's regime was thus fundamentally different from Bourguiba's. In fact, the morality of Bourguiba as 'supreme combatant' (*combattant suprème*) was never questioned, not even when Bourguiba's rule was most contested. Everyone knew about the privileges the top layers of the bureaucracy claimed for themselves but, unlike with Ben Ali, the system itself was never identified as one that functioned essentially to allow a morally corrupt family network to enrich itself illegally and claim absolute power.

BH: But how and when did this perception of immorality spread?
SK: In this case, too, the important moment was in the early 2000s, when the illegal diversion of goods, a corruption racket involving major enterprises, and suspicious accumulation of wealth became

more widely known in the guise of satirical comments denouncing the nepotism of the 'families' around Ben Ali. This rumour, which was impossible to verify then, spread with ease because it was common knowledge that the various representatives of the RCD,[1] the bureaucracy or the police had few scruples when it came to profiting from their positions of power. Quite often, the intricate links between the networks of power, money and delinquency (such as smuggling rings in the border regions) were there for everyone to see.

To illustrate, I think back to the revolt in the cities of the Gafsa region in 2008. This popular movement, which lasted six months, began in the small town of Redeyef and spread to the principal mining centres in the region before hitting a wall of repression. Importantly, for my purposes, this revolt took off when a local job recruitment process was circumvented by company directors, administrative branches of the state and local representatives of the trade union. Of course, unemployment was a key background condition of the revolt, but what sparked and amplified anger to such an extent were the practices of the regime, which were perceived to be contrary to social morality.

In the same vein, I have to mention also, and perhaps above all, the growing role of Leila Ben Ali, a power- and money-hungry woman considered of low moral standards. Even more than the president himself, this woman symbolised the moral corruption of the system. Tunisians were critical of the regime of Ben Ali for his immorality more than his authoritarianism. To put it differently, the regime not only lacked moral authority, it was perceived to be an authority without morals. An authority without moral standing is a form of power that imposes itself on society; it is seen as external to it, so to speak, and whoever possesses it is considered a usurper, driven by his personal interests, which he is willing to satisfy by any means possible. One does not criticise him for inadequate or unjust policies but for threatening society's moral foundation. One does not dismiss him, one brings him to justice. The perception of Ben Ali's power as an authority without morals is undoubtedly key to grasping some of the particularities of the Tunisian revolution, and the widespread consensus that supported it.

BH: Contrary to what many observers presupposed, 'the social question' was not the primary factor in the movement for you.

SK: This is indeed an important point. In my opinion, a strictly socio-economic analysis of the Tunisian revolution is incapable of discerning its deep dynamic. It is true that the movement began in the most deprived regions of the country and social demands were formulated from the beginning (often by groups of politicised militants and trade unions). These demands, important as they were, were not at the heart of the process which led to the departure of the president. The same is true for the question of democracy. Any Tunisian dissident with a degree of experience can testify to the difficulty of translating the concerns of disadvantaged populations into the normative language of democracy, that of parties and civil rights groups. When this language is taken up at a mass scale, one needs to ask oneself what kind of expectations it corresponds to. Neither the socio-economic nor the democratic explanation (nor a combination of the two) suffices to explain the degree to which this sentiment against Ben Ali is shared across social cleavages. To understand this consensus, one needs to make use of a notion that is difficult to define and is often neglected, yet is at the heart of numerous currents of revolt: dignity.

I noted earlier that Ben Ali, his wife and those close to them were perceived to embody the moral corruption of the regime. I now need to add that each Tunisian was forced to be complicit with corruption to a certain degree. This phenomenon led to a form of collective and individual self-degradation. The system of repression and surveillance developed by Ben Ali thus led to a sentiment of indignity as much as, if not more than, fear. Multiple compromises, different ways of paying allegiance to power, even active participation in its networks (all of which were often necessary to find a job, get promoted, open a business, get administrative matters resolved, or simply avoid everyday problems) produced frustrations, humiliations and feelings of disrespect for oneself and others in all social classes.

In Tunisia, power substituted institutionalised contempt for intersubjective and institutional recognition, which are necessary for all forms of ethical hegemony. The degrading of the collective self-image of Tunisians compounded the sense of degradation of each individual. The hero of the revolution, the young

Mohammed Bouazizi who set himself on fire, may have provoked such a widespread sense of identification not because he lived in misery but because he was deliberately humiliated by a municipal bureaucrat who slapped him in the face after confiscating his merchandise. The revolt that followed in the wake of his act of desperation can in this sense be interpreted as carrying forward a demand for social recognition that everyone knew could not be satisfied by the regime and, in fact, required the ousting of Ben Ali as the architect of generalised indignity. Although various slogans chanted during the protests revealed concerns with democracy and economic matters, the Tunisian revolution expressed above all a will to recover a sense of individual and collective self-respect.

BH: You recently wrote *Tunisie. Coercition, consentement, résistance. Le délitement de la cité* (2003, Paris, Karthala). Was the revolution made possible by a disruption in the equilibrium that existed between these three components (coercion, consent and resistance)?

SK: Contrary to superficial representations, Tunisia was not an inert and rather contented society. Only in non-revolutionary periods does there exist a more or less forceful integration of people into mechanisms of domination. But one has to admit that this integration, real as it often is, does not exclude insubordination. Docility, even collaboration, is itself mixed with a lack of discipline, transgression, or direct or masked forms of resistance, which remain hidden most of the time because they are individual or do not take the classic forms of protest or political action. If numerous Tunisians asked themselves every day about how they could profit from the system, many, often the same ones, also asked themselves how to slip through the net and escape requests for collaboration. These were the people who withstood the pressures to join the RCD and its satellite organisations, who 'forgot' to donate to the one of compulsory solidarity funds (Fonds de solidarité nationale, police raffles), who refused to go through the mandatory intermediaries for the purposes of career advancement, or those who struggled to circumvent censorship on the web, those who stayed at home during RCD ceremonies or on election day, those in the office, at home or with friends who reported the latest jokes or rumours about the real or supposed depravities of the ruling families, those who built networks of solidarity among family, in neighbourhoods and regions, the youth who risked clandestine emigration or the others who confronted the police in the stadia. Evasion, subterfuge, individual rebellion, and all the molecular forms of sedition that go along with authoritarian regimes continuously increased during the last years of the Ben Ali regime. To grasp this reality of everyday resistance, it was enough, methodologically speaking, to exhibit more empathy for 'those below' and show less fascination with power and its operations.

By the way, like individual rebellion, collective forms of resistance rarely made it onto the observers' radar. Even though it did not grow in a linear fashion and faced much repression, more or less organised collective resistance has developed for at least ten years. Between 1999 and 2001, after a decade of repression and disarray, the democracy movement in Tunisia reinvigorated itself. The first sign of this was the founding of the Conseil national des libertés en Tunisie in December 1998, which was followed very quickly by the constitution of other independent organisations, the revival of the Tunisian Human Rights League, journalist Taoufik Ben Brik's hunger strike (which was widely reported in France), lawyer activism (the importance of which the mobilisations of the last few weeks have demonstrated), stirrings within the judiciary, the increased resolve of two of the legal opposition parties (PDP[2] and Ettajdid[3]) as new parties like the CPR[4] or the FDTL[5] emerged and PCOT and Ennahda tried to restructure themselves.

These initiatives were covered in Tunisia by the Arab media such as Al Jazeera and stimulated other forms of resistance. They remained largely confined to the traditional sphere of protest and failed to attract new generations of activists. Although the powerlessness of the opposition and the weakness of their influence over the population were often subject to ironic comments, the small margin of manoeuvre these forms of opposition have managed to eke out since 1999, despite persecution and repression, have undoubtedly helped to spread critical information to a growing public opinion. They also facilitated efforts to build spaces and networks of resistance, which, despite their intermittent and muddled character, were not without efficacy (as their participation in various mobilisations, including those at the beginning of the revolution, demonstrated).

It is also important to underline how in the last few years, political dissidence via internet networks emerged and rapidly expanded together with the generalisation of cell-phone usage. In spite of the sophistication of control and censorship, these new tools of communication also made it easier to spread information, create networks and virtual organisational forms which also became vectors of democratic contestation, particularly among youth. Also important to mention is the formation of a radical Islamic scene that broke with the Ennahda party and rejected the regime's policies in its own way.

BH: You speak about a social movement but you only mention political parties!

SK: Be patient, I am getting there. To this awakening of the democracy movement, one has to add the reconstitution of what one can call, for the lack of a better term, social movements, which are difficult to grasp given the scarcity and inaccessibility of information. It seems to me that social forms of resistance re-emerged in two phases. Revolts by students and the unemployed in various cities in the early 2000s, organised strikes in the public sector and private sector enterprises, wildcat strikes and other forms of protest (particularly in the textile and tourist sectors) were expressions of change when compared to the preceding decade. This renewal has manifested itself in particularly striking ways since 2008 in the long struggle of inhabitants in the mining region of Gafsa, which began to spread before being brutally repressed. This was undoubtedly the major turning point. Since then, Tunisia has witnessed other, more limited, protest movements in Skhira, Feriana, Jebeniana and, in the summer of 2010, in Ben Guerdane, as in many small towns in the most disadvantaged regions in the country. In the end, there was Sidi Bouzid and we all know the rest. Despite their sporadic character, the weak media coverage, repression, defeat and the lame compromises that resulted from them, and despite the apparent lack of links between them, the social movements that Tunisia has witnessed in the last decade have helped foment an atmosphere laden with protest, an accumulation of experiences and the construction of informal activist networks of which the Tunisian revolution is a product.

This schematic representation of social mobilisation would be even more incomplete if I did not mention the struggles within the UGTT against the bureaucratic grip of its secretary general, Abdessalam Jrad, and against the trade union leadership's subservience to power. These struggles allowed the most militant labour activists to gain influence in certain sectors (postal service, education and others) and in the local and regional branches of the labour movement. This made it possible for the UGTT to play a more important role in the revolution against the stated positions of its secretary general, particularly in the last week of mobilisation. As we know, the board (*Commission administrative*) of the UGTT ended up supporting the popular demands and the general strikes that proved decisive in setting in motion the revolutionary process, notably in Tunis and Sfax.

BH: Is it already possible to detect the lines of force in future developments?

SK: Although the departure of Ben Ali was probably organised by a few leaders of the RCD and their foreign 'advisers', it was undoubtedly only considered under the pressure of popular mobilisation. The mobilisation was also strong enough to force the departure of the RCD ministers in the first transition government after the president's escape and, more recently, the resignation of the prime minister and other members of government. While the fall of Hosni Mubarak and the revolutionary mobilisations in Libya have shown that the impact of the Tunisian revolution goes much beyond the Tunisian border, it is too early to evaluate the magnitude of internal political upheaval.

It seems clear to me, however, that a satisfactory understanding of current developments is not possible without questioning the modes of analysis that have shaped perspectives on Tunisia. More sustained attention needs to be given to politics from below, the non-institutionalised forms of resistance, and, more generally, the more or less subterranean dynamics at work within the different layers of the population. Finally, and without wanting to unduly isolate and rank each of the multiple factors that have determined the popular explosion in Tunisia (such as the growing economic difficulties and the weight of authoritarianism), it appears important that analyses of political processes and protest movements should pay more careful attention to that intangible need for recognition and dignity.

http://pambazuka.org/en/category/features/73574

This interview was conducted by Béatrice Hibou. It was first published in Politique africaine, no. 121, March 2011. It was translated by Stefan Kipfer.

Notes

1. Bourguiba's renamed Parti socialiste destourien, which was taken over by the Ben Ali regime.
2. Parti démocratique progressiste led by Ahmed Najib Chebbi, a lawyer and now a member of government.
3. The new name of the Tunisian Communist Party after it opened its ranks to democratic and secular oppositional currents.
4. Congrès pour la république, a non-recognised party founded in 2001 by Moncef Marzouki, the former president of the Tunisian Human Rights League (Ligue tunisienne des droits de l'homme).
5. Forum démocratique pour le travail et les libertés, a legal party founded in 1994 by Mustapha Ben Jafaar, a former leader of the Mouvement des democrates socialistes, which split off from Bourguiba's party. The FDTL is a member of the Socialist International.

28

Imperial neurosis and the dangers of 'humanitarian' interventionism

Yash Tandon

2 June 2011

In Chapters 24 and 26 of this book, I made a distinction between colony and neocolony, going beyond Nkrumah's initial analysis of neocolonialism to show that in our times, the contradictions between the neocolonies and the empire are increasing in intensity. I argued that the Arab spring is, in essence, not just a challenge to the Arab dictators, but it is, above all, a challenge to the empire itself.

When the streets revolted against the neocolonial regimes of North Africa and the Arab world, they were revolting, in effect, against the imperial order that is suffocating their democratic aspirations. In other words, in a larger and indeed more fundamental sense, the Arab spring is part of a widening and deepening imperial crisis, which includes other aspects of its global economic crisis and the crisis of its legitimacy and moral authority.

Imperial neurosis

A nightmare scenario for the empire in the Arab region involves three basic ingredients. One is the rise of Iran and what the empire 'perceives' as the Islamic 'fundamentalist' threat (the inverted commas are explained below). The second is a change in the balance of power in the region that in the long run is most certainly going against the security and well-being of Israel, unless the empire and Israel make fundamental changes in their dealings with the Palestinians. And the third is the deepening economic crisis within the capitalist system.

The empire's understanding and responses to the above triple challenges is neurotic. Neurosis is a condition of mind that is based on an irrational phobia and what is recognised in the medical world as an obsessive-compulsive disorder (OCD). This applies to nations as well as to individuals. With nations, the phobia is real; it has real-time effects, especially if it affects powerful countries, as is the case with the present-day empire.

The triple causes of imperial OCD go back to 1979. That is the year when the Iranian revolution ushered in the era of the ayatollahs. That was also the year of the beginning of deep recession in the global capitalist system.

Let us, first, take the economic crisis and the empire's neurotic response to it. The crisis forced the empire to review its global economic strategy. Its 'resolution' around 1985–86 was the neoliberal agenda ushered in under the leadership of Thatcher and Reagan, and then globalised. The question is: what is it about this response that classifies it as neurotic? What made the neoliberal agenda a neurotic response to the economic challenge? The short answer is that the response is neurotic because it is based on a fierce defence of the capitalist system, which has lost its historic justification.

I shall leave a detailed analysis of this complex evolution of the capitalist system for another occasion. Suffice it to say that this particular neurosis has several consequences, two of which are crucial to our analysis here. One is the tightening of control over the political economies of the neocolonies in the third world. And the second is the emerging disintegration of the Euro-American system. On the second we shall not dwell here, except to say that the 2007–08 crisis was inherent within the very dynamics of the capitalist system. In other words, it was inevitable; given the system's internal dynamics, the crisis was unavoidable. It is wrongly identified as a 'financial' crisis, because in fact it is much deeper. The crisis that the Eurozone faces today, for example, is one of its latest manifestations. It requires no genius to understand that what is taking place in Europe is an increasing control of the German, French and British finance capital over the peripheral nations of Europe such as Greece, Ireland, Portugal and Spain, leading, inevitably, to their own 'Arab springs', i.e. popular revolts against the empire of finance capital.

As for the first neurotic response – namely, the tightening of control over the political economies of the neocolonies in the third world – it is more central to our concerns here. For some 30 years, from the 1980s to 2010, the empire of finance capital imposed on these countries an economic structural readjustment. This is a vast subject, but its essence consisted of a harsh regime of budgetary controls; trade liberalisation; centralisation of corporate control over the production, financing, marketing, technology and management of the natural resources of the neocolonies; and monopolisation of scientific knowledge in the form of intellectual property rights vested in the control of transnational corporations. These measures were forced on the recipients of donor funds through debt bondage; the so-called development aid; and the penetration by foreign direct investments through forced capital-flow liberalisation.

But why was this neurotic? What qualifies this action of the empire as neurotic? It was (and is) neurotic because it was an outcome of an OCD in the system, a knee-jerk 'one-solution-fits-all' kind of remedy imposed on all countries that had become victim to financial and economic distress. It was an illusory attempt to bolster a system of global production and distribution that, as earlier mentioned, had become historically irrational. Second, it was principally aimed at resolving empire's own internal crisis of decreasing rates of profitability, increasing threats to accessing global natural resources and, resulting from these, deepening social and class divisions within the imperial countries. It was neurotic, thirdly, because in time, it was to produce, inevitably, a strong counter-reaction from millions of people who were thrown into the pitfalls of poverty, unemployment, crime and mass emigration. The Arab spring was inevitable, and has its roots directly linked to this neurotic response of the empire to try and resolve its deepening internal contradictions.

Equally neurotic is the empire's knee-jerk reaction to the challenge of Islamic 'fundamentalism', worsened by 9/11. This, too, is a vast subject. It has spawned a vast amount of literature, films, talk shows, conferences and popular discussions. The fact is that in terms of realpolitik only Islam is considered as fundamentalist and not, for instance, the extreme expressions of Christianity. This too is a neurotic and irrational response to a phobia that is deeply ingrained in the empire's history and culture. This has led to the many wars against terror in which the empire is currently engaged, for example, in Iraq, Afghanistan, Pakistan, Somalia, Yemen and Indonesia.

One of the major ideological tools of imperial wars is the 'humanitarian' shroud, to which I now turn.

The dangers of humanitarian interventionism

It might sound cynical to say that if there was no good reason to justify imperial wars in our times, the empire would have invented the humanitarian excuse. The truth is that whilst the word humanitarian has a good quality, ethical sound about it, the empire has been utterly cynical in abusing it to legitimise its wars and interventions in the sovereign affairs of other nations. It defies reason to explain its humanitarian intervention, for instance in Yugoslavia, Somalia and Libya and not, for example, in Yemen or Bahrain. Of course, imperial ideologists and legal experts might provide rationales for these aberrations. Nonetheless, the downright cynicism with which the empire uses the humanitarian excuse to legitimise its wars and interventions cannot be explained away by ideological or legalistic obfuscations.

Equally cynical is the empire's abuse of the United Nations, especially the Security Council, where it has disproportionate power and influence, in this instance, Security Council resolution 1674 of 28 April 2006. This resolution reaffirms paragraphs 138 and 139 of the 2005 World Summit Outcome Document containing, among other things, the controversial concept of the 'responsibility to protect', or R2P. However, at the September 2009 session of the General Assembly the Security Council resolution and the idea of R2P were strongly challenged by the president of the General Assembly, the member countries of the Non-Aligned Movement (NAM), and also by Germany and Switzerland. What, then, is this beast or virus that has crept into the UN system?

Briefly, as UN Secretary General Ban Ki-moon had recommended, it is based on a three-pillar approach: 1) the protection responsibilities of the state; 2) international assistance and capacity building; and 3) 'the responsibility of member states to respond collectively in a timely and decisive manner when a state is manifestly failing to provide such protection'. The third pillar is the most controversial, because it includes coercive action under chapter VII of the charter.

But the real question is: how did this virus penetrate the UN system? It is a long story, but the gist of it as follows.

The origins of this doctrine go back to President Bill Clinton's time (1993–2001) when his advisers, especially Secretary of State Madeleine Albright, were looking for a proper ideological cover for what looked like an increasing need for the US to intervene in the collapsing communist regimes in eastern and central Europe and the volatile neocolonial third world.

However, the actual phrase 'responsibility to protect' is traceable to the International Commission on Intervention and State Sovereignty, set up in 2000 and co-chaired by Gareth Evans of Australia and Mohamed Sahnoun of Algeria. In 2004, the then-UN Secretary General Kofi Annan set up a high-level panel on 'Threats, Challenges and Change', which incorporated this phrase among its recommendations and which were debated at the 2005 World Summit. On 16 September 2005 the UN General Assembly adopted a resolution that incorporated what looked like a legitimate function of the UN, namely, the 'responsibility to protect populations from genocide, war crimes, ethnic cleansing and crimes against humanity' (paragraphs 138 and 139). The final step in the evolution of this doctrine was taken on 28 April 2006 when the Security Council, in its resolution 1674, reaffirmed 'the provisions of paragraphs 138 and 139 of the 2005 World Summit Outcome Document'.

At least one had thought that this was the final step, until Ban Ki-moon, in his report to the General Assembly on 12 January 2009, elevated R2P into a principle that he wrongly claimed was 'firmly anchored in well-established principles of international law'. He asked rhetorically whether sovereignty can 'be misused as a shield behind which mass violence could be inflicted on populations with impunity'. But, and this is significant, the third world challenged Ban Ki-moon during the General Assembly debate in July 2009. Egypt, speaking on behalf of the Non-Aligned

Movement, expressed serious concern that the R2P would under-mine the sovereignty of smaller countries – a sentiment echoed by many, among them India, Pakistan, Cuba and Venezuela. Germany too warned against its possible abuse, and Switzerland challenged the legal basis of the R2P idea.

Following the debate, the president of the General Assembly wrote the 'Concept note on responsibility to protect populations from genocide, war crimes, ethnic cleansing and crimes against humanity' for the regular September 2009 General Assembly session, in which he drew attention to the 'four qualifiers to para-graph 139', and asked the important question:

> Can any troops wage a war for human rights without causing more harm than the violations they set out to correct? In terms of the suffering of the population, would this also not be true of sanctions that cause the deaths of the most vulnerable – women and children – from malnutrition and lack of medicines? Will not an association with the use of force also compromise and weaken international humanitarian law?[1]

CARICOM argued that 'a reformed UN Security Council is an important precondition for the implementation of Pillar III'. Eventually, General Assembly resolution 63/308 – 'The respon-sibility to protect' – was unanimously passed and simply took 'note of' the Security Council's report, and decided 'to continue its consideration of the responsibility to protect'. In other words, nothing decisive came out of the crucial General Assembly 2009 regular session, and the Security Council resolution 1674 of 28 April 2006 and the General Assembly debate and resolution of September 2009 remain contested sites on the R2P doctrine.

The most questionable development of the R2P doctrine, however, was during the Libyan crisis. When Western media alarm was raised that Gaddafi was approaching Benghazi around 15 March 2011, and that he might unleash a reign of murder and terror, the empire brought the matter before the Security Council of the UN, and R2P was quickly resurrected from its previous controversial terrain to allow a limited no-fly zone military inter-vention. The rest of the story is well known, and analysed in my previous two chapters on Libya (Chapters 24 and 26 of this book).

In the name of 'protection of the civilians', NATO has overextended the remit of its authority and has been pounding Libya with bombing raids (over 6,000 sorties in the last two months). A full-scale civil war is raging in the country, with one side backed, overtly and covertly, by the empire. This is illegal under the Security Council resolution.

This, then, is the danger of 'humanitarian' intervention. It has a broad, feel-good ethical appeal about it. This can easily beguile even well-intentioned humanists and 'left' intellectuals, not just from the empire but also from the neocolonies, to rally behind a military action that is based, essentially, on realpolitik considerations and cynical manipulation of the doctrine of R2P by the empire to legitimise imperial wars and gross interference in the sovereign affairs of smaller and vulnerable nations.

Conclusion

The humanitarian interventionist doctrine is based on the dubious credentials of the responsibility to protect resolutions within the UN system. But R2P is still a contested terrain. The bulk of the third world has expressed strong opposition to it in the General Assembly and against its endorsement in the Security Council, where the empire has disproportionate power and influence. Libya is a good example of how the empire used scare tactics to resurrect R2P in order to obfuscate its real intentions. The empire is now bombing and supporting one side in a civil war, which is a total violation of its remit, even under the Security Council resolution. These militaristic 'solutions' by the empire are part of its knee-jerk and neurotic OCD reactions to a range of crises the empire has been facing since 1979. The empire's military adventurism must be opposed, and the R2P basis of the doctrine of human interventionism must be questioned, or else in the years and decades to come the world will witness a precipitous erosion of the essential ethical foundations of the global community.

http://pambazuka.org/en/category/features/73728

Note

1. See http://www.un.org/ga/president/63/interactive/protect/conceptnote.pdf.

29

International financial institutions and Egypt

Adam Hanieh

2 June 2011

Although press coverage of events in Egypt may have dropped off the front pages, discussion of the post-Mubarak period continues to dominate the financial news. Over the past few weeks, the economic direction of the interim Egyptian government has been the object of intense debate in the World Bank, International Monetary Fund (IMF) and European Bank for Reconstruction and Development (EBRD). US President Obama's 19 May speech on the Middle East and North Africa devoted much space to the question of Egypt's economic future – indeed, the sole concrete policy advanced in his talk concerned US economic relationships with Egypt. The G8 meeting in France held on 26 and 27 May continued this trend, announcing that up to $20 billion would be offered to Egypt and Tunisia. When support from the Gulf Arab states is factored into these figures, Egypt alone appears to be on the verge of receiving around $15 billion in loans, investment and aid from governments and the key international financial institutions (IFI).

The press releases accompanying the announcement of these financial packages have spoken grandly of 'the transition to democracy and freedom', which, as several analysts have noted, conveniently obfuscates the previous support of Western governments for the deposed dictators in Tunisia and Egypt. I argue, however, that a critique of these financial packages needs to be seen as much more than just a further illustration of Western hypocrisy. The plethora of aid and investment initiatives advanced by the leading powers in recent days represents a conscious attempt to consolidate and reinforce the power of Egypt's dominant class in the face of the ongoing popular mobilisations. They are part of, in other words, a sustained effort to restrain the revolution within the bounds of an 'orderly transition' – to borrow the perspicacious phrase that the US government repeatedly used following the ousting of Mubarak.

At the core of this financial intervention in Egypt is an attempt to accelerate the neoliberal programme that was pursued by the Mubarak regime. The IFI financial packages ostensibly promote measures such as employment creation, infrastructure expansion and other seemingly laudable goals, but in reality, these are premised upon the classic neoliberal policies of privatisation, deregulation and opening to foreign investment. Despite the claims of democratic transition, the institutions of the Egyptian state are being refashioned through this neoliberal drive as an enabling mechanism of the market. Egypt is, in many ways, shaping up as the perfect laboratory of the so-called post-Washington consensus, in which a liberal-sounding pro-poor rhetoric – principally linked to the discourse of democratisation – is used to deepen the neoliberal trajectory of the Mubarak era. If successful, the likely outcome of this – particularly in the face of heightened political mobilisation and the unfulfilled expectations of the Egyptian people – is a society that at a superficial level takes some limited appearances of the form of liberal democracy but, in actuality, remains a highly authoritarian neoliberal state, dominated by an alliance of the military and business elites.

Accelerating structural economic reforms

The most important point to note about the aid packages promised to Egypt is that they do not in any way represent a break from the logic encapsulated in previous economic strategies for the region. In a report to the May G8 summit, the IMF clearly summarised this logic, noting that:

> Overcoming high unemployment will require a substantial increase in the pace of economic growth ... Achieving such growth rates will entail both additional investment and improved productivity. While some increases in public

investment may be required, for instance to improve the quality of infrastructure and services in less developed rural areas, the key role will have to be played by the private sector, including by attracting foreign direct investment. Thus, government policies should support an enabling environment in which the private sector flourishes.

The core argument expressed in this statement is essentially the same message that the IMF and World Bank have been pushing in decades of reports on the Egyptian and Middle East economies.

Egypt's problems stem from the weakness of the private sector and the 'rent-seeking' of state officials. The solution is to open Egypt's markets to the outside world, lift restrictions on investment in key sectors of the economy, liberalise ownership laws, end subsidies to the poor for food and other necessities, and increase market competition. By allowing unfettered markets to operate freely, the private sector will be the key engine of growth and, through this harnessing of entrepreneurial initiative, lead to the creation of jobs and prosperity.

Of course these ideas are simply a restatement of the basic premises of neoliberalism, but it is imperative to acknowledge their continuity with earlier plans – the promised aid to Egypt consciously aims at achieving a specific outcome in line with the previous neoliberal strategy. The concrete policy implications of this were most clearly spelt out in a flagship World Bank report published in 2009, *From Privilege to Competition: Unlocking Private-Led Growth in the Middle East and North Africa*. The report prescribes steps to be taken by all governments in the Middle East, including:

(1) opening protected sectors such as retail and real estate, which have barriers to foreign investors … (2) reducing tariff bands and nontariff barriers; (3) removing protection of state-owned firms by enforcing hard budget constraints and exposing them to open competition; and (4) eliminating anti-export biases.

In order to encourage foreign investment, governments should eliminate 'high minimum capital requirements and restrictions on foreign ownership' and, in countries where state-owned banks exist 'engage in open and transparent privatisation'.

These are the types of policies that we can expect to see in Egypt as this aid begins to flow – in fact, they are the essential pre-requisites for the receipt of this financial support. The mechanisms of this conditionality are discussed further below; at this stage, it is simply important to note that there has been an unassailable link established between aid and the fulfilment of neoliberal reforms. As the Institute of International Finance (IIF), a policy and lobby organisation that brings together the largest financial institutions in the world, noted in early May:

> As momentous as the current security and political restructuring challenges may be, it is absolutely critical that the transition authorities … place a high priority on deepening and accelerating structural economic reforms … transition and subsequent governments must articulate a credible medium-term reform and stabilisation framework … [and] need to focus on creating the legal and institutional environment for fostering entrepreneurship, investment, and market-driven growth.[1]

The IIF went on to bluntly identify this acceleration of structural adjustment as the 'context' in which aid to Egypt would be provided.

Red tape and institutional reform

In addition to these standard neoliberal prescriptions, the other element to the policy logic guiding IFI financial support concerns institutional reform. This reflects a wider shift in the developmental strategy of the IFIs since the 1990s, in which more emphasis has been placed on linking the function of markets with their institutional governance. Within this context, the World Bank and other institutions have emphasised notions such as the rule of law, decentralisation, good governance, separation of the legislative and executive and so forth, which supposedly aim at reducing the rent-seeking capabilities of state officials and guarantee greater transparency in economic affairs.[2]

This emphasis on institutional reform partly reflects a problem of perception faced by the IFIs. The embrace of issues of governance and democracy is explicitly designed to ensure greater legitimacy for neoliberalism, particularly in the wake of the disastrous decades of 1980s and 1990s where the open advocacy of structural adjustment wreaked havoc on much of the South. This policy shift, however, does not represent a turn away from the logic of neoliberalism. Rather, it actually serves to reinforce this logic, by tailoring institutions to the needs of the private sector and removing any ability of the state to intervene in the market. In the Middle East, where authoritarian regimes have been the norm, these calls for institutional reform can be easily portrayed as democratic (and, indeed, they are explicitly framed within a discourse of democratisation). In reality they are profoundly anti-democratic. By limiting democracy to the political sphere and expanding the notion of freedom to include markets, they obfuscate the necessary relations of power within the market, and explicitly block the ability of states to determine the use, ownership and distribution of their economic resources. Democratic control of the economy is thus precluded as a violation of good governance.

In the case of Egypt, the discourse of institutional reform has allowed neoliberal structural adjustment to be presented not just as a technocratic necessity – but as the actual fulfilment of the demands innervating the uprisings. In this sense, neoliberal ideology attempts to reabsorb and fashion dissent in its own image, through rendering Egypt's uprisings within a pro-market discourse. This fundamental message has been repeatedly emphasised by US and European spokespeople over the last weeks: this was not a revolt against several decades of neoliberalism – but rather a movement against an intrusive state that had obstructed the pursuit of individual self-interest through the market.

Perhaps the starkest example of this discursive shift was the statement made by World Bank president Robert Zoellick at the opening of a World Bank meeting on the Middle East in mid-April. Referring to Mohammed Bouazizi, the young peddler from a Tunisian market place who set himself on fire and became the catalyst for the uprising in Tunisia, Zoellick remarked:

> [T]he key point I have also been emphasising and I emphasised in this speech is that it is not just a question of money. It is a question of policy ... keep in mind, the late Mr Bouazizi was basically driven to burn himself alive because he was harassed with red tape ... one starting point is to quit harassing those people and let them have a chance to start some small businesses.

In this discursive reframing of the uprisings, the massive protests that overthrew Mubarak and Ben Ali occurred due to the absence of capitalism rather than its normal functioning. In an ideological sense, this reframing directly confronts the popular aspirations that have arisen through the course of the struggle in Egypt. The political demands heard on the streets of Egypt today – to reclaim wealth that was stolen from the people, offer state support and services to the poor, nationalise those industries that were privatised and place restrictions on foreign investment – can be either disregarded or portrayed as anti-democratic. Precisely because Egypt's uprising was one in which the political and economic demands were inseparable and intertwined, this effort to recast the struggle as pro-market is, in a very real sense, directly aimed at undercutting and weakening the country's ongoing mobilisations.

This understanding of the basic logic presupposed in the IFI financial packages allows us to turn to the precise mechanisms through which structural adjustment is unfolding. There are two common elements to all the financial support offered to Egypt to date – an extension of loans (i.e. an increase in Egypt's external debt) and promised investment in so-called public private partnerships (PPPs). Both these elements are tied to Egypt's implementation of structural adjustment. Strategically, it appears that the initial focus of this structural adjustment will be the privatisation of Egypt's infrastructure and the opening of the economy to foreign investment and trade through PPPs (these are discussed below). In addition to the US government, World Bank and IMF, the other main institutional actor in this process is the EBRD.

Debt

Currently, Egypt's external debt runs at around $35 billion and over the last decade the country has been paying around $3 billion a year in debt service. From 2000 to 2009, Egypt's level of debt increased by around 15 per cent, despite the fact that the country paid a total of $24.6 billion in debt repayments over the same period. Egypt's net transfers on long-term debt between 2000 and 2009, which measures the total difference between received loans and repayments, reached $3.4 billion. In other words, contrary to popular belief, more money actually flows from Egypt to Western lenders than vice versa. These figures demonstrate the striking reality of Egypt's financial relationship with the global economy – Western loans act to extract wealth from Egypt's poor and redistribute it to the richest banks in North America and Europe.

Of course, the decision to borrow this money and enter into this debt trap was not made by Egypt's poor. The vast majority of this debt (around 85 per cent) is public or publicly guaranteed, in other words it is debt that was taken on by the Mubarak government with the open encouragement of the IFIs. Egypt's ruling elite – centred around Mubarak and his coterie – profited handsomely from these transactions (estimated in the many billions). This indicates that much of Egypt's debt is what development economists call odious debt – debt that has been built up by a dictatorial regime without regard to the needs of the population. Mubarak does not hold sole responsibility for this process. The World Bank, IMF and many other lenders continued to encourage this borrowing (and to praise Egypt's economic direction under Mubarak) precisely because it was such a profitable enterprise.

This is the essential background to the discussions around Egypt's foreign debt. In his 19 May speech, Obama made much of a promise to relieve Egypt of up to $1 billion in its debt obligations. Obama described this as the US government's attempt to support 'positive change in the region ... through our efforts to advance economic development for nations that are transitioning to democracy'. In addition to this monetary support, Obama also promised to urge the World Bank, IMF and other countries to help 'stabilise and modernise' Egypt and 'meet its near-term financial needs'.

Putting aside the hubris of this speech, Obama's offer needs to be understood accurately. Contrary to what has been widely reported in the media, this was not a forgiveness of Egypt's debt. It is actually a debt-swap – a promise to reduce Egypt's debt service by $1 billion, provided that money is used in a manner in which the US government approves. This debt-swap confirms the relationship of power that is inherent to modern finance. The US is able to use Egypt's indebtedness as a means to compel the country to adopt the types of economic policies described above. Obama was very explicit about what this meant, stating that:

> The goal must be a model in which protectionism gives way to openness, the reins of commerce pass from the few to the many, and the economy generates jobs for the young. America's support for democracy will therefore be based on ensuring financial stability, promoting reform, and integrating competitive markets with each other and the global economy.

This same policy language has been clearly articulated alongside the loans promised to Egypt by the World Bank and IMF. On 12 May, Caroline Atkinson, director of the External Relations Department at the IMF, announced that the IMF was studying a request from the Egyptian government for $3–4 billion of loans and would 'visit Cairo shortly to begin discussions with the Egyptian authorities on an arrangement'.

Indicating that these loans would come with conditions, Atkinson noted that, 'The size and scope of Fund support will be defined as discussions progress.' An adviser to Egyptian Finance Minister Samir Radwan confirmed this, declaring: 'How the money will be spent will undergo a process of negotiation.' On 24 May this conditionality was set out following an announcement by the World Bank and IMF that they would provide $4.5 billion to Egypt over two years. Noting that 'reforms were as important as money', World Bank President Robert Zoellick explicitly linked the initial $1 billion 'to governance and openness reforms with a further $1 billion available next year dependant on progress.'[3] The remaining $2.5 billion would be invested in development projects and private sector loans (see below).

Unless these loans are refused and the existing debt repudiated, Egypt will find itself in a cul-de-sac from which there is little chance of escape. Foreign debt is not a neutral form of aid but an exploitative social relation established between financial institutions in the North and countries in the South. Trapped in this relationship, countries become dependent upon a continuous stream of new loans in order to service previously accumulated long-term debt. It is a means to deepen the extraction of wealth from Egypt and – precisely because of the continued dependency on financial inflows – serves to chain Egypt to further structural adjustment measures. The Egyptian people are being punished for an indebtedness that they did not create, and that punishment consists of being locked into even greater indebtedness by the institutions that put them there in the first place.

Foreign investment and public private partnerships

Also in his 19 May speech, Obama pledged $1 billion in investments through a US institution known as the Overseas Private Investment Corporation (OPIC). OPIC's mandate is to support US business investment in so-called emerging markets; it provides guarantees for loans (particularly in the case of large projects) or direct loans for projects that have a significant proportion of US business involvement and may face political risk. Perhaps emblematic of OPIC's activities was its first investment in Afghanistan, following soon after the invasion of that country by NATO-led forces in 2001: a new Hyatt hotel in Kabul that would be used as 'a platform for business persons' visiting the country. OPIC was also a key partner in encouraging the free-market ideology that underpinned the economic policy of the Coalition Provisional Authority (CPA) in Iraq following the US-led invasion of 2003.[4] The US government openly asserts the link between OPIC and US foreign policy objectives. This is well encapsulated in the organisation's slogan: 'support[ing] U.S. investment in emerging markets worldwide, fostering development & the growth of free markets'.

Because OPIC's investment depends upon reducing barriers to foreign capital and accelerating the privatisation of state-owned enterprises, its activities are predicated upon, and help to reinforce, the extension of the neoliberal programme described above. In the case of Egypt, this is likely to take place primarily through the use of US government funds to establish public private partnerships. A PPP is a means of encouraging the outsourcing of previously state-run utilities and services to private companies. A private company provides a service through a contract with the government – typically, this may include activities such as running hospitals or schools, or building infrastructure such as highways or power plants. For this, they receive payments from the government or through the users of the service (such as highway tolls). PPPs are thus a form of privatisation, which, in the words of one of their foremost proponents, Emanuel Savas, is 'a useful phrase because it avoids the inflammatory effect of "privatisation" on those ideologically opposed.'[5]

OPIC's intervention in Egypt has been explicitly tied to the promotion of PPPs. An OPIC press release, for example, that followed soon after Obama's speech, noted that the $1 billion promised by the US government would be used 'to identify Egyptian government-owned enterprises investing in public private partnerships in order to promote growth in mutually agreed-upon sectors of the Egyptian economy'.

The focus on PPPs, however, is illustrated even more clearly in investment promised by another international financial institution, the EBRD. The EBRD was established at the time of the fall of the Soviet Union, with the goal of transitioning Eastern Europe to a capitalist economy. As the EBRD's president, Thomas Mirow, put it in the lead up to the bank's discussions on Egypt: 'The EBRD was created in 1991 to promote democracy and market economy, and the historic developments in Egypt strike a deep chord at this bank.'

The EBRD is shaping up to be one of the lead agents of the neoliberal project in Egypt. On 21 May, EBRD shareholders agreed to lend up to $3.5 billion to the Middle East, with Egypt the first country earmarked for receipt of loans in the first half of 2012. This will be the first time since its establishment that the EBRD has lent to the Middle East. Catherine Ashton, the European Union foreign policy chief, has remarked that the EBRD could provide €1 billion annually to Egypt, which would give the institution an enormous weight in the Egyptian economy – as a point of comparison, the total investment value of all PPP projects in Egypt from 1990 to 2008 was $16.6 billion.

Anyone who has any illusions about the goals of the EBRD's investment in Egypt would do well to read carefully the EBRD 2010 transition report. The report presents a detailed assessment of the East European and ex-Soviet republics, measuring their progress on a detailed set of indicators.

These indicators are highly revealing: 1) private sector share of GDP; 2) large-scale privatisation; 3) small-scale privatisation; 4) governance and enterprise restructuring; 5) price liberalisation; 6) trade and foreign exchange system; 7) competition policy;

8) banking reform and interest rate liberalisation; 9) securities markets and non-bank financial institutions; 10) overall infrastructure reform.[6] Only countries that score well on these indicators are eligible for EBRD loans. A research institute that tracks the activity of the EBRD, Bank Watch, noted in 2008 that a country cannot achieve top marks in the EBRD assessment without the implementation of PPPs in the water and road sectors.

As a result, the EBRD intervention probably augurs a massive acceleration of the privatisation process in Egypt, most likely under the extension of PPPs. The current Egyptian government has given its open consent to this process. Indeed, at the EBRD annual general meeting this May, where Egypt was promised funds, a spokesperson of the Egyptian government remarked: 'The current transition government remains committed to the open market approach, which Egypt will further pursue at an accelerated rate following upcoming elections.' The statement noted 'that public private partnerships have much potential as an effective modality for designing and implementing development projects, particularly in infrastructure and service sectors (transport, health, etc.). Therefore we will encourage PPP initiatives.' Moreover, fully embracing the pro-market ideological discourse discussed above, the Egyptian government promised to relax control over foreign investments through committing 'to overcoming the previous shortcomings of excessive government centralisation. In addition, we will build on existing initiatives to achieve a greater level of decentralisation, especially in terms of local planning and financial management'.

Conclusion

The projects and investments mentioned above are not the sole aspects of the IFI-backed neoliberal project in Egypt[7] but, at the most fundamental level, this financial aid confirms a conscious intervention by Western governments into Egypt's revolutionary process. In the very short term, large infrastructure projects and other economic schemes may provide some employment creation, housing, educational training and perhaps the appearance of a return to stability, given the prevailing sense of crisis. This investment, however, is premised upon a profound liberalisation of the Egyptian economy. It will only be undertaken concomitant with measures such as deepening privatisation (undoubtedly in the form of PPPs), deregulation (initially likely to be connected to the opening up of more sectors to foreign investment), the reduction of trade barriers (connected to access to US and European markets), and the expansion of the informal sector (under the banner of cutting red tape). It will necessarily involve, furthermore, a rapid expansion in Egypt's overall indebtedness – tying the country ever more firmly to future structural adjustment packages.

If this process is not resisted, it threatens to negate the achievements of the Egyptian uprising. As the decades of the Egyptian experience of neoliberalism illustrate all too clearly, these measures will further deepen poverty and an erosion of living standards for the vast majority. Simultaneously, the financial inflows will help to strengthen and consolidate Egypt's narrow business and military elites as the only layer of society that stands to gain from further liberalisation of the economy. The expansion of PPPs, for example, will provide enormous opportunities for the largest business groups in the country to take ownership stakes in major infrastructure projects and other privatised service provision. Alongside foreign investors, these groups will gain from the deregulation of labour markets, liberalisation of land and retail activities, and the potential access to export markets in the US and Europe.

These measures also have a regional impact. Their other main beneficiary will be the states of the Gulf Cooperation Council (GCC – Saudi Arabia, Kuwait, United Arab Emirates, Bahrain, Qatar and Oman), who are playing a highly visible and complementary role alongside the IFIs. Saudi Arabia has pledged $4 billion to Egypt – exceeding the amounts promised by the US and EBRD. The Kuwait Investment Authority announced in April that it was establishing a $1 billion sovereign wealth fund that would invest in Egyptian companies. Kuwait's Kharafi Group, which had won PPP contracts in the power sector in Egypt in 2010 and is estimated to have $7 billion invested in Egypt already, announced that it was taking out an $80 million loan for investments in Egypt. Qatar is also reportedly considering investing up to $10 billion, according to its ambassador in Egypt.

As with the investments from Western states, these financial flows from the GCC are dependent upon the further liberalisation of Egypt's economy, most likely through the mechanisms of PPPs. Indeed, Essam Sharaf, Egypt's interim prime minister, and Samir Radwan, finance minister, have both travelled frequently to the GCC states over recent months with the aim of marketing PPP projects, particularly in water and wastewater, roads, education, healthcare and energy. One indication of the direction of these efforts was the announcement by the Dubai and Egyptian stock exchanges to allow the dual listing of stocks on their respective exchanges. This measure will allow privatised companies or investment vehicles to be jointly listed on both exchanges, thus facilitating the increased flows of GCC capital into Egypt.

In essence, the financial initiatives announced over recent weeks represent an attempt to bind social layers such as these – Egypt's military and business elites, the ruling families and large conglomerates of the GCC and so forth – ever more tightly to the Western states. The revolutionary process in Egypt represented an attack against these elements of the Arab world. The uprising cannot be reduced to a question of democratic transition. Precisely because the political form of the Egyptian state under Mubarak was a direct reflection of the nature of capitalism in the country, the uprising implicitly involved a challenge to the position of these elites. The inspiring mobilisations that continue on the Egyptian streets confirm that these aspirations remain firmly held. Western financial aid needs to be understood as an intervention in this ongoing struggle – an attempt to utilise the sense of economic crisis to refashion Egyptian society against the interests of Egypt's majority, and divert the revolution from the goals it has yet to achieve.

http://pambazuka.org/en/category/features/73722

Copyright ©2011 Jadaliyya

This chapter was first published by Jadaliyya, an independent ezine produced by ASI (Arab Studies Institute), a network of writers associated with the *Arab Studies Journal*.

Notes

1. George Abed, David Hedley, Garbis Iradian, Nafez Zouk (2011) 'The Arab World in transition: assessing the economic impact', http://www.iif.com/emr/resources+1200.php, accessed 25 August 2011.
2. For a detailed critique of these notions, see K.S. Jomo and B. Fine (eds) (2006) *The New Development Economics: After the Washington Consensus*, London, Zed Books.
3. This clear message of conditionality makes a mockery of the claim by Egyptian Finance Minister Samir Radwan that: 'We have an Egyptian programme ... I am not accepting any conditionality – none whatsoever.'
4. A fundamental part of this process – likely to be replicated in the case of Egypt – was a focus on encouraging Iraqi business to become increasingly dependent upon US-owned finance capital through the support of US bank and finance lending to small-and-medium enterprises in the country.
5. Emanuel Savas (2005) *Privatisation in the City*, Washington DC, CQ Press: 16.
6. Belarus, for example, was rewarded for its 'removal of price and trade restrictions on many goods and reduction of list of minimum export price' by a rise in its price liberalisation indicator from 3 to 3+. Likewise, Montenegro received the same increase for privatising parts of its power and port sectors.
7. For example, another important vehicle is the Arab Financing Facility for Infrastructure (AFFI), established by the World Bank, International Finance Corporation and the Islamic Development Bank earlier this year to promote investment in the Middle East region. The AFFI aims to raise US$1 billion and will focus on infrastructure, explicitly around PPPs. The AFFI focuses on regional integration projects, and is thereby being used to promote the reduction of trade and tariffs within the region. It is as yet unclear what the AFFI involvement with Egypt will be, but it has been highlighted by the World Bank as a major component of its future activities in the country.

30

Neoliberal threats to North Africa

Patrick Bond

9 June 2011, revised 22 August 2011

A 2008 incident in Carthage spoke volumes about power politics and economic ideology. As he was given the country's main honour, the Order of the Tunisian Republic, on account of his 'contribution to the reinforcement of economic development at the global level', International Monetary Fund (IMF) Managing Director Dominique Strauss-Kahn returned the favour, offering Zine al-Abidine Ben Ali's dictatorship a warm embrace. 'Economic policy adopted here is a sound policy and is the best model for many emerging countries,' said Strauss-Kahn. 'Our discussions confirmed that we share many of the same views on Tunisia's achievements and main challenges. Tunisia is making impressive progress in its reform agenda and its prospects are favourable' (Phillips 2011: 1).

In late May 2011, just days after Strauss-Kahn resigned in disgrace (for other reasons), the IMF (2011a: 1–2) outlined a new set of opportunities in Tunisia and neighbouring countries: 'The spark ignited by the death of Mohammed Bouazizi has irretrievably changed the future course of the countries in the Middle East and North Africa (MENA). But each country will change in its own way and at its own speed. Nor will they necessarily have a common political or economic model when they reach their destination.'

Specifically for Egypt, that destination included two words, 'social justice', which began appearing frequently in official statements. The IMF's $3 billion loan offer to Egypt on 4 June would have added to an existing $33 billion in foreign debt inherited from Hosni Mubarak's regime, which a genuinely new, free democracy would have grounds to default on because of its 'odious' nature in legal and technical terms. To legitimise that debt requires new loans that have an aura of relevance. However, to everyone's surprise, on 25 June, the IMF loan was rejected in favour of financing by the GCC and Islamic Development Bank.

IMF mission head in Egypt Ratna Sahay (2011: 1) had claimed on 2 June: 'We share the draft budget's overarching goal aimed at promoting social justice. The measures go in the right direction of supporting economic recovery, generating jobs and assisting low-income households, while maintaining macroeconomic stability.' Three days later, acting Managing Director John Lipsky (IMF Survey 2011: 1) reiterated: 'We are optimistic that the programme's objectives of promoting social justice, fostering recovery, and maintaining macroeconomic stability and generating jobs will bring positive results for the Egyptian people.' The same day, said Sahay (IMF Survey 2011: 1): 'Following a revolution and during a challenging period of political transition, the Egyptian authorities have put in place a home-grown economic program with the overarching objective of promoting social justice.'

Egyptians may disagree, for the following week, the new government of Essam Sharaf began implementing a controversial law banning strikes. The minister of finance, Samir Radwan, promised a continuation of neoliberal policies and on 9 June cancelled a proposed capital gains tax after pressure from the stock market. It is not known whether the IMF was surreptitiously involved in these decisions, a few weeks prior to the rejection of the institution's $3 billion loan.

Beyond the incongruous rhetoric embracing democracy and social justice, there appears to be very little difference in what is being advocated to Arab democrats today and what was advocated to Arab dictators yesterday. For in September 2010, *IMF Survey Magazine* (Toujas-Bernate and Bhattacharya 2010: 1) praised Ben Ali for his commitment 'to reduce tax rates on businesses and to offset those reductions by increasing the standard Value Added Tax (VAT) rate'. A few weeks later, on 27 December, informal street trader Mohammed Bouazizi was subject to a police attack – his fruit cart was overturned, which caused such frustration he publicly self-immolated – presumably because he was not contributing to the 18 per cent VAT rate with his survivalist home-production business. There may have been other reasons, but this is typically one rationale offered by authorities for disrupting street traders across the world, and Tunisia's informal sector has been measured at nearly half the gross domestic product in recent decades (Easton 2001: 22).

If the IMF leadership praised the dictatorship, insisted on austerity and advocated squeezing poor people for more taxes, what business does it have today in giving similar decisive advice in Tunisia, or anywhere in the Middle East and North Africa, or for that matter Europe (from Ireland to Greece) or anywhere at all? What can we learn about IMF thinking in Tunisia, Egypt and Libya? And should we be hopeful by the Egyptian military's rejection of the loan?

Tunisia as 'best model'

In its 2010 Tunisia review, called an Article IV consultation, the IMF (2010a: 1, 12, 13) approved Ben Ali's policies of 'enhancing its business environment and improving the competitiveness of its economy', including a preferential trade agreement with West Africa and 'free-trade agreements with the Central African Economic and Monetary Community. Bilateral negotiations with the European Union are also under way to extend the association agreement to services, agricultural products, and processed food; the agreement currently provides for free trade for industrial products.' In addition, the IMF (2010a: 13) appreciated Tunisia's 'reforms to labour market policies, the educational system, and public employment services that will serve to facilitate labour mobility'. The IMF applauded the Tunis authorities for 'reforming the social security system' (i.e. payment cuts to retirees that might 'buttress the pension system's financial sustainability'), exploring 'ways to contain subsidies of food and fuel products', and 'undertaking reforms to make the tax regime more business friendly' including, as noted above, commitments 'to reduce tax rates on businesses and to offset those reductions by increasing the standard VAT rate' (the VAT is a consumption tax and thus explicitly regressive insofar as low-income people are hit by the state for a larger share of their income).

A further IMF (2010a: 14) objective was 'consolidating the financial strength of banks, enhancing the role of banks in the economy, restructuring the public banking system, and bolstering the presence of Tunisian banks abroad. The aim, ultimately, is to transform Tunisia into a banking services hub and a regional financial market'. That in turn required 'inflation targeting' (a technique to depoliticise monetarist policy especially for the purpose of raising interest rates) and 'convertibility of the dinar and capital account liberalisation by 2014'.

This was economic liberalisation without much disguise, at a time of declining tourism revenues and textile trades. In contrast, there was no IMF conditionality aimed at reforming the dictatorship and halting widespread corruption by Ben Ali and his wife's notorious Trabelsi family, or lessening the two families' extreme level of business concentration, or ending the regime's reliance upon murderous security forces to defend Tunisian crony capitalism, or lowering the hedonism for which Ben Ali had become famous. According to Wikileaks (Cole 2011), even the notoriously lax-on-dictatorship US State Department was disgusted by the consumption norms of the Ben Ali and Trabelsi families, and their control of half the national economy. In this sense, the typical way in which African 'IMF riots' degenerated in prior decades was avoided, as a deep democratic social movement emerged (in a parallel to similar movements of the 1990s in Latin America). Whether or not it is strong enough to prevent the post-dictatorship government from adopting neoliberal measures at its core remains to be seen.

Egypt

The IMF (2010b) offered a strikingly similar line of argument in Egypt in its April 2010 Article IV consultation statement, praising the Mubarak dictatorship for implementing neoliberal policies prior to the global financial meltdown, and then after a brief moment of rising budget deficits and loose monetary policy, insisting on a return to the Washington consensus forthwith. On the one hand the IMF (2010b: 10) document complained about the crisis-induced postponement of 'key fiscal reforms – introducing the property tax, broadening the VAT, and phasing out energy subsidies', but offered an upbeat endorsement of the ruling regime:

> Five years of reforms and prudent macroeconomic policies created the space needed to respond to the global financial crisis, and the supportive fiscal and monetary policies of the past year have been in line with staff's advice. The authorities remain committed to resuming fiscal consolidation broadly in keeping with past advice to address fiscal vulnerabilities … Such adjustment will be crucial to maintain investor confidence, preserve macroeconomic stability, and create scope for future countercyclical fiscal policy. (IMF 2010b: 1, 4)

In addition to expanding public private partnerships (PPPs, a euphemism for services privatisation and outsourcing), the IMF (2010b: 4) named its priorities: 'adopting as early as possible a full-fledged VAT, complementing energy subsidy reform with better-targeted transfers to the most needy, and containing the fiscal cost of the pension and health reforms'. Although the IMF noted just once that 'Transparency International cites accountability and transparency, and weaknesses in the legal/regulatory system as key reasons for Egypt remaining 111th of 180 countries on its Corruption Perception Index', it immediately followed this observation with a non-sequitur:

> Decisive action to continue the earlier reform momentum should focus on addressing the remaining structural weaknesses. In addition to sound macroeconomic policies, efforts should focus on: Resuming privatisation and increasing the role of carefully structured and appropriately priced PPPs should assist fiscal adjustment and mobilise private resources for infrastructure investment. (IMF 2010b:24)

The word governance does not appear in the IMF (2010b: 35) document, nor, interestingly, did the IMF express concern about Egypt's then $33 billion foreign debt: 'The composition and small size of Egypt's external debt makes it relatively resilient to adverse external shocks.' The IMF (2010b: 44) also noted, in 2010, that 'The relationship between Egypt and the World Bank Group has been transformed and markedly improved over the last few years as a result of the progress Egypt has made in implementing reforms.'

So it was that in Egypt in early 2011, just as in Tunisia, the IMF was caught flatfooted by the popular uprising and, relatedly, by the immediate problems of rapid capital flight and fiscal/financial stress that resulted. By late May 2011, in its G8 report, IMF staff had recovered and conceded:

> The January revolution has raised the aspirations of Egypt's population at a time when the economy is taking a hit from domestic unrest in the short term, the ensuing uncertainty, and large global and regional shocks (e.g. the rise in commodity prices and the violence in Libya). The political shock triggered substantial capital outflows, which in addition to the decline in tourism revenue, remittances, and exports, have led to a loss of foreign exchange reserves of about US$15 billion in the four months to end-April. (2011a: 9)

In that document, IMF (2011a: 9) staff worried that 'managing popular expectations and providing some short-term relief measures will be essential to maintain social cohesion in the short term', and that this would come at a price: 'external and fiscal financing gaps of $9–12 billion ... which would need to be filled with exceptional support from Egypt's multilateral and bilateral development partners, particularly given the limited scope for adjustment in the short term'. The 'limited scope' reflected the breath of democracy in Egypt, but the assumption seemed to be that investments of $1 billion in debt relief (leaving $33 billion to repay) and additional grants would permit Cairo to restore good relations with Washington and to get over the hump of the democratic revolution with its 'reform' agenda intact. And even if the $3 billion IMF loan was rejected after deliberation and protest, the other Gulf states that will step in with financing have the same basic interests in status quo political economy.

As political economist Adam Hanieh concluded just after the G8 summit and allied Arab states pledged $15 billion to Egypt:

> The plethora of aid and investment initiatives advanced by the leading powers in recent days represents a conscious attempt to consolidate and reinforce the power of Egypt's dominant class

in the face of the ongoing popular mobilisations. They are part of, in other words, a sustained effort to restrain the revolution within the bounds of an 'orderly transition' – to borrow the perspicacious phrase that the US government repeatedly used following the ousting of Mubarak. At the core of this financial intervention in Egypt is an attempt to accelerate the neoliberal programme that was pursued by the Mubarak regime. (Hanieh, Chapter 29 of this book: 238–9)

Libya

The same neoliberal pro-dictator narrative was established in Libya, for example, in the IMF's (2010c: 7) October 2010 pronouncements in which Mu'ammar Gaddafi's mass firing of 340,000 civil servants was celebrated: 'About a quarter have reportedly found other sources of income and are no longer receiving transfers from the state budget. The mission recommends that the retrenchment program be accelerated.'

The IMF's last full Article IV consultation for Libya was published on 15 February 2011, just before civil war broke out. Implying that Gaddafi was safe from the Arab spring, the IMF noted that 'Recent developments in neighbouring Egypt and Tunisia have had limited economic impact on Libya so far', and flattered Tripoli on a variety of fronts:

> An ambitious program to *privatise banks and develop the nascent financial sector is underway* … Structural reforms in other areas have progressed. The passing in early 2010 of a number of far-reaching laws bodes well for *fostering private sector development and attracting foreign direct investment* … Executive Directors agreed with the thrust of the staff appraisal. They welcomed Libya's strong macroeconomic performance and the progress *on enhancing the role of the private sector* and supporting growth in the non-oil economy. The fiscal and external balances remain in substantial surplus and are expected to strengthen further over the medium term, and the outlook for Libya's economy remains favorable [emphasis added]. (IMF 2011b: 2–3)

This optimistic report and others like it annoyed two *New York Times* reporters (Briancon and Foley 2011):

Less than two weeks ago, the IMF's executive board, its highest authority, assessed a North African country's economy and commended its government for its 'ambitious reform agenda'. The IMF also welcomed its 'strong macroeconomic performance and the progress on enhancing the role of the private sector', and 'encouraged' the authorities to continue on that promising path. By unfortunate timing, that country was Libya. The fund's mission to Tripoli had somehow omitted to check whether the 'ambitious' reform agenda was based on any kind of popular support. Libya is not an isolated case. And the IMF doesn't look good after it gave glowing reviews to many of the countries shaken by popular revolts in recent weeks.

MENA economies under Washington's thumb

Although not objecting to the IMF's neoliberal ideology, the *New York Times* reporters cited similar upbeat language in its reviews of Bahrain, Algeria and Egypt, worrying that 'the toppling of unpopular regimes will make it difficult for their successors to adopt the same policies. In the future, the IMF might want to add another box to check on its list of criteria: democratic support' (Briancon and Foley 2011). Indeed, Tunisia, Egypt and Libya were not isolated mistakes, but reflected an approach to the entire Middle East and North Africa region. As Masood Ahmed, IMF director for the Middle East and Central Asia Department, argued in the November 2010 *International Economic Bulletin of the Carnegie Endowment for International Peace*, the countries in his portfolio:

> must, first and foremost, boost their competitiveness. Sound macroeconomic policies – in particular, fiscal consolidation – will help, but governments will also need to make greater efforts to improve the business climate. Unfortunately, many of these countries are still characterised by burdensome regulatory systems, weak institutions, and a dominating public sector. Countries must also enhance labour market functioning by improving education (to better match the supply of, and demand for, certain skill sets) and ensuring that wages better reflect market conditions. Finally, trade tariffs need to come down. (Ahmed 2010: 1)

Of course, this kind of dogmatic Washington consensus advice was often balanced, in the IMF's 2010 Article IV consultations, with language to the effect that 'pro-growth reforms' and 'shared', 'pro-poor' development and social policies would also be pursued. But as the World Bank's MENA Regional Economic Update of May 2011 showed, the support for social policy was within tight fiscal limitations, which many MENA countries were breaking:

> as governments want to reduce unemployment and ease the burden of high commodity prices, social protection has expanded rapidly in the region. While some measures are desirable, especially those targeted at protecting the most vulnerable, there is a risk that many of these policies are broad and will be very costly. In particular, expansion of public sector employment is costly and difficult to reverse. (World Bank 2011a: 27–8)

However, the harsh reality (borne out through social revolutions) that growth was weak and not being shared meant that by May 2011, the IMF's new language was much more sober:

> In MENA, prolonged instability, resulting from unmet political and social targets or spillover effects and lack of clarity about the future political transition, is the most serious risk to the short-term regional economic outlook. Prolonged tensions would amplify the negative impact on capital inflows and domestic financial exchanges, tourism receipts and remittances, and in turn on investment, output, and employment … Prolonged unrest would also threaten MENA's social policy design and fiscal health, as revenues would remain weak and expenditure would be elevated, especially if commodity prices remain strong. (IMF 2011a: 27)

But imposing a new round of Washington consensus policies risks what even World Bank (2009: 1) chief and Africa economist Shanta Devarajan in 2009 termed 'the spectre of political instability and social unrest', a point we take up again in the conclusion. For Devarajan, 'market-based reforms, which were painful in the first place but which African countries implemented because they could see the impact they were having on growth, are likely to lose political support because they no longer deliver results'. At the same press briefing, the bank's Africa vice-president, Obiageli Ezekwesili, worried, 'It is precisely in a season of crisis like this that African governments must stay the course of market-based reforms' (World Bank 2009: 1).

The possibility of MENA governments not taking Ezekwesili's advice and diverting further into Keynesian territory, including imposing exchange controls, was sufficiently strong (especially in North Africa) that a journalist at the April 2011 IMF (2011c) spring meetings dared pose it to Strauss-Kahn: 'Do you have any fears that there is perhaps a far left movement coming through these revolutions that want more, perhaps, closed economies?' For Strauss-Kahn, this was a 'Good question. Good question. There's always this risk, but I'm not sure it will materialise.' For Strauss-Kahn, the bottom-line slogan for his questioner was predictable enough: 'We're in a globalised world, so there is no domestic solution.'

The Bretton Woods institutions and the G8

For anyone worried about the ways neoliberalism will undermine popular aspirations in the Middle East and North Africa, the World Bank and IMF documents released in late May give enormous cause for concern. The two institutions have long been implicated in third world corruption, to the extent that odious debts owed by poor economies are increasingly subject to questioning (the way that Ecuador did in 2009 while defaulting on $9 billion in loans it should not have had to repay). But while repaying foreign debt under conditions of crisis is one of the central tasks that the bank and IMF paymasters have taken on since the early 1980s, there is also a crucial ideological role played by the two in continually reinventing neoliberalism, which in the case of MENA in 2011, requires a conflation of political and economic 'reform'.

The bank's 27 May document, 'Towards a new partnership for inclusive growth in the Middle East and North Africa (MENA) region' is exemplary, if only to illustrate either amnesia or chutzpah:

Economic reforms had started in several countries during the last decade. But in the context of declining state legitimacy, low levels of political participation, nepotism, perceptions of

261

corruption and predation, and little accountability, reforms were too partial to take real hold or to transform sclerotic intuitions. Often they were perceived to increase inequality, and benefit the politically connected elite. (World Bank 2011b: 4)

A more honest rewriting of this paragraph might be:

Economic austerity was imposed by the IMF and bank starting in several countries during the 1970s, and was amplified subsequently across the lower-income MENA countries. Political corollaries to Washington's support for the ruling regimes included their declining state legitimacy, low levels of political participation, nepotism, perceptions of corruption and predation, and little accountability. Austerity was implemented by the societies' sclerotic ruling intuitions, so as to increase inequality and benefit the politically connected elite.

Because the politically connected elite will take extreme measures to remain in power, as the Gaddafi family showed in the weeks after February 2011, the bank probably knows that socio-political and environmental problems in the Arab world will intensify and that citizens' movements will oppose the kinds of policies that drove Mohammed Bouazizi to suicide. Nevertheless, the bank's main objective appears to be making Arab economies more vulnerable:

The wave of self-confidence and self-assertion now sweeping the Arab world, and the refutation of any notion of Arab 'exceptionalism', could lay the foundation for an even deeper partnership between the Arab countries, the World Bank Group, and other partners in the Arab World Initiative. The time could be ripe for Arab regional cooperation, and for the more vigorous pursuit of inclusive globalisation. (World Bank 2011b: 24)

In general the agenda of Washington in both political and economic terms is to use state instability created by popular protest to lock in more extreme forms of neoliberalism via globalisation. The IMF, for example, argues that:

close to 60 per cent of MENA exports are directed to Europe – reflecting proximity and long-standing linkages – which implies that MENA has not inserted itself into the global economy and has not been benefiting from the high growth rates achieved in other emerging markets. (IMF 2011a: 3)

If the new governments pursue this path, then very short-term increases in state spending to quell unrest will be permitted by the IMF, it appears:

> With mostly limited fiscal space, MENA oil importers confront the immediate challenge of preserving macroeconomic stability while building social cohesion. Additional spending in the short term is understandable and necessary to ensure social cohesion. Nonetheless, oil importers cannot afford to strain public finances, in order not to derail – over the medium term – the pursuit of the new inclusive growth agenda. To this end, they will need to partially offset some of the additional cost of higher subsidies and other support measures through cuts elsewhere. In the same vein, they will also need to avoid introducing measures that would raise spending on a permanent basis. To preserve market confidence and prevent further escalation of the cost of funding, governments should detail credible plans for unwinding emergency measures. (IMF 2011a: 7)

Those plans, according to the IMF, should include:

- Revisiting the role of the public sector and providing space for a vibrant private sector
- Improving further the business climate
- Developing financial systems with a wider reach
- Fostering trade integration
- Strengthening the functioning of labour markets. (IMF 2011a: 8)

Interestingly, the IMF offered one brief mea culpa in its May 2011 document:

> The success of such a partnership will require the international community to draw lessons from the shortcomings of previous approaches that generated weak country ownership and resulted in scepticism amongst many stakeholders in the region. For the IMF, this means addressing important socio-economic dimensions that thus far have not been sufficiently

brought to the fore in its policy advice, and to work with other stakeholders to build broader support within the region. (IMF 2011a: 15)

Yet the authors of the report appeared to have added this as a formality, because the 'socio-economic dimensions' will worsen if neoliberal policies are implemented, and, moreover, there was no mea culpa on the IMF's support to tyrants.

As a result of these multiple attacks by the IMF and World Bank on North Africa and the entire region, democracy activists will fruitfully compare notes and unite to forcefully challenge Washington's political and economic agenda. After all, the World Bank regional economic survey of May 2011 linked resistance quite explicitly to neoliberal policy (albeit with 'unmet targets' as a discursive substitute for dictatorial behaviour):

In MENA, prolonged instability, resulting from unmet political and social targets or spillover effects and lack of clarity about the future political transition, is the most serious risk to the short-term regional economic outlook. Prolonged tensions would amplify the negative impact on capital inflows and domestic financial exchanges, tourism receipts and remittances, and in turn on investment, output, and employment. Construction, manufacturing, tourism and financial institutions are most likely to suffer losses with further deterioration of the situation. A renewed loss of investors' confidence would translate into increased cost of capital further dampening growth prospects. Prolonged unrest would also threaten MENA's social policy design and fiscal health, as revenues would remain weak and expenditure would be elevated, especially if commodity prices remain strong. (World Bank 2011b: 27)

Prolonged unrest

The prospect for a new round of political protest centred on economic justice is therefore worth taking seriously. Such protest is especially important given that the world's mainstream media has apparently bought into an increased role for the IMF and World Bank in 'supporting' the Arab spring. When Strauss-Kahn began reacting to the crisis in January, Philip Lim's was a fairly typical, uncritical report:

As Egyptian protesters gathered in their thousands demanding the departure of President Hosni Mubarak, Strauss-Kahn said: 'The IMF is ready to help in defining the kind of economic policy that could be put in place.' In a speech in Singapore, he said rampant unemployment and a growing income gap was a 'strong undercurrent of the political turmoil in Tunisia and of rising social strains in other countries'. Nationwide demonstrations last month led to the ouster of Tunisian strongman Zine El Abidine Ben Ali, and massive street protests are raging in Egypt seeking an end to Mubarak's more than 30-year rule. 'As tensions between countries increase, we could see rising protectionism – of trade and of finance,' Strauss-Kahn said. 'And as tensions within countries increase, we could see rising social and political instability within nations – even war.' (Lim 2011)

The Western media exhibits a relatively low awareness of the 'social and political instability' threat from neoliberalism. Austin Mackell's *Guardian* report on May 25 was one of the few to express concern about new IMF loans offered to Egypt and Tunisia:

Given the IMF's history, we should expect these to have devastating consequences on the Egyptian and Tunisian people. You wouldn't guess it though, from the scant and largely fawning coverage the negotiations have so far received.

The pattern is to depict the IMF like a rich uncle, showing up to save the day for some wayward child. This Dickensian scene is completed with the IMF adding the sage words that this time it hopes to see growth on the 'streets' not just the 'spreadsheets'. It is almost as if the problem had been caused by these regimes failing to follow the IMF's teachings...

Beginning in the 1990s, IMF-led structural adjustment programmes saw the privatisation of the bulk of the Egyptian textile industry and the slashing of its workforce from half a million to a quarter-million. What is more, the workers who were left faced – like the rest of Egypt – stagnant wages as the price of living rocketed. Though you would not know it from Western coverage, the long and gallant struggle of these workers, particularly the strike of the textile workers of Mahalla el-Kubra, is credited by many Egyptian activists as a crucial step on the Egyptian people's path towards revolution...

During this transition period, forces like the IMF will seek to lock in and enlarge the neoliberal project before there is an accountable government to complain about it...

These new loans from the IMF threaten to bind the newly democratic Egypt and Tunisia in much the same way. Once more, local elites could collaborate with the institutions at the helm of global capitalism to screw the broader population. If this occurs, these revolutions will be robbed of much of their meaning, and a terrible blow will be dealt to the broader Arab spring. (Mackell 2011)

Predictably, the *New York Times* reported on the Bretton Woods institutions' capacity to 'stabilise' MENA countries just after the G8 meeting:

At a series of working sessions that lasted until the early morning hours Friday, representatives of the Group of 8 expressed concern that the democracy movement in the Arab world could be 'hijacked' by Islamic radicals if the West did not help stabilize the economies of the two countries that touched off the Arab spring...

How much aid the Western powers would ultimately provide, and how effective any aid would be during volatile political transitions in the two countries, remained uncertain. The group's official communiqué promised $20 billion, which would be a major infusion of funds...

Democracy, the leaders said, could be rooted only in economic reforms that created open markets, equal opportunities and jobs to lower staggeringly high unemployment rates, especially among restless youths...

Officials cautioned that the projected $20 billion in aid from international financial institutions would come in phases and be contingent on democratic and economic reforms. The pledge, an aide to President Obama said, was 'not a blank check' but 'an envelope that could be achieved in the context of suitable reform efforts'. (Alderman 2011)

To be fair, the *New York Times* reporter (Alderman 2011) did add, 'There is a fear, shared by both the American administration and democracy activists, that plunking down large dollar pledges upfront would risk funneling money into the hands of institutions, including the Egyptian military, which could misuse or simply siphon it off.' But as for the actual policies suggested by Washington, there is no dispute, as noted above in the *New York Times* report on IMF favouritism to dictators.

To expect or demand more from the IMF and World Bank is to miss the point: they are still instruments of global corporate policy, and indeed also of Western geopolitical interests. As Iranian revolutionary Mohammad-Reza Shalgooni put it in his series on revolution and counter-revolution in the Arab world, in Egypt and Tunisia:

> the military establishment has generally proceeded in harmony with general U.S. policy vis-à-vis the Arab Revolution, and their main objective has been to prevent (or abort when possible) any radicalisation of the revolution … It was the U.S. that decided to remove the military in both these countries from an all-out confrontation with the millions-strong masses of people, and to keep them intact (as institutions), to be preserved as levers for controlling the situation in the subsequent stages of the revolution … while pressing these dictatorships behind closed curtains to avoid blood baths on a mass scale, in the final analysis, they decided that in order to preserve the ruling regimes, they would sacrifice the dictators themselves. (Shalgooni 2011)

What forces might overthrow the ruling regimes, with or without dictators, in the event North African neoliberalism gathers pace? There is certainly awareness amongst the current army elites that the earlier round of neoliberal 'reform' was a factor in the recent revolts, according to Emad Mekay of *InterPress Service*:

> Anger at Egypt's privatisation programme, involving the transfer of billions of dollars worth of public assets to private hands, aided the Egyptian revolution that elbowed the Western-backed Hosni Mubarak out of office in February, a top army general said. Major General Mohammed al-Assar, a leading member of the Supreme Council of the Armed Forces, a group of top military generals who are running the country until a civilian leadership is elected, said the military brass were deeply opposed to the privatisation programme. That in turn eased their decision to side with the Egyptian public against the 30-year autocratic rule of Mubarak. Al-Assar told state television on Wednesday that the army has been against the 'plans to

sell Egypt' and viewed them as a threat to social peace. He said that Field Marshal Mohammed Tantawi, the council's president and minister of defence, had repeatedly raised objections to the privatisation programme, as shown in the minutes of several cabinet meetings he attended. His opinion was often over-ruled by Mubarak and other top officials who had favoured following economic prescriptions from Western countries.

Many of those officials stood to gain from the sale of public enterprises. Prodded by the Washington-based trio – the United States Agency for International Development (USAID), World Bank, and International Monetary Fund (IMF) – Egypt under Mubarak adopted an aggressive programme to sell public companies to both local and foreign investors since the early 1990s. The programme peaked between 1996 and 1999 with the sale of at least some 30 profitable public companies a year. (Mekay 2011)

Even if this sort of analysis is not widely considered by most Western commentators as logical within the context of North Africa's democratic revolution, the need for genuine (not IMF) social justice is often remarked upon by the region's activists and writers. For example, Joseph Massad warns:

Moves to limit economic protests and labour strikes are ongoing in Egypt and Tunisia. Once elections are held to bring about a new class of servants of the new order, we will hear that all economic demands should be considered 'counter-revolutionary' and should be prosecuted for attempting to 'weaken' if not 'destroy' the new 'democracy'. If, as is becoming more apparent, the US strikes alliances with local Islamist parties, we might even hear that economic protests and opposition to neoliberal imperial economic policies are 'against Islam'. The US-imposed 'democracy' to come, assuming even a semblance of it will be instituted, is precisely engineered to keep the poor down and to delegitimise all their economic demands. (Massad 2011)

For Samir Amin, the opportunity to contest Washington's agenda represents continuity in potential, thanks to the revolution's profound socio-economic roots:

The youth and the radical left sought in common three objectives: restoration of democracy (ending the police/military regime), the undertaking of a new economic and social policy favourable to the popular masses (breaking with the submission to demands of globalised liberalism), and an independent foreign policy (breaking with the submission to the requirements of US hegemony and the extension of US military control over the whole planet). The democratic revolution for which they call is a democratic social and anti-imperialist revolution. Although the youth movement is diversified in its social composition and in its political and ideological expressions, it places itself as a whole on the left. Its strong and spontaneous expressions of sympathy with the radical left testify to that. (Chapter 31 of this book: 278)

One webzine supporting the revolution, *GlobalFairNet* (2011), reported of the proposed $3 billion IMF loan that 'Egyptians were largely sceptical, with the deal receiving negative feedback from online citizens and activists.' And, indeed, as one small reflection of the potential for wider conscientisation, a Facebook group was started in early June, 'dedicated to resisting attempts to highjack our new republic through imposing monetary, economic, or political regulations on Egypt via the IMF or any other lending institution'. Those attempts were rebuffed, according to *Christian Science Monitor* journalist Dan Murphy:

Among the leftist activists who helped organise and drive the Egyptian revolution, there were howls of fury over the IMF loan when it was first agreed (and over ongoing contacts between Egypt and the World Bank). These folks view both organisations as tools of economic imperialism, and any ties with the institutions as threats to Egyptian sovereignty.

It's unclear how popular the left will be at the ballot box. But the growing importance of labor unions in Egypt in recent years, the fact that some of the most effective protest organisers around Tahrir Square during the revolution were from the left, and the general drift of Egyptian society indicates they'll have a much bigger voice then they've had in decades.

If I had to guess, I would say Egypt's ruling military junta decided it wasn't worth it to have a confrontation over the IMF loan. (Murphy 2011)

By late July, Radwan – sacked from his job due to youth pressure two weeks earlier – explaining Egypt's rejection of the loan (which he had himself negotiated) in explicitly political terms: 'People are still affected by the past, when the IMF used to impose harsh conditions … The military council said it doesn't want to burden the democratically elected government with debt.' Explained protest leader Wael Khalil, 'For years we have been told that this is the IMF doctrine: cut budget deficits, reduce spending and liberalise markets' (Shahine and Rastello 2011).

This is a hopeful sign of potential power. Nevertheless until now, moving from social media to a more thorough-going social revolution has been a step too steep for Africans since the era of structural adjustment, notwithstanding the leaps taken by so many Latin Americans in the last decade. Perhaps 2011 will be seen as the year that step became possible, as the popular uprisings in Tunisia and Egypt were soon followed by major socio-economic protests in various other African countries, including Senegal, Uganda, Swaziland, Kenya, Botswana and South Africa. In Zimbabwe, 45 arrests occurred in February when Robert Mugabe's police force broke up a meeting (International Socialist Organisation of Zimbabwe) in which films from Tunisia and Egypt were shown, with six leaders held for a month and tortured. This is the kind of tribute to North African democratic revolutions which reminds of the inspiration of a marvellous example.

http://pambazuka.org/en/category/features/73932

This chapter also appeared in the *Review of African Political Economy*, 130, September 2011

References

Ahmed, M. (2010) 'Middle East and North Africa: protecting social cohesion and economic stability', *International Economic Bulletin of the Carnegie Endowment for International Peace*, Washington, http://www.imf.org/external/np/vc/2011/051911.htm, accessed 1 September 2011

Alderman, L. (2011) 'Aid pledge by Group of 8 seeks to bolster Arab democracy', *New York Times*, 27 May

Amin, S. (2012) '2011: an Arab springtime?', in Manji, F. and Ekine, S. (eds) *African Awakening: The Emerging Revolutions*, Oxford, Pambazuka Press

Briancon, P. and Foley, J. (2011) 'IMF reviews praised Libya, Egypt and other nations', *New York Times*, 23 February

Cole, J. (2011) 'New Wikileaks: US knew Tunisian government rotten corrupt, supported Ben Ali anyway', Informed Comment blog,

16 January, http://www.juancole.com/2011/01/new-wikileaks-us-knew-tunisian-gov-rotten-corrupt-supported-ben-ali-anyway.html, accessed 1 September 2011

Easton, S. (2001) 'The size of the underground economy: a review of the estimates', unpublished paper, Simon Fraser University, http://www.sfu.ca/~easton/Econ448W/TheUndergroundEconomy.pdf, accessed 1 September 2011

GlobalFairNet (2011) 'IMF deal sparks controversy', 6 June, http://www.globalfair.net/en/content/egypt-imf-deal-sparks-controversy

Hanieh, A. (2012) 'International finance institutions and Egypt', in Manji, F. and Ekine, S. (eds) *African Awakening: The Emerging Revolutions*, Oxford, Pambazuka Press

IMF Survey (2011) 'IMF outlines $3 billion support plan for Egypt', 5 June, http://www.imf.org/external/pubs/ft/survey/so/2011/NEW060511A.htm, accessed 1 September 2011

International Monetary Fund (2010a) 'Tunisia: 2010 Article IV consultation', IMF Country Report No. 10/282, Washington, September

International Monetary Fund (2010b) 'Arab Republic of Egypt: 2010 Article IV consultation', IMF Country Report No. 10/94, Washington, April

International Monetary Fund (2010c) 'The Socialist People's Libyan Arab Jamahiriya – 2010 Article IV consultation, preliminary conclusions of the mission', Washington, 28 October

International Monetary Fund (2011a) 'Economic transformation in MENA: delivering on the promise of shared prosperity', paper presented to the G8 summit, Deauville, France, 27 May

International Monetary Fund (2011b) 'The Socialist People's Libyan Arab Jamahiriya – Article IV consultation', Public Information Notice No. 11/23, Washington, 15 February

International Monetary Fund (2011c) Press conference, Washington DC, 6 April

Lim, P. (2011) 'Tackle inequality or risk war', *Agence France Presse*, 1 February

Mackell, A. (2011) 'The IMF versus the Arab spring', *Guardian*, 25 May

Massad, J. (2011) 'Under the cover of democracy', Al Jazeera, 8 June, http://english.aljazeera.net/indepth/opinion/2011/06/2011689456174295.html, accessed 1 September 2011

Mekay, E. (2011) 'Privatisation aided Egypt revolt, army says', *InterPress Service*, 8 April, http://www.ips.org/africa/2011/04/privatisation-aided-egypt-revolt-army-says/, accessed 1 September 2011

Murphy, D. (2011) '$3 billion loan with almost zero interest? No thanks says Egypt', *Christian Science Monitor*, 26 June, http://www.csmonitor.com/World/Backchannels/2011/0628/3-billion-loan-with-almost-zero-interest-No-thanks-says-Egypt, accessed 1 September 2011

Phillips, L. (2011) 'EU socialists, conservatives, play "dictator badminton" over Tunisia', *EUObserver*, 18 January, http://euobserver.com/9/31663, accessed 1 September 2011

Sahay, R. (2011) 'Statement by Deputy Director of the Middle East and Central Asia Department and head of the IMF mission in Egypt',

International Monetary Fund Press Release No. 11/211, Washington, 2 June, http://www.imf.org/external/np/sec/pr/2011/pr11211.htm, accessed 1 September 2011

Shahine, A. and Rastello, S. (2011) 'IMF "harsh" legacy may block Mideast loans after Egypt's $3 billion U-turn', *Bloomberg News*, 2 August, http://www.bloomberg.com/news/2011-08-01/imf-s-harsh-legacy-blocks-middle-east-loans-after-egypt-u-turn.html, accessed 1 September 2011

Shalgooni, M.R. (2011) 'US role in the Arab counter-revolution', *Raah-e Kargar*, 22 May, http://rahekargar.net/

Toujas-Bernate, J. and Bhattacharya, R. (2010) 'Tunisia weathers crisis well, but unemployment persists', Washington, IMF Middle East and Central Asia Department, 10 September, http://www.imf.org/external/pubs/ft/survey/so/2010/car091010a.htm, accessed 1 September 2011

World Bank (2009) 'Africa likely to be worst hit by the financial crisis', press conference, Washington DC, 23 April, http://web.worldbank.org/WBSITE/EXTERNAL/COUNTRIES/AFRICAEXT/SOMALIAEXTN/0,,contentM DK:22154832~menuPK:50003484~pagePK:2865066~piPK:2865079~theSit ePK:367665,00.html, accessed 1 September 2011

World Bank (2011a) 'Middle East and North Africa region: regional economic update – MENA facing challenges and opportunities', Washington, 27 May

World Bank (2011b) 'Towards a new partnership for inclusive growth in the Middle East and North Africa Region', Washington, 27 May

31

2011: an Arab springtime?

Samir Amin

9 June 2011

The year 2011 began with a series of shattering, wrathful explosions from the Arab peoples. Is this springtime the inception of a second 'awakening of the Arab world?' Or will these revolts bog down and finally prove abortive – as was the case with the first episode of that awakening, which was evoked in my book *L'Eveil du Sud* (2008)? If the first hypothesis is confirmed, the forward movement of the Arab world will necessarily become part of the movement to go beyond imperialist capitalism on the world scale. Failure would keep the Arab world in its current status as a submissive periphery, prohibiting its elevation to the rank of an active participant in shaping the world.

It is always dangerous to generalise about the 'Arab world', thus ignoring the diversity of objective conditions characterising each country of that world. So I will concentrate the following reflections on Egypt, which is easily recognised as playing, and having always played, a major role in the general evolution of its region.

Egypt was the first country in the periphery of globalised capitalism that tried to 'emerge'. Even at the start of the 19th century, well before Japan and China, the Viceroy Mohammed Ali had conceived and undertaken a programme of renovation for Egypt and its near neighbours in the Arab Mashreq.[1] That vigorous experiment took up two-thirds of the 19th century and only belatedly ran out of breath in the 1870s, during the second half of the reign of the Khedive Ismail. The analysis of its failure cannot ignore the violence of the foreign aggression by Great Britain, the foremost power of industrial capitalism during that period. In the naval campaign of 1840, by taking control of the

Khedive's finances during the 1870s and finally by military occupation in 1882, England fiercely pursued its objective: to make sure that a modern Egypt would fail to emerge. Certainly the Egyptian project was subject to the limitations of its time since it manifestly envisaged emergence within and through capitalism, unlike Egypt's second attempt at emergence – which we will discuss further on. That project's own social contradictions, like its underlying political, cultural and ideological presuppositions, undoubtedly had their share of responsibility for its failure. The fact remains that without imperialist aggression those contradictions would probably have been overcome, as they were in Japan.

Beaten, emergent Egypt was forced to undergo nearly 40 years (1880–1920) as a servile periphery, whose institutions were refashioned in service to that period's model of capitalist/imperialist accumulation. That imposed retrogression struck, over and beyond its productive system, the country's political and social institutions. It operated systematically to reinforce all the reactionary and medievalist cultural and ideological conceptions that were useful for keeping the country in its subordinate position.

The Egyptian nation – its people, its elites – never accepted that position. This stubborn refusal in turn gave rise to a second wave of rising movements which unfolded during the next half-century (1919–67). Indeed, I see that period as a continuous series of struggles and major forward movements. It had a triple objective: democracy, national independence, social progress. Three objectives – however limited and sometimes confused were their formulations – inseparable one from the other. An inseparability identical to the expression of the effects of modern Egypt's integration into the globalised capitalist/imperialist system of that period. In this reading, the chapter (1955–67) of Nasserist systematisation is nothing but the final chapter of that long series of advancing struggles, which began with the revolution of 1919–20.

The first moment of that half-century of rising emancipation struggles in Egypt had put its emphasis – with the formation of the Wafd in 1919 – on political modernisation through adoption (in 1923) of a bourgeois form of constitutional democracy (limited monarchy) and on the reconquest of independence. The form of democracy envisaged allowed progressive secularisation – if not secularism in the radical sense of that term – whose symbol was the flag linking cross and crescent (a flag that reappeared in the demonstrations of January and February 2011). 'Normal' elections then allowed, without the least problem, not merely for Copts to be elected by Muslim majorities but for those very Copts to hold high positions in the state.

The British put their full power, supported actively by the reactionary bloc comprising the monarchy, the great landlords and the rich peasants, into undoing the democratic progress made by Egypt under Wafdist leadership. In the 1930s the dictatorship of Sedki Pasha, abolishing the democratic 1923 constitution, clashed with the student movement then spearheading the democratic anti-imperialist struggles. It was not by chance that, to counter this threat, the British embassy and the royal palace actively supported the formation in 1927 of the Muslim Brotherhood, inspired by Islamist thought in its most backward Salafist version of Wahhabism as formulated by Rachid Reda – the most reactionary version, anti-democratic and against social progress, of the newborn political Islam.

The conquest of Ethiopia undertaken by Mussolini, with world war looming, forced London to make some concessions to the democratic forces. In 1936 the Wafd, having learnt its lesson, was allowed to return to power and a new Anglo-Egyptian treaty was signed. The Second World War necessarily constituted a sort of parenthesis. But a rising tide of struggles had resumed on 21 February 1946 with the formation of the worker–student bloc, reinforced in its radicalisation by the entry on stage of the communists and of the working-class movement. Once again the Egyptian reactionaries, supported by London, responded with violence and to this end mobilised the Muslim Brotherhood behind a second dictatorship by Sedki Pasha – without, however, being able to silence the protest movement. Elections had to be held in 1950 and the Wafd returned to power. Its repudiation of the 1936 treaty and the inception of guerrilla actions in the Suez Canal zone were defeated only by setting fire to Cairo (January 1952), an operation in which the Muslim Brotherhood was deeply involved.

A first *coup d'état* in 1952 by the Free Officers, and above all a second coup in 1954 through which Nasser took control, were taken by some to crown the continual flow of struggles and by others to put it to an end. Rejecting the view of the Egyptian awakening advanced above, Nasserism put forth an ideological discourse that wiped out the whole history of the years from 1919 to 1952 in order to push the start of the Egyptian revolution to July 1952. At that time many among the communists had denounced this discourse and analysed the *coups d'état* of 1952 and 1954 as aimed at putting an end to the radicalisation of the democratic movement. They were not wrong, since Nasserism only took the shape of an anti-imperialist project after the Bandung conference of April 1955. Nasserism then contributed all it had to give: a resolutely anti-imperialist international posture (in association with the pan-Arab and pan-African movements) and some progressive (but not socialist) social reforms. The whole thing was done from above, not only without democracy (the popular masses being denied any right to organise by and for themselves) but even by abolishing any form of political life. This was an invitation to political Islam to fill the vacuum thus created. In only ten short years (1955–65) the Nasserist project used up its progressive potential. Its exhaustion offered imperialism, henceforward led by the United States, the chance to break the movement by mobilising to that end its regional military instrument: Israel. The 1967 defeat marked the end of the tide that had flowed for a half-century. Its reflux was initiated by Nasser himself, who chose the path of concessions to the right (the *infitah* or opening, an opening to capitalist globalisation, of course) rather than the radicalisation called for by, among others, the student movement (which held the stage briefly in 1970, shortly before and then after the death of Nasser). His successor, Sadat, intensified and extended the rightward turn and integrated the Muslim Brotherhood into his new autocratic system. Mubarak continued along the same path.

The following period of retreat lasted, in its turn, almost another half-century. Egypt, submissive to the demands of globalised liberalism and to US strategy, simply ceased to exist as an active factor in regional or global politics. In its region the major US allies – Saudi Arabia and Israel – occupied the foreground. Israel was then able to pursue the course of expanding its colonisation of occupied Palestine with the tacit complicity of Egypt and the Gulf countries.

Under Nasser Egypt had set up an economic and social system that, though subject to criticism, was at least coherent. Nasser wagered on industrialisation as the way out of the colonial inter-national specialisation which was confining the country in the role of cotton exporter. His system maintained a division of incomes that favoured the expanding middle classes without impoverish-ing the popular masses. Sadat and Mubarak dismantled the Egyp-tian productive system, putting in its place a completely incoher-ent system based exclusively on the profitability of firms, most of which were mere subcontractors for the imperialist monopolies. Supposed high rates of economic growth, much praised for 30 years by the World Bank, were completely meaningless. Egyptian growth was extremely vulnerable. Moreover, such growth was accompanied by an incredible rise in inequality and by unem-ployment afflicting the majority of the country's youth. This was an explosive situation. It exploded.

The apparent stability of the regime, boasted of by successive US officials such as Hillary Clinton, was based on a monstrous police apparatus counting 1,200,000 men (the army numbering a mere 500,000), free to carry out daily acts of criminal abuse. The imperialist powers claimed that this regime was protecting Egypt from the threat of Islamism. This was nothing but a clumsy lie. In reality the regime had perfectly integrated reactionary politi-cal Islam (on the Wahhabite model of the Gulf) into its power structure by giving it control of education, the courts and the major media (especially television). The sole permitted public speech was that of the Salafist mosques, allowing the Islam-ists, to boot, to pretend to make up the opposition. The cynical duplicity of the US establishment's speeches (Obama no less than Bush) was perfectly adapted to its aims. The de facto support for political Islam destroyed the capacity of Egyptian society to confront the challenges of the modern world (bringing about a catastrophic decline in education and research), while by occa-sionally denouncing its abuses (such as assassinations of Copts) Washington could legitimise its military interventions as actions in its self-styled war against terrorism.

The regime could still appear tolerable as long as it had the safety valve provided by mass emigration of poor and middle-class workers to the oil-producing countries. The exhaustion of that system (Asian immigrants replacing those from Arabic countries) brought with it the rebirth of opposition movements.

The workers' strikes in 2007 (the strongest strikes on the African continent in the past 50 years), the stubborn resistance of small farmers threatened with expropriation by agrarian capital, and the formation of democratic protest groups among the middle classes (such as the Kefaya and April 6 movements) foretold the inevitable explosion – expected by Egyptians but startling to foreign observers. And thus began a new phase in the tide of emancipation struggles, whose directions and opportunities for development we are now called on to analyse.

The components of the democratic movement

The 'Egyptian revolution' now underway shows that it is possible to foresee an end to the neoliberal system, shaken in all its political, economic and social dimensions. This gigantic movement of the Egyptian people links three active components: youth repoliticised by their own will in modern forms that they themselves have invented; the forces of the radical left; and the forces of the democratic middle classes.

The youth (about one million activists) spearheaded the movement. They were immediately joined by the radical left and the democratic middle classes. The Muslim Brotherhood, whose leaders had called for a boycott of the demonstrations during their first four days (sure, as they were, that the demonstrators would be routed by the repressive apparatus), only accepted the movement belatedly once its appeal, heard by the entire Egyptian people, was producing gigantic mobilisations of 15 million demonstrators.

The youth and the radical left sought in common three objectives: restoration of democracy (ending the police/military regime), the undertaking of a new economic and social policy favourable to the popular masses (breaking with the submission to demands of globalised liberalism), and an independent foreign policy (breaking with the submission to the requirements of US hegemony and the extension of US military control over the whole planet). The democratic revolution for which they call is a democratic social and anti-imperialist revolution.

Although the youth movement is diversified in its social composition and in its political and ideological expressions, it places itself as a whole on the left. Its strong and spontaneous expressions of sympathy with the radical left testify to that.

The middle classes as a whole rally around only the democratic objective, without necessarily objecting thoroughly to the market (such as it is) or to Egypt's international alignment. Not to be neglected is the role of a group of bloggers who take part, consciously or not, in a veritable conspiracy organised by the CIA. Its animators are usually young people from the wealthy classes, extremely Americanised, who nevertheless present themselves as opponents of the established dictatorships. The theme of democracy, in the version required for its manipulation by Washington, is uppermost in their discourse on the net. That fact makes them active participants in the chain of counter-revolutions, orchestrated by Washington, disguised as democratic revolutions on the model of the East European colour revolutions. But it would be wrong to think that this conspiracy is behind the popular revolts. What the CIA is seeking is to reverse the direction of the movement, to distance its activists from their aim of progressive social transformation and to shunt them onto different tracks. The scheme will have a good chance of succeeding if the movement fails in bringing together its diverse components, identifying common strategic objectives and inventing effective forms of organisation and action. Examples of such failure are well known – look at Indonesia and the Philippines. It is worthy of note that those bloggers – writing in English rather than Arabic(!) – setting out to defend American-style democracy in Egypt, often present arguments serving to legitimise the Muslim Brotherhood.

The call for demonstrations enunciated by the three active components of the movement was quickly heeded by the whole Egyptian people. Repression, extremely violent during the first days (more than a thousand deaths), did not discourage those youths and their allies (who at no time, unlike in some other places, called on the Western powers for any help). Their courage was decisive in drawing 15 million Egyptians from all the districts of big and small cities, and even villages, into demonstrations of protest lasting days (and sometimes nights) on end. Their overwhelming political victory had as its effect that fear switched sides. Obama and Hillary Clinton discovered that they had to dump Mubarak, whom they had hitherto supported, while the army leaders ended their silence and refused to take over the task of repression – thus protecting their image – and wound up deposing Mubarak and several of his more important henchmen.

The generalisation of the movement among the whole Egyptian people represents a positive challenge in itself. For this people, like any other, are far from making up a homogeneous bloc. Some of its major components are without any doubt a source of strength from the perspective of radicalisation. The 5-million-strong working class's entry into the battle could be decisive. The combative workers, through numerous strikes, have advanced further in constructing the organisations they began in 2007. There are already more than 50 independent unions. The stubborn resistance of small farmers against the expropriations permitted by abolition of the agrarian reform laws (the Muslim Brotherhood cast its votes in parliament in favour of that vicious legislation on the pretext that private property was sacred to Islam and that the agrarian reform had been inspired by the devil, a communist!) is another radicalising factor for the movement. What is more, a vast mass of 'the poor' took active part in the demonstrations of February 2011 and often participate in neighbourhood popular committees in defence of the revolution. The beards, the veils, the dress-styles of these poor folk might give the impression that in its depths Egyptian society is Islamic, even that it is mobilised by the Muslim Brotherhood. In reality, they erupted onto the stage and the leaders of that organisation had no choice but to go along. A race is thus underway: who – the brotherhood and its (Salafist) Islamist associates or the democratic alliance – will succeed in forming effective alliances with the still-confused masses and even (a term I reject) 'getting them under discipline'?

Conspicuous progress is happening in Egypt in constructing the united front of workers and democratic forces. In April 2011 five socialist-oriented parties (the Egyptian Socialist Party, the Popular Democratic Alliance – made up of a majority of the membership of the former loyal-left Tagammu party – the Democratic Labour Party, the Trotskyist Socialist Revolutionary Party and the Egyptian Communist Party – which had been a component of Tagammu) established an Alliance of Socialist Forces through which they committed themselves to carrying out their struggles in common. In parallel, a national council (Maglis Watany) was established by all the active political and social forces of the movement (the socialist-oriented parties, the diverse democratic parties, the independent unions, the peasant organisations, the networks of young people, numerous social associations). The council has about 150 members, the Muslim Brotherhood and the right-wing parties refusing to participate and thus reaffirming their well-known opposition to continuation of the revolutionary movement.

Confronting the democratic movement: the reactionary bloc

Just as in past periods of rising struggle, the democratic social and anti-imperialist movement in Egypt is up against a powerful reactionary bloc. This bloc can perhaps be identified in terms of its social composition (its component classes, of course), but it is just as important to define it in terms of its means of political intervention and the ideological discourse serving its politics.

In social terms, the reactionary bloc is led by the Egyptian bourgeoisie taken as a whole. The forms of dependent accumulation operative over the past 40 years brought about the rise of a rich bourgeoisie, the sole beneficiary of the scandalous inequality accompanying that globalised liberal model. They are some tens of thousands – not of innovating entrepreneurs as the World Bank likes to call them but of millionaires and billionaires, all owing their fortunes to collusion with the political apparatus (corruption being an organic part of their system). This is a comprador bourgeoisie (in the political language current in Egypt, the people term them corrupt parasites). They make up the active support for Egypt's placement in contemporary imperialist globalisation as an unconditional ally of the United States. Within its ranks this bourgeoisie counts numerous military and police generals, civilians with connections to the state and to the dominant National Democratic Party created by Sadat and Mubarak, and of religious personalities – the whole leadership of the Muslim Brotherhood and the leading sheikhs of the Al-Azhar University are all billionaires. Certainly, there still exists a bourgeoisie of active small-and-medium entrepreneurs. But they are the victims of the racketeering system put in place by the comprador bourgeoisie, usually reduced to the status of subordinate subcontractors for the local monopolists, themselves mere transmission belts for the foreign monopolies. In the construction industry this system is the general rule: the large organisations snap up the state contracts and then subcontract the work to the small ones. That authentically entrepreneurial bourgeoisie is in sympathy with the democratic movement.

The rural side of the reactionary bloc has no less importance. It is made up of rich peasants who were the main beneficiaries of Nasser's agrarian reform, replacing the former class of wealthy landlords. The agricultural cooperatives set up by the Nasser regime included both rich and poor peasants and so they mainly worked for the benefit of the rich. But the regime also had measures to limit possible abuse of the poor peasants. Once those measures had been abandoned, by Sadat and Mubarak on the advice of the World Bank, the rural rich went to work to hasten the elimination of the poor peasants. In modern Egypt the rural rich have always constituted a reactionary class, now more so than ever. They are likewise the main sponsors of conservative Islam in the countryside and, through their close (often family) relationships with the officials of the state and religious apparatuses (in Egypt the Al-Azhar University has a status equivalent to an organised Muslim church), they dominate rural social life. What is more, a large part of the urban middle classes (especially the army and police officers but likewise the technocrats and medical/legal professionals) stem directly from the rural rich.

This reactionary bloc has strong political instruments in its service: the military and police forces, the state institutions, the privileged National Democratic political party (a de facto single party) that was created by Sadat, the religious apparatus (Al Azhar), and the factions of political Islam (the Muslim Brotherhood and the Salafists). The military assistance (amounting to some $1.5 billion annually) extended by the US to the Egyptian army never went toward the country's defensive capacity. On the contrary, its effect was dangerously destructive through the systematic corruption that, with the greatest cynicism, was not merely known and tolerated but actively promoted. That aid allowed the highest ranks to take over for themselves some important parts of the Egyptian comprador economy, to the point that 'Army Incorporated' (Sharika al geish) became a common-place term. The high command, who made themselves responsible for directing the transition, is thus not at all neutral despite its effort to appear so by distancing itself from the acts of repression.

The civilian government, chosen by and obedient to it and made up largely of the less-conspicuous men from the former regime, has taken a series of completely reactionary measures aimed at blocking any radicalisation of the movement. Among those measures are a vicious anti-strike law (on the pretext of economic revival), and a law placing severe restrictions on the formation of political parties, aimed at confining the electoral game to the tendencies of political Islam (especially the Muslim Brotherhood), which are already well organised thanks to their systematic support by the former regime.

Despite all that, the attitude of the army remains, at bottom, unforeseeable. In spite of the corruption of its cadres (the rank and file are conscripts, the officers professionals), nationalist sentiment has still not disappeared entirely. Moreover, the army resents having in practice lost most of its power to the police. In these circumstances, and because the movement has forcefully expressed its will to exclude the army from political leadership of the country, it is very likely that the high command will seek in future to remain behind the scenes rather than present its own candidates in the coming elections.

Though it is clear that the police apparatus has remained intact (their prosecution is not contemplated) like the state apparatus in general (the new rulers all being veteran regime figures), the National Democratic Party vanished in the tempest and its legal dissolution has been ordered. But we can be certain that the Egyptian bourgeoisie will make sure that its party is reborn under a different label or labels.

Political Islam

The Muslim Brotherhood make up the only political force whose existence was not merely tolerated but actively promoted by the former regime. Sadat and Mubarak turned over to them control of three basic institutions: education, the courts and television. The Muslim Brotherhood have never been and never can be moderate, let alone democratic. Their leader – the *murchid* (Arabic for guide or führer) – is self-appointed and its organisation is based on the principle of disciplined execution of the leader's orders without any sort of discussion. Its top leadership is entirely made up of extremely wealthy men (thanks, in part, to financing by Saudi Arabia – which is to say, by Washington), its secondary leadership of men from the obscurantist layers of the middle classes, its rank and file by lower-class people recruited through the charitable services run by the brotherhood (likewise financed by the Saudis), while its enforcement arm is made up of militias (the *baltaguis*) recruited among the criminal element.

The Muslim Brotherhood are committed to a market-based economic system of complete external dependence. They are in reality a component of the comprador bourgeoisie. They have taken their stand against large strikes by the working class and against the struggles of poor peasants to hold on to their lands. So the Muslim Brotherhood are moderate only in the double sense that they refuse to present any sort of economic and social programme – thus accepting reactionary neoliberal policies without question – and that they are submissive de facto to the enforcement of US control over the region and the world. They are thus useful allies for Washington (and does the US have a better ally than their patron, the Saudis?), which now vouches for their democratic credentials.

Nevertheless, the United States cannot admit that its strategic aim is to establish Islamic regimes in the region because it needs to maintain the pretence that it is afraid of this. In this way it legitimises its permanent war against terrorism, which in reality has quite different objectives: military control over the whole planet in order to guarantee that the US–Europe–Japan triad retains exclusive access to its resources. Another benefit of that duplicity is that it allows it to mobilise the Islamophobic aspects of public opinion. Europe, as is well known, has no strategy of its own in the region and is content from day to day to go along with the decisions of Washington. More than ever, it is necessary to point out clearly the true duplicity in US strategy, which has quite effectively manipulated the opinions of its deceived public. The United States (with Europe going along) fears more than anything a really democratic Egypt, which would certainly turn its back on its alignments with economic liberalism and with the aggressive strategy of NATO and the United States. The US will do all it can to prevent a democratic Egypt, and to that end will give full support (hypocritically disguised) to the false Muslim Brotherhood alternative, which has been shown to be only a minority within the movement of the Egyptian people for real change.

The collusion between the imperialist powers and political Islam is, of course, neither new nor particular to Egypt. The Muslim Brotherhood, from its foundation in 1927 up to the present, has always been a useful ally for imperialism and for the local reactionary bloc. It has always been a fierce enemy of the Egyptian democratic movements. And the multibillionaires currently leading the brotherhood are not destined to go over to the democratic cause. Political Islam throughout the Muslim world is quite assuredly a strategic ally of the United States and its NATO minority partners. Washington armed and financed the Taliban, whom they called freedom fighters, in their war against the national/popular regime (termed communist) in Afghanistan before, during and after the Soviet intervention. When the Taliban shut the girls' schools created by the communists there were democrats and even feminists at hand to claim that it was necessary to respect traditions.

In Egypt the Muslim Brotherhood are now supported by the traditionalist Salafist tendency, who are also generously financed by the Gulf states. The Salafists (fanatical Wahhabites, intolerant of any other interpretation of Islam) make no bones about their extremism, and they are behind a systematic murder campaign against Copts. It is scarcely conceivable that such operations could be carried out without the tacit support (and sometimes even greater complicity) of the state apparatus, especially of the courts, which have mainly been turned over to the Muslim Brotherhood. This strange division of labour allows the Muslim Brotherhood to appear moderate: which is what Washington pretends to believe. Nevertheless, violent clashes among the Islamist religious groups in Egypt are to be expected. That is because Egyptian Islam has historically been mainly Sufist, the Sufi brotherhoods even now grouping 15 million Egyptian Muslims. Sufism represents an open, tolerant, Islam – insisting on the importance of individual beliefs rather than on ritual practices (they say 'there are as many paths to

God as there are individuals'). The state powers have always been deeply suspicious of Sufism although, using both the carrot and the stick, they have been careful not to declare open war against it.

The Wahhabi Islam of the Gulf states is at the opposite pole from Sufism: it is archaic, ritualist, conformist, declared enemy of any interpretation other than repetition of its own chosen texts, enemy of any critical spirit – which is, for it, nothing but the devil at work. Wahhabite Islam considers itself at war with, and seeks to obliterate, Sufism, counting on support for this from the authorities in power. In response, contemporary Sufis are secularistic, even secular; they call for the separation of religion and politics (the state power and the religious authorities of Al Azhar recognised by it). The Sufis are allies of the democratic movement. The introduction of Wahhabite Islam into Egypt was begun by Rachid Reda in the 1920s and carried on by the Muslim Brotherhood after 1927. But it only gained real vigour after the Second World War, when the oil rents of the Gulf states, supported by the United States as allies in its conflict with the wave of popular national liberation struggles in the 1960s, allowed a multiplication of their financial wherewithal.

US strategy: the Pakistan model

The three powers that dominated the Middle East stage during the period of the ebb tide (1967–2011) were the United States, boss of the system, Saudi Arabia and Israel: three very close allies, all sharing the same dread that a democratic Egypt would emerge. Such an Egypt could only be anti-imperialist and welfarist. It would depart from globalised liberalism, would render insignificant the Gulf states and the Saudis, would reawaken popular Arab solidarity and force Israel to recognise a Palestinian state.

Egypt is a cornerstone in the US strategy for worldwide control. The single aim of Washington and its allies Israel and Saudi Arabia is to abort the Egyptian democratic movement, and to that end they want to impose an Islamic regime under the direction of the Muslim Brotherhood – the only way for them to perpetuate the submission of Egypt. The 'democratic speeches' of Obama are there only to deceive a naive public opinion, primarily that of the United States and Europe.

There is much talk of the Turkish example in order to legitimise a government by the Muslim Brotherhood, but that is just
a smokescreen. For the Turkish army is always there behind the
scene, and though scarcely democratic and certainly a faithful ally
of NATO, it remains the guarantor of secularism in Turkey. Washington's project, openly expressed by Hillary Clinton, Obama and
the think tanks at their service, is inspired by the Pakistan model:
an Islamic army behind the scenes and a civilian government run
by one or more elected Islamic parties. Plainly, under that hypothesis, the Islamic Egyptian government would be recompensed for
its submission on the essential points (perpetuation of economic
liberalism and of the self-styled peace treaties permitting Israel
to get on with its policy of territorial expansion) and enabled,
as demagogic compensation, to pursue its projects of Islamisation of the state and of politics and of assassinating Copts. Such
is the beautiful democracy Washington has designed for Egypt.
Obviously, Saudi Arabia supports the accomplishment of that
project with all its (financial) resources. Riyadh knows perfectly
well that its regional hegemony (in the Arab and Muslim worlds)
requires that Egypt be reduced to insignificance, which is to be
done through 'Islamisation of the state and of politics' – in reality,
a Wahhabite Islamisation with all its effects, including anti-Copt
pogroms and the denial of equal rights to women.

Is such a form of Islamisation possible? Perhaps, but at the
price of extreme violence. The battlefield is Article 2 of the overthrown regime's constitution. This article, which stipulates that
'sharia is the origin of law', was a novelty in the political history of
Egypt. Neither the 1923 constitution nor that of Nasser contained
anything of the sort. It was Sadat who put it into his new constitution, with the triple support of Washington ('traditions are to
be respected'), Riyadh ('the Koran is all the constitution needed')
and Tel Aviv ('Israel is a Jewish state').

The project of the Muslim Brotherhood remains the establishment of a theocratic state, as is shown by its attachment to Article
2 of the Sadat/Mubarak constitution. What is more, the organisation's most recent programme further reinforces that medievalist
outlook by proposing to set up a council of ulemas, empowered
to assure that any proposed legislation be in conformity with the
requirements of sharia. Such a religious constitutional council

would be analogous to the one that, in Iran, is supreme over the elected government. It is the regime of a religious, single super-party, all parties standing for secularism becoming illegal. Their members, like non-Muslims (Copts), would thus be excluded from political life. Despite all that, the authorities in Washington and Europe talk as though the recent opportunist and disingenu-ous declaration by the brotherhood that it was giving up its theo-cratic project (its programme staying unchanged) should be taken seriously. Are the CIA experts unable to read Arabic?

The conclusion is inescapable: Washington would see the brotherhood in power, guaranteeing that Egypt remain in its grip and that of liberal globalisation, rather than that power be held by democrats who would be very likely to challenge the subal-tern status of Egypt. The recently created Party of Freedom and Justice, explicitly on the Turkish model, is nothing but an instru-ment of the brotherhood. It offers to admit Copts, which signifies that they have to accept the theocratic Muslim state enshrined in the brotherhood's programme if they want the right to partici-pate in their country's political life. Going on the offensive, the brotherhood is setting up unions and peasant organisations and a rigmarole of diversely named political parties, whose sole objec-tive is to foment division in the now-forming united fronts of workers, peasants and democrats – to the advantage, of course, of the counter-revolutionary bloc.

Will the Egyptian democratic movement be able to strike that article from the forthcoming new constitution? The question can be answered only by going back to an examination of the political, ideological, and cultural debates that have unfolded during the history of modern Egypt.

In fact, we can see that the periods of rising tide were character-ised by a diversity of openly expressed opinions, leaving religion (always present in society) in the background. It was that way during the first two-thirds of the 19th century (from Mohamed Ali to Khedive Ismail). Modernisation themes (in the form of enlightened despotism rather than democracy) held the stage. It was the same from 1920 to 1970: open confrontation of views among bourgeois democrats and communists staying in the fore-ground until the rise of Nasserism. Nasser shut down the debate, replacing it with a populist pan-Arab, though also modernising, discourse. The contradictions of this system opened the way for a return of political Islam. It is to be recognised, contrariwise, that in the ebb-tide phases such diversity of opinion vanished, leaving the space free for a medievalism, presented as Islamic thought, that arrogates to itself a monopoly over government-authorised speech. From 1880 to 1920 the British built that diversion channel in various ways, notably by exiling (mainly to Nubia) all modernist Egyptian thinkers and actors who had been educated since the time of Mohamed Ali. But it is also to be noted that the opposition to British occupation also placed itself within that medievalist consensus. The Nadha (begun by Afghani and continued by Mohamed Abdou) was part of that deviation, linked to the Ottomanist delusion advocated by the new Nationalist Party of Moustapha Kamil and Mohammad Farid. There should be no surprise that toward the end of that epoch this deviation led to the ultra-reactionary writings of Rachid Reda, which were then taken up by Hassan el Banna, the founder of the Muslim Brotherhood.

It was the same again in the ebb-tide years 1970–2010. The official discourse (of Sadat and Mubarak), perfectly Islamist (as proven by their insertion of sharia into the constitution and their yielding essential powers to the Muslim Brotherhood) was equally that of the false opposition, the only one tolerated, which was sermonising in the mosque. It is because of this that Article 2 might seem solidly anchored in general opinion (the 'street' as American pundits like to call it). The devastating effects of the depolarisation systematically enforced during the ebb-tide periods are not to be underestimated. The slope can never be easily re-ascended. But it is not impossible. The current debates in Egypt are centred, explicitly or implicitly, on the supposed cultural (actually, Islamic) dimensions of this challenge. And there are signposts pointing in a positive direction: the movement making free debate unavoidable – only a few weeks sufficed for the brotherhood's slogan 'Islam is the Solution' to disappear from all the demonstrations, leaving only specific demands about concretely transforming society (freedom to express opinions and to form unions, political parties and other social organisations; improved wages and workplace rights; access to landownership, to schools, to health services; rejection of privatisations and calls for nationalisations and). A signal that does not mislead: in April elections to the student organisation, where five years ago (when its discourse was the only permitted form of supposed opposition) the brotherhood's candidates had obtained a crushing 80 per cent majority, their share of the vote fell to 20 per cent.

Yet the other side likewise sees ways to parry the democracy danger. Insignificant changes to the Mubarak constitution (continuing in force), proposed by a committee made up exclusively of Islamists chosen by the army high command and approved in a hurried April referendum (an official 23 per cent negative vote, but a big affirmative vote imposed through electoral fraud and heavy blackmail by the mosques), obviously left Article 2 in place. Presidential and legislative elections under that constitution are scheduled for September/October 2011. The democratic movement contends for a longer democratic transition, which would allow its discourse actually to reach those big layers of the Muslim lower classes still at a loss to understand the events. But as soon as the uprising began, Obama made his choice: a short, orderly (that is to say without any threat to the governing apparatus) transition, and elections that would result in victory for the Islamists. As is well known, elections in Egypt, as elsewhere in the world, are not the best way to establish democracy, but are often the best way to set a limit to democratic progress.

Finally, some words about corruption. Most speech from the transition regime concentrates on denouncing it and threatening prosecution (Mubarak, his wife, and some others are arrested, but what will actually happen remains to be seen). This discourse is certainly well received, especially by the major part of naive public opinion. But they take care not to analyse its deeper causes and to teach that corruption (presented in the moralising style of American speech as individual immorality) is an organic and necessary component in the formation of the bourgeoisie. And not merely in the case of Egypt and of the Southern countries in general, where if a comprador bourgeoisie is to be formed the sole way for that to take place is in association with the state apparatus. I maintain that at the stage of generalised monopoly capitalism, corruption has become a basic organic component in the reproduction of its accumulation model: rent-seeking monopolies require the active complicity of the state. Its ideological discourse (the 'liberal virus') proclaims 'state hands off the economy' while its practice is 'state in service to the monopolies'.

The storm zone

Mao was not wrong when he affirmed that actually existing (which is to say, naturally imperialist) capitalism had nothing to offer to the peoples of the three continents (the periphery made up of Asia, Africa and Latin America – a 'minority' consisting of 85 per cent of world population) and that the South was a 'storm zone', a zone of repeated revolts potentially (but only potentially) pregnant with revolutionary advances toward the socialist transcendence of capitalism.

The Arab spring is enlisted in that reality. The case is one of social revolts potentially pregnant with concrete alternatives that in the long run can register within a socialist perspective. This is why the capitalist system, monopoly capital dominant at the world level, cannot tolerate the development of these movements. It will mobilise all possible means of destabilisation, from economic and financial pressures up to military threats. It will support, according to circumstances, either fascist and fascistic false alternatives or the imposition of military dictatorships. Not a word from Obama's mouth is to be believed. Obama is Bush with a different style of speech. Duplicity is built into the speech of all the leaders of the imperialist triad (the US–Western Europe–Japan).

I do not intend in this chapter to examine in as much detail each of the ongoing movements in the Arab world (Tunisia, Libya, Syria, Yemen and others). The components of the movement differ from one country to the other, just like the forms of their integration into imperialist globalisation and the structures of their established regimes.

The Tunisian revolt sounded the starting gun, and surely it strongly encouraged the Egyptians. Moreover, the Tunisian movement has one definite advantage: the semi-secularism introduced by Bourguiba can certainly not be called into question by Islamists returning from their exile in England. But at the same time the Tunisian movement seems unable to challenge the extraverted development model inherent in liberal capitalist globalisation.

Libya is neither Tunisia nor Egypt. The ruling group (Gaddafi) and the forces fighting it are in no way analogous to their Tunisian and Egyptian counterparts. Gaddafi has never been anything but a buffoon, the emptiness of whose thought was reflected in his notorious *Green Book*. Operating in a still-archaic society, Gaddafi could indulge himself in successive nationalist and socialist speeches with little bearing on reality, and the next day proclaim himself a liberal. He did so to please the West, as though the choice of liberalism would have no social effects. But it had and, as is commonplace, it worsened living conditions for the majority of Libyans. Those conditions then gave rise to the well-known explosion, of which the country's regionalists and political Islamists took immediate advantage. For Libya has never truly existed as a nation. It is a geographical region separating the Arab West from the Arab East (the Maghreb from the Mashreq). The boundary between the two goes right through the middle of Libya. Cyrenaica was historically Greek and Hellenistic, then it became Mashreqian. Tripolitania, for its part, was Roman and became Maghrebian. Because of this, regionalism has always been strong in the country. Nobody knows who the members of the National Transition Council in Benghazi really are. There may be democrats among them, but there are certainly Islamists, some among the worst of the breed, as well as regionalists. The president of the National Transition Council is Mustafa Muhammad Abdeljelil, the judge who condemned the Bulgarian nurses to death, was rewarded by Gaddafi, and named minister of justice from 2007 to February 2011. For that reason the prime minister of Bulgaria, Boikov, refused to recognise the council, but his argument was not followed up by the US and Europe.

From its outset the movement in Libya took the form of an armed revolt fighting the army rather than a wave of civilian demonstrations. And right away that armed revolt called NATO to its aid. Thus a chance for military intervention was offered to the imperialist powers. Their aim is surely neither protecting civilians nor democracy but control over oilfields and acquisition of a major military base in the country. Of course, ever since Gaddafi embraced liberalism the Western oil companies have had control over Libyan oil. But with Gaddafi nobody can be sure of anything. Suppose he were to switch sides tomorrow and start to play ball with the Indians and the Chinese? But there is something else more important. Currently, the United States needs to find a place in Africa for its AFRICOM (the US military command for Africa, an important part of its alignment for military control over the world but which is still based in Stuttgart). With the African Union refusing to accept it, until now no African country has dared to do so. A lackey emplaced in Tripoli (or Benghazi) would surely comply with all the demands of Washington and its NATO lieutenants.

The components of the Syrian revolt have yet to make their programmes known. Undoubtedly, the rightward drift of the Baathist regime, gone over to neoliberalism and singularly passive with regard to the Israeli occupation of the Golan, is behind the popular explosion. But CIA intervention cannot be excluded: there is talk of groups penetrating into Diraa across the neighbouring Jordanian frontier. The mobilisation of the Muslim Brotherhood, which had been behind earlier revolts in Hama and Homs, is perhaps part of Washington's scheme, seeking an eventual end to the Syria/Iran alliance that gives essential support to Hezbollah in Lebanon and Hamas in Gaza.

In Yemen the country was united through the defeat of progressive forces that had governed independent South Yemen. Will the movement mark a return to life of those forces? That uncertainty explains the hesitant stance of Washington and the Gulf states.

In Bahrain the revolt was crushed at birth by massacres and intervention by the Saudi army, without the dominant media (including Al Jazeera) having much to say about it. As always, the double standard.

The Arab revolt, though its most recent expression, is not the only example showing the inherent instability of the storm zone. A first wave of revolutions, if that is what they are to be called, had swept away some dictatorships in Asia (the Philippines, Indonesia) and Africa (Mali) that had been installed by imperialism and the local reactionary blocs. But there the United States and Europe succeeded in aborting the potential of those popular movements, which had sometimes aroused gigantic mobilisations. The United States and Europe seek in the Arab world a repetition of what happened in Mali, Indonesia and the Philippines: to change everything in order that nothing changes. There, after the popular movements had got rid of their dictators, the imperialist powers undertook to preserve their essential interests by setting up governments aligned with their foreign-policy interests and with neoliberalism. It is noteworthy that in the Muslim countries (Mali, Indonesia) they mobilised political Islam to that end.

In contrast, the wave of emancipation movements that swept over South America allowed real advances in three directions: democratisation of state and society; adoption of consistent anti-imperialist positions; and entry onto the path of progressive social reform.

The prevailing media discourse compares the democratic revolts of the third world to those that put an end to East European socialism following the fall of the Berlin Wall. This is nothing but a fraud, pure and simple. Whatever the reasons (and they were understandable) for those revolts, they signed on to the perspective of an annexation of the region by the imperialist powers of Western Europe (primarily to the profit of Germany). In fact, reduced thenceforward to the status of developed capitalist Europe's peripheries, the countries of Eastern Europe are still on the eve of experiencing their own authentic revolts. There are already signs foretelling this, especially in the former Yugoslavia.

Revolts, potentially pregnant with revolutionary advances, are foreseeable nearly everywhere in Asia, Africa and South America, which more than ever remain the storm zone, by that fact refuting all the cloying discourse on 'eternal capitalism' and the stability, the peace, the democratic progress attributed to it. But those revolts, to become revolutionary advances, will have to overcome many obstacles: on the one hand they will have to overcome the weaknesses of the movement, arrive at positive convergence of its components, and formulate and implement effective strategies; on the other they will have to turn back the interventions (including military interventions) of the imperialist triad. Any military intervention of the United States and NATO in the affairs of the Southern countries must be prohibited no matter its pretext, even seemingly benign humanitarian intervention. Imperialism seeks to permit neither democracy nor social progress to those countries. Once it has won the battle, the lackeys whom it sets up to rule will still be enemies of democracy. One can only regret profoundly that the European left, even when it claims to be radical, has lost all understanding of what imperialism really is.

The discourse currently prevailing calls for the implementation of international law authorising, in principle, intervention whenever the fundamental rights of a people are being trampled. But the necessary conditions allowing for movement in that direction are just not there. The international community does not exist. It amounts to the US embassy, followed automatically by those of Europe. No need to enumerate the long list of worse-than-unfortunate interventions (Iraq, for example) with criminal outcomes, nor to cite the double standard common to them all (obviously one thinks of the trampled rights of the Palestinians and the unconditional support of Israel, of the innumerable dicta-torships still being supported in Africa).

Springtime for the people of the South and autumn for capitalism

The springtime of the Arab peoples, like that which the peoples of Latin America have been experiencing for two decades now and which I refer to as the second wave of awakening of the Southern peoples – the first having unfolded in the 20th century until the counteroffensive unleashed by neoliberal capitalism/imperialism – takes on various forms, running from explosions aimed against precisely those autocracies participating in the neoliberal ranks to challenges by emerging countries to the international order. These springtimes thus coincide with the autumn of capitalism, the decline of the capitalism of globalised, financialised, generalised monopolies. These movements begin, like those of the preceding century, with peoples and states of the system's periphery regain-ing their independence, retaking the initiative in transforming the world. They are thus, above all, anti-imperialist movements and so are only potentially anti-capitalist. Should these movements succeed in converging with the other necessary reawakening, that of the workers in the imperialist core, a truly socialist perspec-tive could be opened for the whole human race. But that is in no way a predestined historical necessity. The decline of capitalism might open the way for a long transition toward socialism, but it might equally well put humanity on the road to generalised barbarism. The ongoing US project of military control over the planet by its armed forces, supported by their NATO lieutenants, the erosion of democracy in the imperialist core countries, and the medievalist rejection of democracy within Southern countries in revolt (taking the form of fundamentalist semi-religious delusions disseminated by political Islam, political Hinduism, political Buddhism) all work together toward that dreadful outcome. At the current time the struggle for secularist democratisation is crucial for the perspective of popular emancipation, crucial for opposition to the perspective of generalised barbarism.

http://pambazuka.org/en/category/features/73902

This chapter was translated by Shane Henry Mage and first appeared in *Monthly Review*.

Note

1. Mashreq means 'East', that is, eastern North Africa and the Levant.

Bibliography

Achcar, Gilbert (2009) *Les Arabes et la Shoah*, Arles, Actes Sud (for the best analysis of the components of political Islam – Rachid Reda, the Muslim Brotherhood, the modern Salafists)

Achcar, Gilbert (2011) *Le choc des barbaries*, Bruxelles, Cairo and Paris, Complexe (concerning the relationship between the North/South conflict and the opposition between the beginning of a socialist transition and the strategic organisation of capitalism)

Amin, Samir (1976) *La nation arabe*, Paris, Editions de Minuit

Amin, Samir (2006) *A Life Looking Forward: Memories of an Independent Marxist*, London, Zed Books

Amin, Samir (2008) *L'Eveil du Sud*, Paris, Le temps des cerises (for my interpretations of the achievements of the viceroy Muhammad Ali (1805–1848) and of the Khedives who succeeded him, especially Ismail (1867–1879); of the Wafd (1920–1952); of the positions taken by Egyptian communists in regard to Nasserism; and of the deviation represented by the Nahda from Afghani to Rachid Reda)

Amin, Samir (2008) The *World We Wish to See*, New York, Monthly Review Press

Amin, Samir (2011) *Ending the Crisis of Capitalism or Ending Capitalism?*, Oxford, Pambazuka Press

Amin, Samir (2011) *The Law of Worldwide Value*, New York, Monthly Review Press

Amin, Samir (2011) 'The trajectory of historical capitalism and Marxism's tricontinental vocation', *Monthly Review*, 62(9)

Riad, Hassan (1964) *L'Egypte nassérienne*, Paris, Editions de Minuit

32

Libya – the true costs of war

Charles Abugre

28 July 2011

The invasion of Libya was planned and the opportunity to execute it was highly propitious.

They say time heals emotional wounds. If that is so, why do I not feel less enraged as the days go by since the outrageous invasion of Libya under ludicrous false pretences four months ago? Yes, Libya is under invasion from air and sea bombardments, directed by foreign special forces on Libyan soil. The purpose of the invasion is regime change. The bombs that are killing people and laying Tripoli to waste have one purpose only: to help a rebel group which the invaders formed and armed to overthrow the Gaddafi regime. The air bombardments were initiated in the false expectation that once bombs started falling in Tripoli, Libyans in Tripoli would rise up against Gaddafi and in this murky situation, the armed group would march in from Benghazi and take power. As time goes by, the strategy gets desperate. It has now become 'anything to kill or oust Gaddafi and his sons will do'. This is reminiscent of the 1960s when the same actors used not-so-dissimilar tactics to overthrow governments they did not like. The plan failed, which is why four months into the carnage, Gaddafi still pops out of the hole he is hiding in to scream insults at his invaders.

The invasion was planned. In the case of the US, involvement went as far back as George Bush Jr's 'war on the axis of evil'. In the case of the French, active planning may have been happening since October 2010. The planning ensured that weapons and forces were at the ready in Benghazi when the moment came. This is why the civil protest in Benghazi, which started in a similar manner to the Tunisian and Egyptian uprisings of unarmed civilians, turned into an armed rebellion in two days, and in less than a month, the NATO/French invasion had began. The incredible speed of these events was far from spontaneous.

That there are British, Dutch, French and Italian special forces, among others, on the ground – not just in Benghazi but all over the country – is neither debatable nor denied. We know that much from the reports of the British media and from the incompetent ways in which the Netherlands and Britain sought to introduce their special forces into the insurgency in the early days. Recall the helicopter full of British special forces that landed in the middle of the rebel troops, who promptly captured and displayed them before realising that they were 'friendly forces'. Days later, the Dutch were even more inept. They ended up being captured by the Gaddafi forces, who displayed them before the world's media and then released them. You should have the seen the glee in the face of Gaddafi's son.

But the penetration of special forces into Libya, if we are to believe Franco Bechis, the Italian journalist writing in the 24 March edition of *Libero*,[1] may have begun as far back as 16 November 2010 when a train arrived in Benghazi ostensibly carrying French businessmen seeking to invest in Libya's agriculture. A large number of these businessmen were in fact soldiers. According to Franco Bechis, quoting *Maghreb Confidential*, active planning for regime change by the French began on 21 October 2010 when Nuri Mesmar, Gaddafi's chief of protocol and his closest chum, arrived in Paris for surgery. However, Mesmar was not met by doctors but by the French secret service and Sarkozy's closest aides. Mesmar was also responsible for the Ministry of Agriculture. On 16 November, Mesmar agreed a strategy to drop troops in Libya under the guise of a business delegation. Two days later, a planeload of people, including soldiers, landed in Benghazi where they met, among others, Libyan military commanders in order to encourage them to desert. One of those who agreed to do so was Colonel Gehan Abdallah, whose militia subsequently led the rebellion. Where did this information come from? The Italian intelligence service.

The role of Nuri Mesmar is as old as the story of Brutus and Caesar in Shakespeare and reminds one of how Captain Blaise

Campoare of Burkina Faso was used by the French to overthrow and execute his closest friend, Thomas Sankara.

But it was not only from France that the armed rebellion was planned. The head of the Libyan National Transitional Council, Colonel Khalifa, arrived from the US on 14 March to lead the armed rebellion a month after it began. Colonel Khalifa had been living in the United States since the 1980s, apparently working as an agent for the CIA, according to Pierre Pean's 2001 book *The African Handling*.[2] The 31 March edition of the *Wall Street Journal* carries a story which says that 'The CIA officials acknowledge that they have been active in Libya for several weeks, like other Western Intelligence Services.' Khalifa, Mesmar and others will be joined in the leadership of the provisional government by some of the most murderous individuals in the Gaddafi regime, for example Jalil Mustafa Abud, who until the uprising was the minister for justice and was on the list of Amnesty International's most egregious human rights violators.

Ludicrous false pretences

I used the phrase 'ludicrous false pretences' to describe the excuses publicly sold to a gullible press, decidedly. Why? The core of UN Security Council Resolution 1973 claims to aim at 'protecting civilians'. There are two sets of principles from which the need to protect civilians could have been drawn. One is the principle of holding all combatants responsible in respect of the Geneva Convention. This principle is covered by UN Security Council Resolutions 1265, 1296, and 1820 among others. Armed combatants from both sides who violate the Geneva Convention will be held liable, under these resolutions, and could suffer sanctions and by extension could be liable to face the International Criminal Court (ICC) to the extent that the violations qualify as crimes against humanity or are genocidal. These resolutions, however, do not legalise external military intervention.

The second is the principle of the 'responsibility to protect' (R2P). This is based on the concept of 'borderless' security, which was the title of the report of the International Commission on Intervention and State Sovereignty (ICISS) released in December 2001 and subsequently adopted as an operative principle by the

UN. This commission, chaired by Gareth Evans and Mohamed Sahnoun, undertook to study the relationship between 1) the rights of sovereign states, upon which the greater part of international relations has been built, and 2) the so-called right of humanitarian intervention, which has been exercised sporadically – in Somalia, Bosnia and Kosovo but not Rwanda – and with varying degrees of success and international controversy. The report addressed 'the question of when, if ever, it is appropriate for states to take coercive – and in particular military – action, against another state for the purpose of protecting people at risk in that other state'.[3]

The conclusion was that the priority should be the protection of human beings not state sovereignty. As a result, if human security – physical safety and dignity – was threatened by the state or by its severe inability to address the situation, the international community had the responsibility to act including through armed intervention. R2P places humanitarian law above that of sovereignty. The R2P was heavily lobbied for, especially by Western humanitarian organisations, who celebrated its adoption by the UN. However, others have warned of the danger of this principle for a number of reasons. First, placing humanitarian law above the right to sovereignty is dangerous because human rights are based on citizenship, which in turn rests on sovereignty. Second, the R2P principle opens the door to selective interventions and justice by those who control the UN Security Council. It also creates legal and political dependence on the Security Council and militarily powerful countries, thereby undermining the very foundations for long-term justice and peace which rest on domestic political processes. Resolution 1973 was crafted on the basis of R2P, thereby 'legalising' the invasion. Invasion is what the NATO countries wanted not simply in order to minimise the harm done to civilians by Gaddafi's forces but for regime change.

Was an invasion necessary on humanitarian grounds? This is debatable because the answer lies with the counterfactual, which is the issue of whether or not Gaddafi's forces would have bombed Benghazi to bits, as claimed. What we now know is that the Gaddafi air forces did not target civilian settlements in Benghazi when they flew and that according to Amnesty International the claim of mass rape by Gaddafi's forces could not be verified on the ground. We also know that the suppression of the 15 February civilian uprising by Gaddafi was not the first of its kind; the last major suppression happened in 2006. Like other North African and Middle Eastern dictators, Gaddafi put down the 2006 uprising violently, shooting a few people and arresting others. There were no mass murders and at the time his actions received the tacit support of America, in particular, as a legitimate response to an Al Qaeda influence. But the plain truth is that the situation was no longer a civilian uprising after two days; it was an armed insurgency and every state has the right to confront armed insurgency with arms. We have seen this time and again in the US, whether the authorities are responding to religious fanatics or drug gangs in black neighbourhoods.

Was there a better way to save lives? Yes, if given the chance. We know that the former president of Brazil, Lula de Silva, offered to lead a mission to mediate a ceasefire. This was supported by Latin American countries, the African Union and even the weak-kneed Arab League. Gaddafi had agreed the idea of a ceasefire, including an international force to observe it. The offer was turned down by NATO and their vassals in Benghazi. The African Union mission was humiliated in Benghazi and the Western media hosted discussions that ridiculed the AU initiatives. Peace was given no chance because the agenda is regime change, *not* the protection of civilians.

If military intervention is the better route to protecting civilians, why has NATO not invaded Yemen, where a wholly non-violent uprising is being brutally suppressed with live bullets? Robert Gates, until recently the US defence secretary, is reported to have said, about Yemen that 'I do not think it's my role to intervene in the internal affairs of Yemen'.[4] Could it be because the Yemeni leader is 'our bloody dictator'? After all, he is fighting a war against left-wing separatists 'we' do not like and Yemen plays host to America's fifth fleet. How about Bahrain, the tiny kingdom where the royal family owns most of the islands that make up the kingdom and where, with the support of Saudi troops, large numbers of unarmed demonstrators have been gunned down? Is there even mention of hauling the sultan to the ICC? This is the selective use of the R2P that many have feared.

Is the military intervention saving lives? Clearly not. How

do aerial bombardments of civilian settlements and atrocities by rebels armed by NATO constitute saving civilians' lives? Are the Benghazi civilians more civilian than the civilians in Tripoli and other places? The history of Western military invasions that were ostensibly meant to save lives shows that they tend to claim lives. Take Iraq, where a million or so have died directly from bombs and indirectly from sectarian violence, while a million more have been displaced. Not even Saddam's several years of murderous rule managed to achieve that feat. Or take Afghanistan, or Somalia or even the Balkan interventions.

Are these invaders capable of false pretences to justify armed interventions? Yes; the evidence abounds. The story of lies and deceitfulness that was sold to the same gullible media to justify the invasion of Iraq is well known. George Bush and Tony Blair were in no doubt that Saddam Hussein had no weapons of mass destruction. Once the decision was made to invade Iraq, everything was done to provoke a justification for invasion. Before the invasion of Afghanistan on the pretext of going after Osama bin Laden and Al Qaeda, the ruling Taliban had offered to hand over bin Laden to an international tribunal if the Americans provided evidence of his involvement in the 9/11 bombing of the Twin Towers in New York. There are similar stories relating to the bombardment of Yugoslavia.

Why regime change?

So, if the North African uprisings that spilled over into Libya provided the enabling conditions for regime change planned long before, and if saving lives was not the real purpose of the military intervention, why are they so desperate to remove Colonel 'Brother' Mu'ammar Gaddafi and his family from power?

There are many theories.

Retribution

Different governments harbour different grievance against 'The Brother'. Some say Sarkozy is seeking to cover up an embarrassment: the allegation that his presidential election campaign was substantially funded by the Gaddafi family. This could cause him a legal headache if the lethargic French legal system were to ever to come to life. Papi Silvio (Berlusconi) was embarrassed by Gaddafi when he pitched his tent in Milan at the time the Italian prime minister was facing a public outcry over his womanising. Surrounded by his 'liberated' women guards, Gaddafi is said to have declared himself as their protector to a room full of angry Italian women. The British and the Americans may have more serious grievances in the form of the downing of the Pan Am flight over Lockerbie. It is probably the same sense of grievance that led many African governments to acquiesce to UN resolution 1973. Many would love to see the back of this weird man, who prowled their territories in a manner that made them small in the eyes of their people. But it is simply not wise to embarrass, let alone anger, those with bigger military might.

Supporting a legitimate independence struggle

In the *New Eastern Outlook* journal,[5] Dmitry Isayev quotes Berlusconi as saying that the war in Libya is Cyrenaica's (eastern Libya's) war of independence, presumably from the colonisation of western Libya, perhaps much in the same way as South Sudan has separated from the rest of Sudan. Berlusconi's Italy is therefore clear that it is supporting a separatist movement. While it is unlikely that his NATO counterparts will welcome this perspective of the war, Berlusconi's view does have resonance. The armed insurrection is launched from Benghazi (the capital of the east), which for several centuries was the seat of the monarchy. While the monarchy lasted Cyrenaica controlled the oil resources, a thriving port and fishing grounds, and therefore the wealth. This monarchy was overthrown by Gaddafi in 1969 with the support of clans from the west. Since then the east has been marginalised, politically and economically. But if the purpose of the war is to separate the two Libyas, how does this gel with Security Council Resolution 1973, which is meant merely to protect civilians?

Geopolitical interests

In the 23 June 2011 issue of Pambazuka News,[6] Ismael Hossein-Zadeh suggests that NATO is going after Gaddafi because of his insubordination, which threatens its strategic interests and its very sense of power. One area of unforgiveable insubordination is

Gaddafi's (and his Syrian counterpart's) refusal – they are the only two 'Arab nations' – to be absorbed into NATO/US/French strategic security arrangements for the control of the Mediterranean sea basin and the Middle East. 'Libya and Syria have also not participated in NATO's almost ten-year-old Operation Active Endeavour naval patrols and exercises in the Mediterranean sea and neither is Libya a member of NATO's Mediterranean Dialogue military partnership, which includes most regional countries: Israel, Jordan, Egypt, Tunisia, Algeria, Morocco and Mauritania.' Libya's Gaddafi also opposed the US Africa Command (AFRICOM).

These are serious infractions because of the strategic importance of the Mediterranean region. Staying out means Gaddafi cannot be trusted when it comes to the security of Israel – a country you do not mess around with. Staying out means an important source of oil, gas and mineral deposits cannot be relied upon in strategic planning. Staying out also means, leaving a crack for other non-NATO countries, especially China, Brazil, India and Russia, to find serious footing in the region. Staying out constitutes a serious geopolitical risk.

The concern to contain India and China is not a throwaway point. Questioned on his view about what really motivates the invasion of Afghanistan, Henry Kissinger, the famed US foreign secretary of the cold war era, says that 'trends supported by Japan and China, to create a free-trade area in Asia – an opposing block of the most populous nations in the world with great resources and some of the most industrial nations will be inconsistent with American national interests. For this reason, America must maintain a presence in Asia…'.[7] This is consistent with the views of Zbigniew Brzezinski, Jimmy Carter's foreign secretary, the man understood to have discovered and mentored Barack Obama into the presidency. He considers Euro-Asia to be the 'chessboard on which the battle takes place for global primacy'.[8] The Mediterranean is a core part of Euro-Asia. Speaking on 28 March, Barrack Obama says of the Libyan invasion 'when our interests and values are at stake, we have a responsibility to act … America has an important strategic interest in preventing Gaddafi from defeating those who oppose him'.[9]

Strategic economic interests

In my view there are three areas in which strategic economic interests express themselves: economic policies that influence the accumulation, ownership and movement of capital, goods and services; the control over natural resources, indirectly or directly; and the power of long-term debt. In the Pambazuka article, Ismael makes the point that the control of oil matters but NATO countries already exercise control through the presence of their companies. The problem is that Gaddafi has refused to privatise the oil wells and so exercises effective control. That is dangerous, in the same way that Hugo Chavez is. Gaddafi keeps an open door policy with regard to foreign companies. Such a policy risks letting China into Libya in a big way, thereby complicating the strategic security question. As George Bush once said, 'If you are not with us then you are against us.' Obama has merely retained this view.

Alongside control over natural resources is control over policies. Neoliberalism may be dead in academic circles, but not in realpolitik. If it were, Goldman Sachs would not be running US economic policy. Gaddafi has been extremely naughty in this area as well. If you look at the World Bank's world development indices, you find that Libya has not borrowed from the World Bank and the IMF in years, even after the sanctions were lifted. Libya's economy is heavily state owned. The country has a life expectancy and quality of life comparable to the richest countries. This is against the grain. Worst still, Libya is actively supporting and putting aside resources to realise the dreams of three major pan-African institutions – the African Monetary Fund, the African Investment Bank and the African Central Bank – so Libya could be said to be undermining the Bretton Woods institutions controlled by the NATO countries. Breaking the stranglehold that the Bretton Woods institutions have over Africa could also mean weakening the geopolitical influence of NATO countries over the continent. Moreover, Libya has become an investment competitor in Africa. The Libya African Portfolio has a rolling kitty of $8 billion, channelled into investments ranging from telecommunications, the hospitality industry, some manufacturing, and retail of oil and gas. Libya is effectively redeploying some of its sovereign wealth funds away from purchasing US government bonds into investments in Africa. That cannot be totally encouraged given the US government's dependence on petrodollars for selling their bonds.

War as a means of transferring badly needed capital out of Libya

The military bombardments of Libya have already resulted in the shifting of capital from Libya to the invaders, who have immediately seized the assets of the Libyan people owned by Libyan public institutions and rechannelled them into expenditure. This expenditure will most likely be on military hardware and other logistics in support of the war. The US impounded around $30 billion, which Ismael suggests had been earmarked as a contribution to the building of the pan-African institutions mentioned earlier. Britain impounded undisclosed bank accounts and assets, including £700 million worth of Libyan dinars printed by the British firm De La Rue, which they are likely to give to the rebels. The procurements in support of the war effort will most likely be from these countries and will therefore serve as a fiscal stimulus in these economies. In advance of the war, Libyan 'opposition' figures will have quietly shifted their ill-gotten wealth abroad, some into the tax havens controlled by the invading countries. We will never know how much.

But perhaps the most significant and long-term means of inducing capital from Libya will be as reparation payments for the war. The cost of every munition that was fired, wildly or on target, by the Libyan rebels and by NATO; the cost of every missile fired from the air or seas; the cost of every spy plane that flew over Libyan airspace; the cost of every soldier mobilised for the war effort; the cost of intelligence, special analysts and contractors will all be paid for by the Libyan people with their oil and gas for decades into the future. And this will not be cheap. Newspapers in Britain speculate that if the war continues to the autumn, Britain may spend upwards of $1.6 billion. At the end of May, the British armed forces estimated that they had flown 1,500 sorties, attacked 300 targets, fired at least 20 tomahawk missiles, each costing $1 million. A tornado bomber flying a 3,000-mile round trip from its base to Tripoli and back costs $300,000 per flight. A C17 transport plane costs over $60,000 per hour to fly. The British say they have over 1,000 personnel involved in the operation. The cost to the US taxpayer is estimated to top a $1 billion by autumn 2011. In March, the US had 75 aircrafts involved in the operation and the *Financial Times* reports that on the first day of the operation, the US had spent $110 million. If the Kosovo war is a guide, by the end of the third month, the US had spent $2.4 billion in the operation. Add the cost of the other NATO and Arab partners, and it is conceivable that by end of July, the cost of the Libyan Invasion will approach, if not exceed, $10 billion and counting. The British prime minister, David Cameron, said plainly on TV that whatever the outcome of the war, Libya will have to pay the cost of the UK's participation. Add the cost of reparations and compensation for mercenaries and plain theft by many of the crooks constituting the provisional government, and the Libyan people will find themselves tens of billions of dollars out of pocket.

The long-term beneficial effects of war to the victors

Note that the power of debt is not simply the volume of money one owes and transfers but also the effect on power relations. Libya will forever be subordinated to its creditors, even if the debt is odious. It will have to open up its policymaking to the creditors, open up its banks, import more and privatise assets including natural resources. As the vanquished, it will be forced to join those organisations it previously shunned and conform. The destruction is equally beneficial for the victors: for after the war comes the reconstruction. This is great for the victors' construction firms, the suppliers of building material, architects, engineers. The suffering banks of Europe and America will be energised by massive lending for the reconstruction effort, exacerbating the debt burden of the Libyan people but widening the profit margins of investment banks and the army of rent-seekers that follow them – accountants, lawyers, gamblers. War, especially in an oil-rich country, cannot be bad for economies that are in the doldrums.

Impact on the rest of Africa

I characterised the invasion as wicked and heartless, which was also quite deliberate. It is wicked because of the selfishness of the agenda underpinning the invasion, its lack of concern for the impact on the Libyan people. The invasion will undoubtedly turn Libyans from a proud people who know little abject poverty (in spite of Gaddafi's dictatorship and several years of economic sanctions) into a typical sub-African type – a few wealthy people swimming in increasing pools of desperately poor people with severely wounded pride. It is not inconceivable that various armed factions will emerge however this madness ends. Centuries-old tribal and clan divisions will have been widened not narrowed. Racial bigotry will spread, having been unleashed by the media propaganda about black African support to Gaddafi. Libya will never be the same again and seeing what is happening in Iraq, Libya's change will not be for the good for a long time to come.

But the wicked effects are not limited to the boundaries of Libya. Anything between 500,000 and one million workers from across Africa south of the Sahara have been displaced, adding to the already overflowing pool of the unemployed. The president of Niger estimated the displaced Nigerien workforce to be in the neighbourhood of 200,000. Is anybody intending to compensate for these losses? The effect of this displacement is not simply that it aggravates the already scary poverty situation but also that it has the potential to exacerbate the insecurity in these fragile zone, especially the area stretching from Mauritania, across Niger, Mali, Chad, Sudan, Ethiopia, Somalia, Eritrea and Djibouti. These areas are fragile and volatile in several respects – ecologically, economically, socially and in their potential for armed conflicts. The potential for violent conflict will be made worse by the increased availability of arms of all sorts – the type that are now being dropped all over the place by NATO.

The invasion is also heartless because it has deprived Africa of investment resources and undermined the creation of institutions that are critical if the poorest continent is to transform its economies and overcome suffering and the indignity of poverty. It has transformed the African Union from one representing all of

Africa to one effectively representing Africa south of the Sahara in the manner that Libya has been characterised by the invaders as an Arab country, a characterisation that the rebel group seems to carry proudly on its chest.

Way forward

Too much water has passed under the bridge. The Gaddafi family must leave power. Indeed, no-one anywhere should have the legitimacy to rule and exert power over the resources of a land without being democratically elected. This applies to Gaddafi and his family just as much as to the rag-tag bunch that calls itself the interim government, especially as we know that it is made up of some of the most unsavoury elements in the Gaddafi government.

This means that negotiation is not on the cards for NATO. The NATO invaders have been forced to acknowledge this, particularly since their hope of speedily toppling Gaddafi has not materialised. The African Union plan for a negotiated settlement remains the most credible – an immediate ceasefire; humanitarian intervention and protection in all parts of Libya; an external observer force; an interim government made up of both sides; a timetable for political parties to form, electioneering to happen and elections to take place; a legal process to investigate, try and punish the guilty – and, if I may add, a no-reparations and no-debt-claims commitment by the invading forces. This should have been the way forward from day one, were the Lula mission and the AU strategy followed.

The bottom line is that war was solely unwarranted. But my greatest sadness and shame was to be part of a United Nations that hastened to beat the war drums and cheer on the battle rather than sing the songs of peace. A sad time indeed. So how else can one describe what is going on in Libya other than as a wicked, heartless folly?

http://pambazuka.org/en/category/features/75252

Notes

1. Economics NewsPaper.com, http://economicsnewspaper.com/economics/ understanding-the-war-in-libya-11018.html, accessed 15 September 2011.
2. Economics NewsPaper.com, http://economicsnewspaper.com/policy/

french/secret-financing-from-africa-sarkozy-too-66736.html, accessed 15 September 2011.

3. International Commission on Intervention and State Sovereignty (ICISS) (2001) *The Responsibility to Protect*, Ottawa, International Development Research Centre: vii, http://www.iciss.ca/report-en.asp, accessed 15 September 2011.

4. Reuters (2011) 'US concerned about Yemen instability, Qaeda fight', http://www.reuters.com/article/2011/03/22/us-yemen-usa-gates-idUSTRE72L3CL20110322, accessed 15 September 2011.

5. Dmitry Isayev (2011) 'The economics of the Libyan war and NATO's crisis', *New Eastern Outlook*, 17 May, http://journal-neo.com/?q=node/6532, accessed 15 September.

6. Ismael Hossein-Zadeh (2011) 'Why regime change in Libya?', Pambazuka News, 23 June, http://pambazuka.org/en/category/features/74278, accessed 15 September.

7. Henry Kissinger (2001) *Does America Need a Foreign Policy?*, New York, NY, Simon and Schuster, www.economicsnews.com.

8. Zbigniew Brzezinski (1997) *The Grand Chessboard: American Primacy and Its Geostrategic Imperatives*, New York, NY, Basic Books.

9. *The Telegraph*, http://www.telegraph.co.uk/news/worldnews/africaandindianocean/libya/8412809/Libya-Barack-Obama-speech-in-full.html.

Appendix – Further readings from Pambazuka News

This book contains only a selection of the rich archive of analyses, reports and reviews carried in Pambazuka News. The following reviews of independent media – blogs, Twitter, newsletters and interviews – were also published in Pambazuka News during the first half of 2011. They can be read online and provide a week-by-week timeline of events and analysis across the continent.

Patrick Burnett (3 February 2011) 'Egypt: a revolution reflected', http://pambazuka.org/en/category/features/70631

Patrick Burnett (24 February 2011) 'Gaddafi's overthrow: telling the story online', http://pambazuka.org/en/category/features/71189

Sokari Ekine (17 March 2011) 'Libya, Egypt, Cameroon, Côte d'Ivoire: confusion remains', http://pambazuka.org/en/category/features/71800

Sokari Ekine (24 March 2011) 'Haiti and the endless revolution', http://pambazuka.org/en/category/features/71989

Sokari Ekine (30 March 2011) 'Côte d'Ivoire, Egypt and Libya: contested battles for support and attention', http://pambazuka.org/en/category/features/72119

Sokari Ekine (7 April 2011) 'Uprising, imperialism and uncertainty', http://pambazuka.org/en/category/features/72342

Sokari Ekine (14 April 2011) 'Swaziland: Mswati, you are on your own…', http://pambazuka.org/en/category/features/72563

Sokari Ekine (21 April 2011) 'Libya: five principles of war propaganda', http://pambazuka.org/en/category/features/72764

Sokari Ekine (2 June 2011) ' "Defiant in the face of brutality": uprisings in East and Southern Africa', http://pambazuka.org/en/category/features/73738

Sokari Ekine (9 June 2011) 'Maghreb uprisings: truth is "impossible to find" ', http://pambazuka.org/en/category/features/73928

Sokari Ekine (16 June 2011) 'Mauritania: 'A simple citizen demanding his rights" ', http://pambazuka.org/en/category/features/74110

Sokari Ekine (23 June 2011) 'Egypt: The old repression resurfaces', http://pambazuka.org/en/category/features/74282

Sokari Ekine (30 June 2011) 'Senegal on the rise: "Ne touche pas à ma constitution!" ', http://pambazuka.org/en/category/features/74491

Index

Ending the Crisis of Capitalism or Ending Capitalism?

Samir Amin

2010
paperback
978-1-906387-80-8
also available in pdf, epub
and Kindle formats

With his usual verve and sharpness Samir Amin, renowned radical economist, explores the systemic crisis of capitalism leading to the 2008 financial collapse, lays bare the relationship between dominating oligopolies and the globalisation of the world economy and analyses the attempts by the threatened plutocracies of the US, Europe and Japan to impose domination on the peoples of the South through intensifying military intervention. The current crisis, he argues, is a profound crisis of the capitalist system itself, bringing forward an era in which wars, and perhaps revolutions, will once again shake the world.

Amin presents an alternative strategy for the way forward which, by building on advances made by progressive forces in Latin America, would allow for a more humane society through both the North and the South working together.

'An earnest and acute analysis of the failures of capitalism in the contemporary world.'

Tom Odhiambo, University of Nairobi

Ending Aid Dependence

Yash Tandon

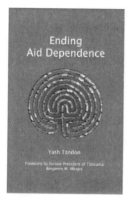

Developing countries can liberate themselves from aid that pretends to be developmental but is not. This book cautions against the collective colonialism of rich donor countries. Ending aid dependence requires a radical shift in the mindset and the development strategy of countries dependent on aid.

2008
paperback
978-1-906387-31-0
also available in pdf, epub
and Kindle formats

'Yash Tandon shows that "aid" is an instrument of imperialism's strategy of domination ... which he strongly contrasts with proposals for "another aid", one rooted in the principles of international and anti-imperialist solidarity.'

Samir Amin, director of the Third World Forum

'The message of this book needs to be seriously considered and debated by all those that are interested in the development of the countries of the South.'

Benjamin W. Mkapa, former President of Tanzania (1995-2005)

Women and Security Governance in Africa

Edited by 'Funmi Olonisakin and Awino Okech

2011
paperback
978-1-906387-89-1
also available in pdf, epub
and Kindle formats

When the path-breaking United Nations Resolution 1325 on women, peace and security was adopted in 2000, it was the first time that the security concerns of women in situations of armed conflict and their role in peace building were placed on the agenda of the UN Security Council.

In the field of international security, discussions on women and children are often relegated to the margins. This book addresses a broader debate on security and its governance in a variety of contexts while making the argument that the single most important measure of the effectiveness of security governance is its impact on women. But this is more than a book about women. Rather it is a book about inclusive human security for Africans, which cannot ignore the central place of women.

'In the first volume of its kind, some of the best and most engaging African intellectuals and activists have gathered to expose the fallacies of the current security paradigm to show how "security for women" must entail, at least in large part, "security by women".'

Professor Eboe Hutchful, chair of the African Security Network

'We need fresh perspectives and new ways of visioning governance in Africa so that women's security becomes an intrinsic measure of development and peace. This important collection of insights from across the continent leads the way.'

Winnie Byanyima, director of UNDP Gender Team

 Order your copy from www.pambazukapress.org